MIMI'S HEIRLOOM SEWING
Book Two

By Mildred Turner

Illustrations by Rebekah Russell and Tina Davis

Printed by Groves Printing Co.
Asheville, North Carolina

COVER

Monica Marie Whyte, 5-year-old daughter of Edward and Lorraine Whyte is featured wearing a dress designed and made by Cassie Sheffield and photographed by Phillip C. Sheffield all of Tampa, Florida.

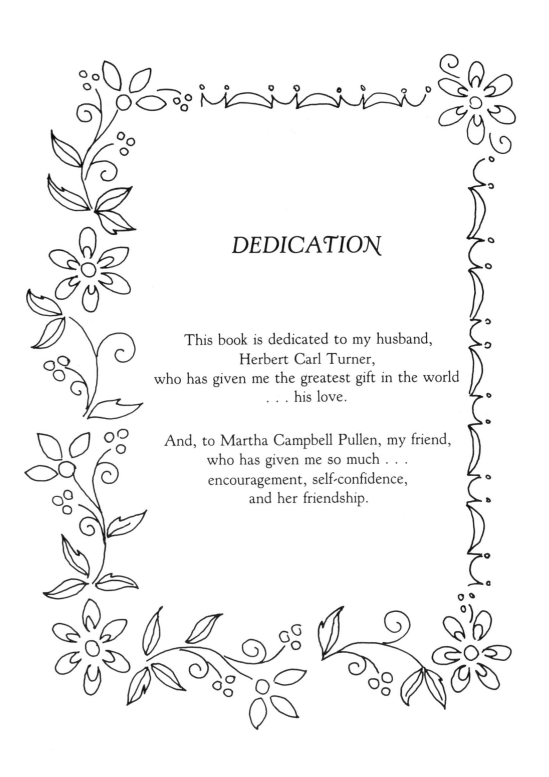

DEDICATION

This book is dedicated to my husband,
Herbert Carl Turner,
who has given me the greatest gift in the world
. . . his love.

And, to Martha Campbell Pullen, my friend,
who has given me so much . . .
encouragement, self-confidence,
and her friendship.

ACKNOWLEDGEMENTS

There are so many people to whom I am grateful. So many people that have meant so much to me personally and have had a great influence in my life. It scares me to mention names for fear that I shall leave one out . . . probably the one that has meant the most to me. But, I do feel such a debt of gratitude that I must express my deep appreciation to some.

A special thanks to Cassie Sheffield. She designed and made the dress which Monica wears on the front of this book. Her husband, Philip C. Sheffield, spent much time taking pictures so that I could pick one for the front of this book. Philip has been nominated twice for the Pulitzer Prize and has pictures hanging in The Hague in Holland. Cassie and Philip have one daughter, Susan Lynn, and live in Tampa, Florida. I am still overwhelmed that Cassie spent the many hours stitching and Philip, out of his busy schedule, to photograph Monica (with a rabbit, yet) so that I could have a beautiful cover for my book. Thank you both. And, a thank you to Lorraine and Edward Whyte for allowing Monica Marie to model. She was most patient to sit in the hot sun so that Philip was able to get just the right "shot."

To my friends – Susan York, Ruth Walther, Margaret Blackwell, Frances Satterfield, Becky Davis, Patsy Underwood, Kathy McMakin, Becky Lambert, Janice Ferguson, Lane Edwards, and Beth Bryson . . . whose love and loyal support are far greater than I deserve.

To my assistant, Alma Best, I owe a special debt. She is most efficient, kind, understanding, and loyal . . . I am both appreciative and thankful. A thank you to Shirley Edwards and Alma, who daily do much of the work I should be doing and thereby allowing me more time for teaching engagements.

To Martha Pullen, I am most grateful! She has encouraged me and without that support, I do not believe that Mimi's Machine Heirloom Sewing, Book I, or Mimi's Heirloom Sewing, Book II would have ever been published. Thank you, Martha.

I am also most grateful to my children. Even though two of my sons live far away (Kevin in Germany and Bryan in California), they have been very close in spirit. They have been most understanding with me and my neglect as far as writing them letters. They have been very supportive, allowing my grandchildren to wear clothes when I have tried a new design, fabric or an idea. Their wives, Pam and Sandy, have been the daughters I never had. My grandchildren, Jennifer, Michael, Elizabeth, and Joshua are a joy and delight unto my soul. My youngest son, Matthew, deserves special recognition, as I spent much time doing un-motherly "things." I love you and appreciate you . . . thank you for being you. A big thank you to Matthew's friends, Charlotte, Gina, Kim, Laura and Christy for their youthful perspective on "heirloom sewing." And, I must not leave out my nieces! They are most special to me and have been most generous with their love and support and have shared so much of their life with me . . . I love you Beth, Jean, Carol and Sally.

Last, but most important! A "special" thank you to my husband. Without his encouragement, assistance and love this book would not have even been started!

And, the deep gratitude which I feel for my Lord and Savior leaves me without words. All the talent I have, everything which I am and all that I do comes from HIM. It is to His Glory that this book is written.

Mildred Turner

Contents

TECHNIQUES

ZIG AND ZAG

When reading directions for any of the techniques, I will refer to Zig when the needle is on the left side and Zag when the needle swings to the right. **fig. 1, 2 and 3.**

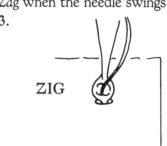

ZIG **fig. 1**

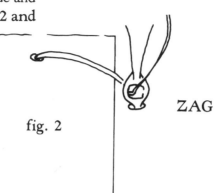

fig. 2 ZAG

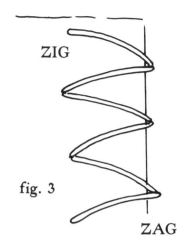

ZIG

fig. 3

ZAG

ROLL AND WHIP *By Machine*

1. Trim the edge of the fabric so that you have a clean cut edge — no fuzzies!

2. Set the Zigzag Stitch of your machine so that the needle catches about ⅛" to a scant ¼" of the fabric edge on the left and clears the raw edge of the fabric on the right side. **fig. 1.**

Setting For Roll and Whip

ELNA 7000
"B" Foot
Selector Stitch # 2
Width Setting 3.7
Length Setting .8

Bernina 1130
3 Foot
2 Zigzag Stitch
Width Setting 3.5
Length Setting 1

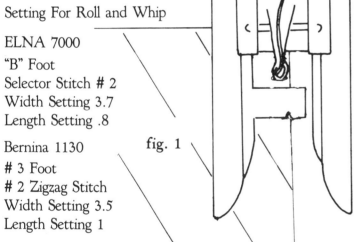

fig. 1

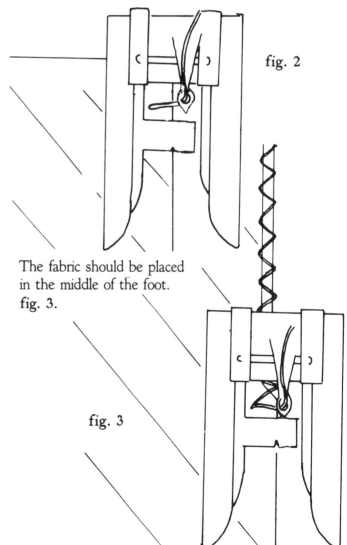

fig. 2

The fabric should be placed in the middle of the foot. **fig. 3.**

fig. 3

Note: All machines which have a Zigzag Stitch will roll and whip. All machines will do heirloom sewing if they zigzag; however, I am putting only the Elna and Bernina settings for some of the techniques, as they are the only machines which are available to me. Some machines will make a prettier roll and whip than others. Some machines will do some things which others will not. But, if you get to know your machine, you will be able to get it to do more than you think.

Make sure that the needle completely clears the fabric edge on the right side. This allows the fabric to roll. **fig. 2.**

ROLL AND WHIP

MOCK FRENCH ROLL

1. Turn raw edge under ⅛" to ¼" and press . . . you can finger press as you go. The finished "rolled" hem will be half this width.

   a. Insert needle through the fold. Knot will be hidden this way. **fig. 1.**

c. Return to the top fold and take ¼" stitch in the fold. **fig. 3A and fig. 3B.**

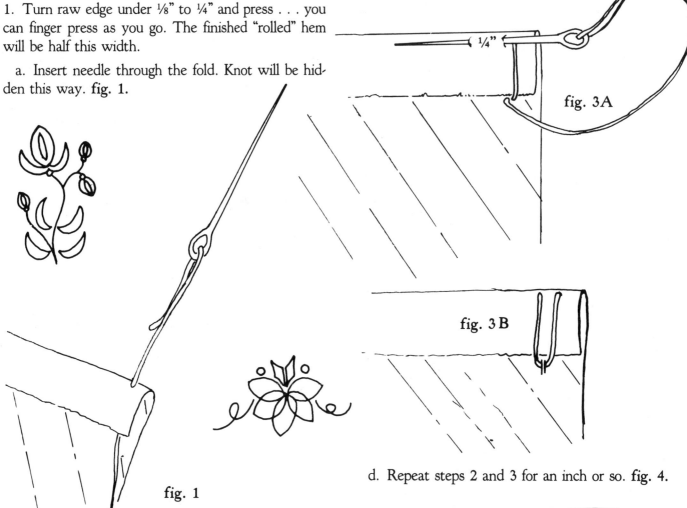

fig. 3A

fig. 3 B

fig. 1

b. Move directly below the fold and pick up one or two threads. Do not catch threads from the folded down piece. **fig. 2.**

d. Repeat steps 2 and 3 for an inch or so. **fig. 4.**

fig. 4

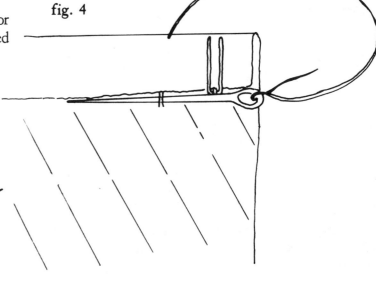

fig. 2

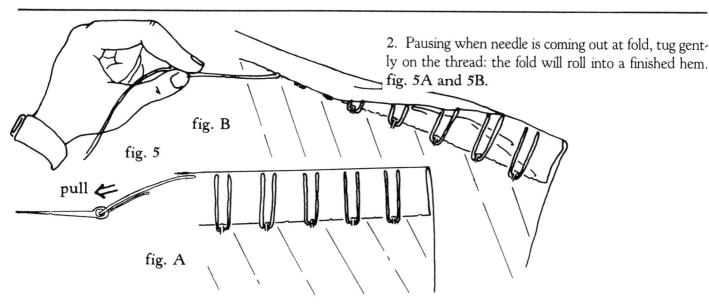

2. Pausing when needle is coming out at fold, tug gently on the thread: the fold will roll into a finished hem. fig. 5A and 5B.

fig. B

fig. 5

pull ⬅

fig. A

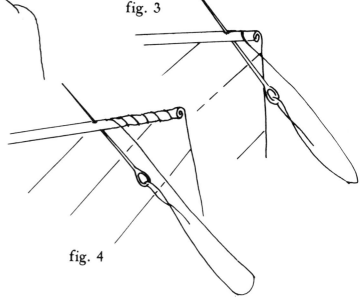

fig. 3

fig. 4

fig. 1

This technique requires practice, but it is well worth the effort if you are in need of a hand rolled hem.

1. Hold the top of the fabric so that the thumbs and index fingers catch the very top threads.

With both thumbs, roll the top thread over two or three times, rolling toward you. Do not try to roll with just one thumb, as you can not roll as tightly or as straight as you can when you use both thumbs. fig. 1.

2. Now, start back at the beginning of the rolled hem and roll the hem very tight. Place the needle under the roll and not through it. Roll only an *inch or two* at a time, whipping the hem as you roll. Hold the rolled fabric with your thumb and index finger of your left hand. Getting the first stitches started are the hardest of all.

3. To begin, slide the needle under the roll and out of the top of the roll. fig. 2 and fig. 3.

4. Keep the needle at about a 45° angle and encase the roll but *DO NOT GO* into or through the back of the material. Make your stitches about ⅛" apart. fig. 4.

5. The needle will sew toward the hand holding the rolled fabric edge. And, you will need to roll the seam often. It is sometimes easier to make the material roll by moistening the finger. You may hold the fabric to be rolled over and around your finger if it makes it easier. fig. 5.

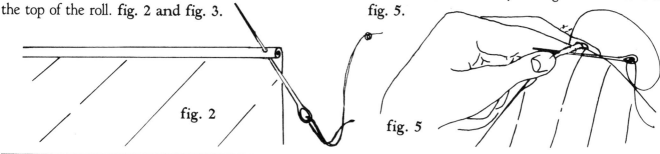

fig. 2

fig. 5

HOW TO ROLL AND WHIP A BIAS OR CURVED EDGE

THE CONCAVE CURVE _____
(or the neck edge of a dress)

1. Straight Stitch ⅛" from the seam allowance line. This line of stitching will be closest to the raw edge. **fig. 1.**

2. Lightly spray starch and press. (Do not iron, as you do not wish to stretch the bias edge.) Trim just as close to the line of stitching as possible without cutting into the stitch line. **fig. 2.**

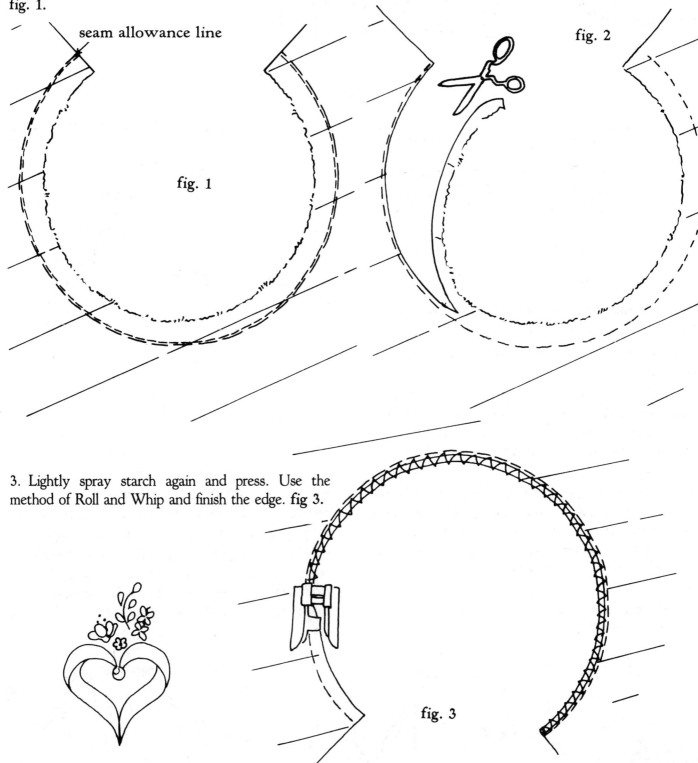

seam allowance line

fig. 1

fig. 2

3. Lightly spray starch again and press. Use the method of Roll and Whip and finish the edge. **fig 3.**

fig. 3

CONVEX CURVE
The technique is the same as for the Concave Curve

1. Machine Stitch using a very tiny stitch ⅛" outside of the seam allowance edge of the fabric. **fig. 1.**

2. Lightly spray starch and press. Trim just as close as you can without cutting into the line of stitching. **fig. 2.**

3. For example, if you are going to Roll and Whip the top edge of a sleeve, it is good to use quilting thread, as the quilting thread can be introduced at the point where you need for the gathers to start. **fig. 3.**

4. After you have rolled and whipped the edge, pull the quilting thread to gather the sleeve. **fig. 4.**

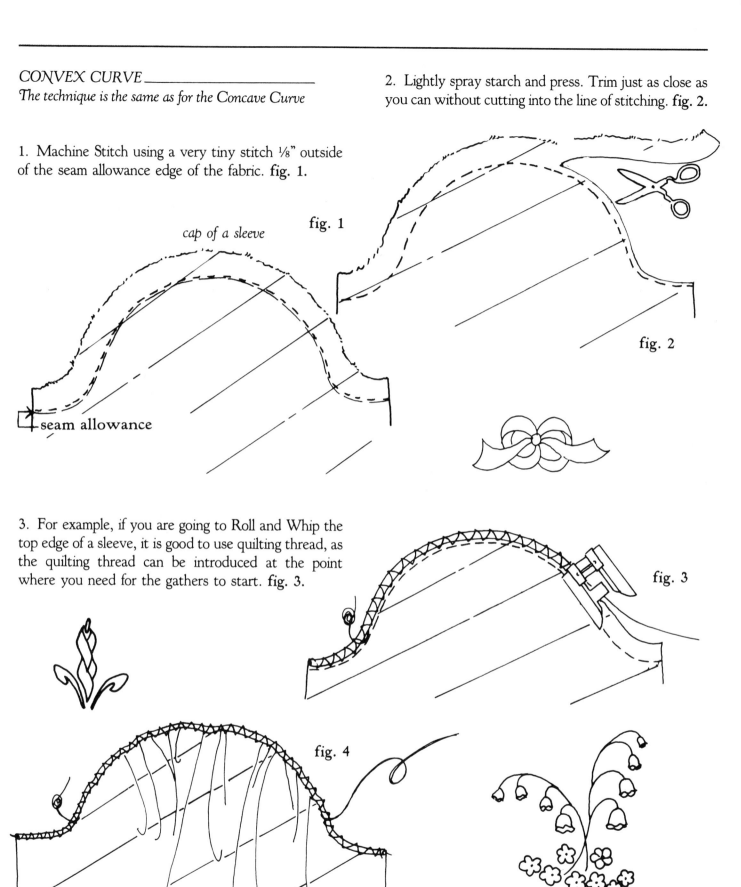

cap of a sleeve   fig. 1

seam allowance

fig. 2

fig. 3

fig. 4

ROLL, WHIP AND GATHER –

METHOD 1 – QUILTING THREAD

1. Make a BIG knot in the end of a piece of quilting thread which is longer than the strip of fabric. **fig. 1**.

2. Place the quilting thread under the presser foot and hold the quilting thread along the raw edge of the fabric. **fig. 2**.

3. Make sure that the needle clears the fabric edge as well as the quilting thread which is lying along side of the fabric. **fig. 3**.

4. The Zigzag Stitch will roll the raw edge of the fabric over the thread and encase it into the roll. **fig. 4**.

Machine Setting For Roll, Whip and Gather to make it look like a Hand Rolled, Whipped and Gathered edge:

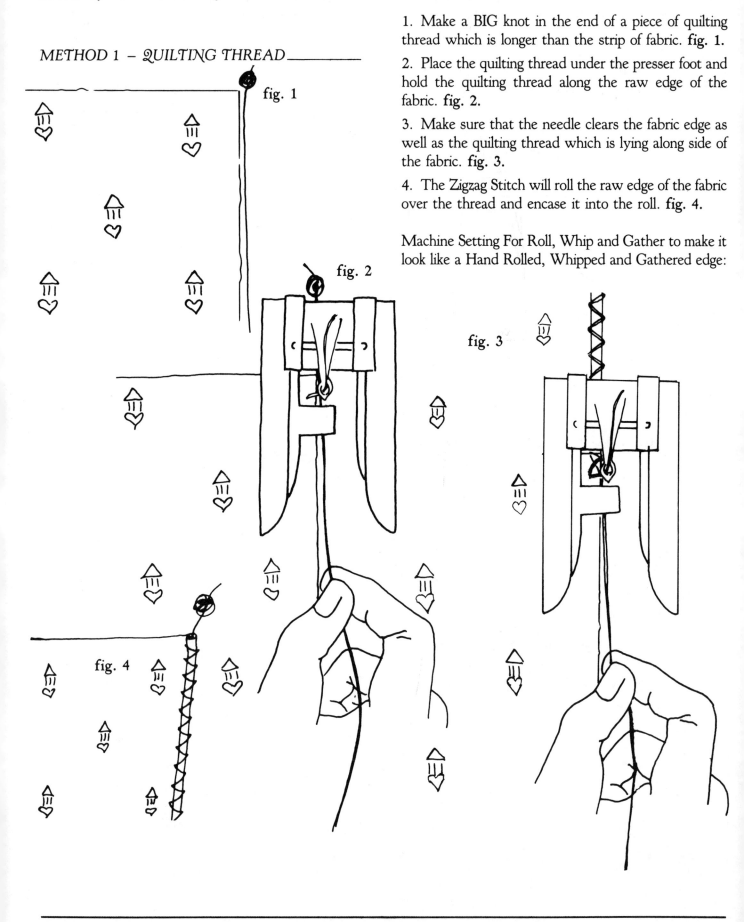

fig. 1

fig. 2

fig. 3

fig. 4

METHOD 2 – TWO THREAD PULL

This is an excellent method when using short strips of fabric which need to be rolled, whipped and gathered.

1. Pull both the top thread and the bobbin thread out of the sewing machine toward you. Pull the two threads the full length of the fabric strip to be gathered. **fig. 1.**

2. Place the fabric under the presser foot and hold the two threads along the fabric edge. **fig. 2.**

3. Zigzag, making sure that the needle clears the fabric edge. **fig. 3.**

4. Pull the two threads to gather the fabric. **fig. 4.**

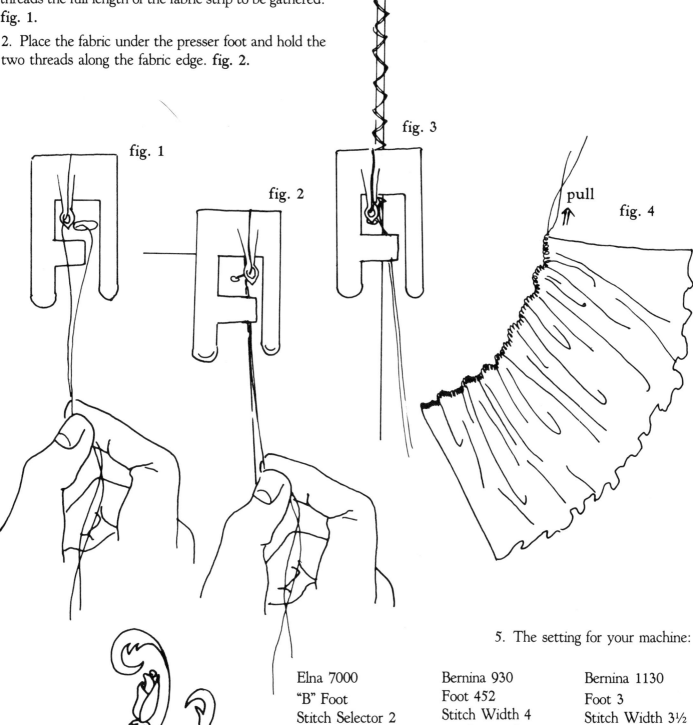

fig. 1

fig. 2

fig. 3

pull
fig. 4

5. The setting for your machine:

Elna 7000	Bernina 930	Bernina 1130
"B" Foot	Foot 452	Foot 3
Stitch Selector 2	Stitch Width 4	Stitch Width 3½
Width 3.5	Stitch Length 1½	Stitch Length 1½
Stitch Length 1.2		

Set the stitch length long enough so that when you straight stitch you will be able to pull up the threads and have nice gathers.

1. Make one row of long machine stitching. **fig. 1.**

2. Carefully zigzag over this so that the needle is off the fabric edge on the right and just encasing the basting line of stitching on the left side. **fig. 2.**

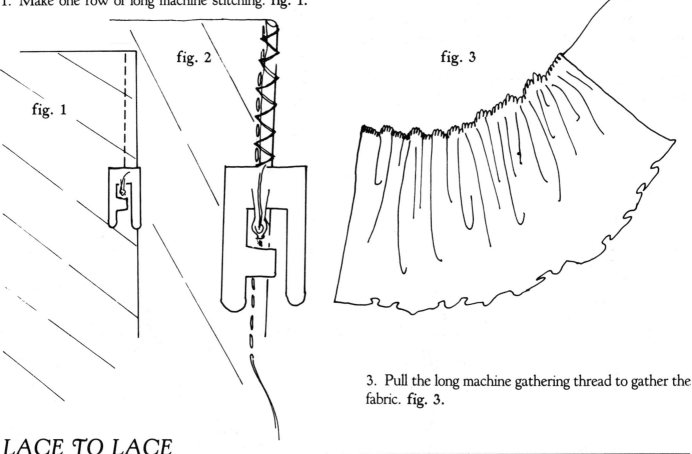

fig. 2

fig. 1

fig. 3

3. Pull the long machine gathering thread to gather the fabric. **fig. 3.**

LACE TO LACE _____

METHOD 1
SIDE-BY-SIDE OR BUTT METHOD

Place the laces side-by-side and right sides up. **fig. 1.** Set the machine width so that the needle will encompass the lace heading of each strip of lace as it Zigzags.

The width of the stitch will be determined by the width of the lace heading. You want the width of the stitch to be just wide enough to encase both of the lace headings. **fig. 2.**

The length is really a personal choice; however, I like to use the length of 1.2 on the Elna # 7000, and 1½ on the Bernina 1130.

I use the "A" Foot on the Elna 7000, and the # 10 when doing Lace to Lace on the Bernina 1130.

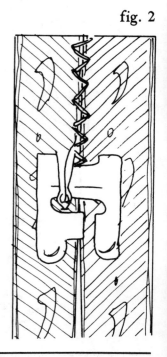

fig. 2

fig. 1

METHOD 2
STACK METHOD OR RIGHT SIDES TOGETHER

Place the lace right sides together. One on top of the other. Zigzag the laces together, making sure that the needle catches the entire lace heading of both pieces of lace. Press the lace back flat. **fig. 3.**

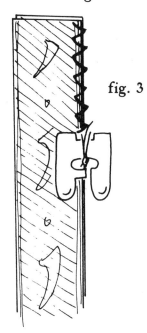

fig. 3

METHOD 3
USING THE STRAIGHT STITCH OF THE SEWING MACHINE

If studying some antique clothing where lace has been joined together, you will find that many garments were joined together using the straight stitch of the sewing machine. The lace edges are slightly overlapped and a very short stitch length used. **fig. 4 and 5.**

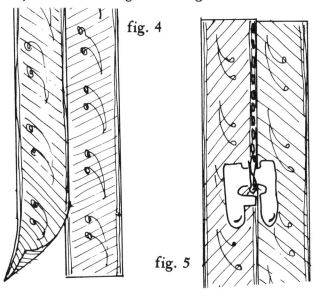

fig. 4

fig. 5

METHOD 4
LACE TO LACE WITH FAGOTING BY HAND

1. Baste two strips of lace to paper, leaving about ¼" between the two lace edges.

Note: If working with lace in straight lines, graph paper is ideal for pinning the lace to; and if working with the laces in a curve, draw the placement on paper before beginning.

2. To begin, tie off the thread by making a small knot in the thread and bring the threaded needle up in the lace heading. **fig. 6.** Notice the holes in the lace and use them as a grid for making the stitches. Stitch in each hole or every other hole in the lace, depending on the desired effect.

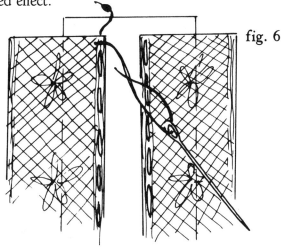

fig. 6

a. On the right side, the thread is held below the needle. The needle enters from the right side and points to the left. **fig. 7.**

fig. 7

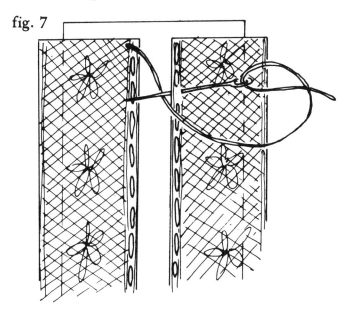

b. On the left side, the thread is down and behind the needle as the needle enters the left side of lace heading pointing to the right. **fig. 8.**

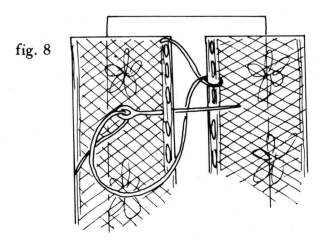

fig. 8

Complete the fagoting by moving with each stitch and alternating stitches at the lace edges. **fig. 9.**

Fasten off with a back stitch or two. Remove the basting thread.

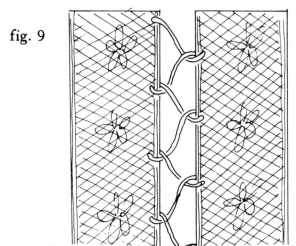

fig. 9

Note: Fagoting may be used between Lace and Lace, Lace and Fabric, Ribbon and Ribbon or Lace and Ribbon, or Lace and a Bias Strip. (Example would be a round collar. Fagoting is used between two finished edges.)

METHOD 5
Elna 7000 - Stitch Selector # 747

Use a stabilizer (a wash-away stabilizer is excellent) under the lace. Place the lace onto the stabilizer about ⅛" apart. Use the Stitch Selector # 747, a wing needle and increase the tension to about 7 or 9. If you need to baste the lace to hold in place, do so.

STRAIGHT EDGE LACE TO ENTREDEUX

METHOD 1

1. Trim one side of the entredeux. **fig. 1.**

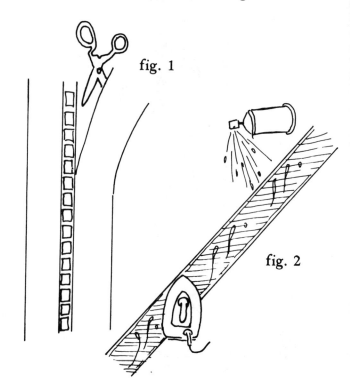

fig. 1

fig. 2

2. Lightly spray starch and press the lace. **fig. 2.**

3. Butt the entredeux's trimmed edge, side-by-side, with the lace edge. **fig. 3.**

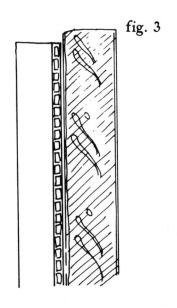

fig. 3

4. Set the length so that the needle goes into each hole of the entredeux and swings just wide enough to encase the heading of the lace. **fig. 4.**

The Elna 7000 length will be .8 for regular entredeux. The needle will go into each and every hole of the entredeux with this length.

The 1130 Bernina length will be just slightly below the 1 mark.

Note: Remember, the width of the lace heading will require different width settings, depending on the width of the lace heading.

5. Zigzag the lace to the entredeux.

6. Press.

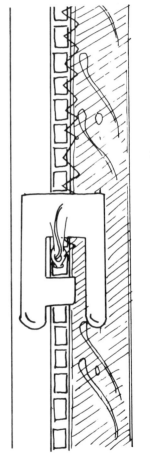

fig. 4

METHOD 2 _____

1. Trim one side of the entredeux.

2. Lightly spray starch and press the lace and entredeux.

3. Place the entredeux's trimmed edge, right sides to the right side of the lace, with the lace edge even with the entredeux. Entredeux on top facing up.

4. Set the length so that the needle goes into each hole of the entredeux and swings wide enough to clear the heading of the lace. **fig. 1.**

Machine setting for the length will be the same each time you use regular entredeux. .8 for the Elna 7000 and just below the 1 mark for the 1130 Bernina.

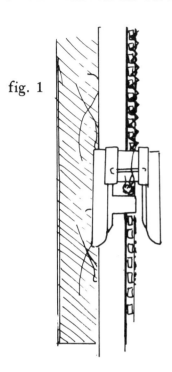

fig. 1

GATHERED LACE TO ENTREDEUX

METHOD 1 _____

1. Gather the lace by pulling the *very top* thread in the lace heading. **fig. 1.**

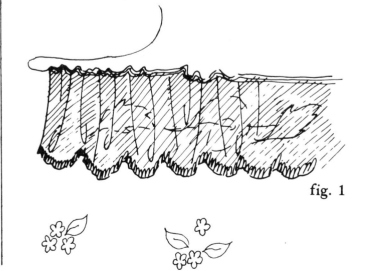

fig. 1

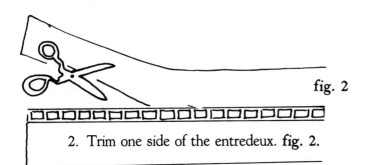

fig. 2

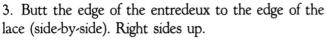

2. Trim one side of the entredeux. **fig. 2.**

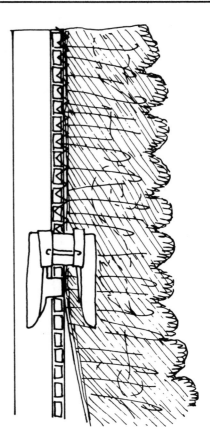

fig. 3

3. Butt the edge of the entredeux to the edge of the lace (side-by-side). Right sides up.

4. Zigzag with a stitch width that goes into each hole of the entredeux and encompasses the lace heading. **fig. 3.**

METHOD 2

1. Gather the lace by pulling the top thread in the lace heading. **fig. 1.**

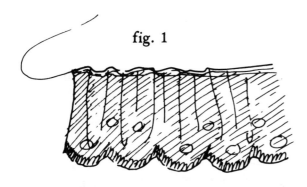

fig. 1

fig. 2

2. Trim one side of the entredeux. **fig. 2.**

3. Place the entredeux's trimmed edge *on top* of the lace, right sides together and the edges even. Entredeux does not need to be clipped.

4. Zigzag together going into each hole of the entredeux and off the edge. **fig. 3.**

fig. 3

METHOD 1 _____

1. The setting for your machine will be the same as the setting for the Roll and Whip.

2. Trim all fuzzies from the fabric edge.

3. Place the right side of the lace onto the right side of the fabric, leaving about ⅛" to ¼" of the fabric edge showing. In other words, the lace edge will be about ¼" from the fabric's raw edge. **fig. 1.**

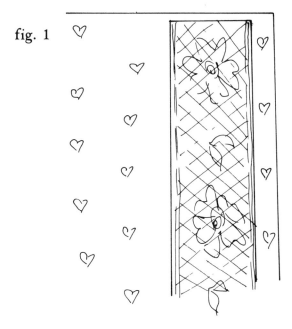

fig. 1

4. Zigzag, encompassing the entire lace heading, and the needle clearing the fabric edge. The fabric edge will roll and completely fold into the lace heading as you stitch. **fig. 2 and fig. 3.** _____

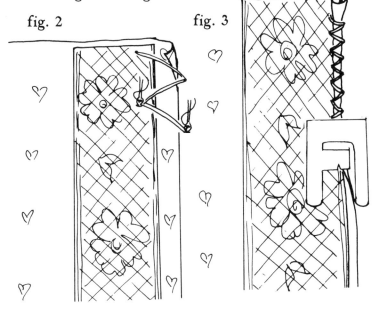

fig. 2   fig. 3

Note: REMEMBER ⅛" to ¼" of the fabric edge is exposed. If you put the edge of the lace even with the fabric edge, the lace will probably pull away from the fabric.

5. Press the lace and fabric open with the seam toward the fabric. **fig. 4.**

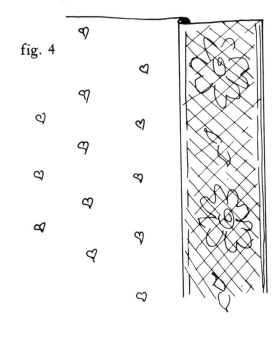

fig. 4

METHOD 2 _____

1. Roll and Whip the fabric edge. **fig. 1.**

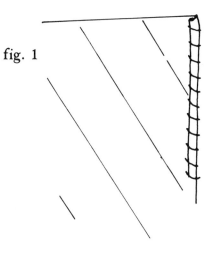

fig. 1

2. Place the right side of the lace edge to and even with the right side of the rolled and whipped fabric edge. **fig. 2.**

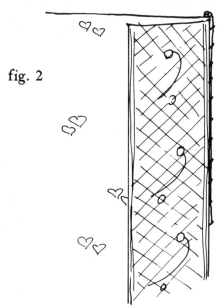

fig. 2

3. Zigzag Stitch. The needle will encompass the lace heading and the rolled fabric edge as it zigs to the left, and will clear the edge as it zags to the right. **fig. 3.** Finished. **fig. 4.**

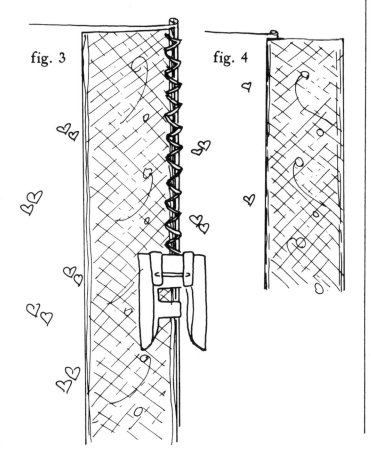

fig. 3

fig. 4

METHOD 3

1. Place the lace edge ¼" from the raw edge of the fabric. The wrong side of the lace will be to the right side of the fabric. **fig. 1.**

fig. 1

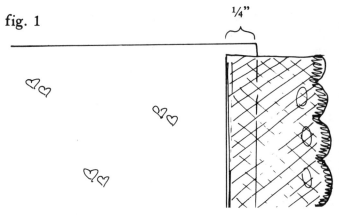

¼"

2. Straight Stitch on the lace heading using very tiny stitches. **fig. 2.**

fig. 2

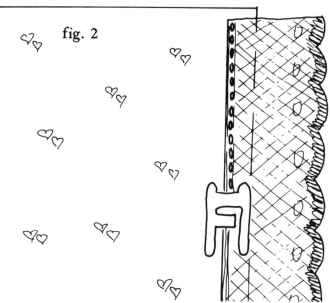

3. Fold the lace edge back, leaving the raw edge of the fabric exposed. Trim to ⅛". **fig. 3.**

fig. 3

4. Roll and Whip the fabric edge, or finish the edge so that the fabric will not ravel out. **fig. 4**.

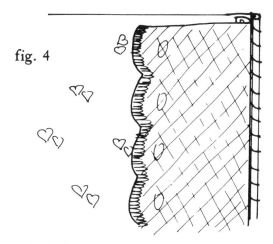

fig. 4

5. Finished. **fig. 5**.

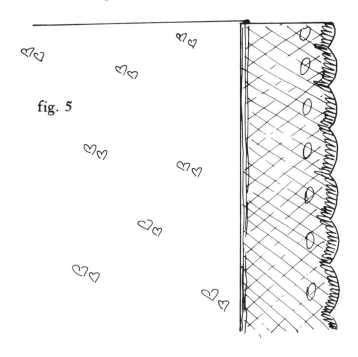

fig. 5

METHOD 4 _____
FAGOTING

1. Baste the fabric and the lace to paper or some sort of medium which will stabilize the two.

Leave about ¼" between the fabric edge and the edge of the lace. You may leave more or less, but the ¼" looks very pretty.

2. Work the Fagoting Stitch between the fabric edge and the edge of the lace. Begin with the thread on the left with the knot in the fabric. **fig. 1**.

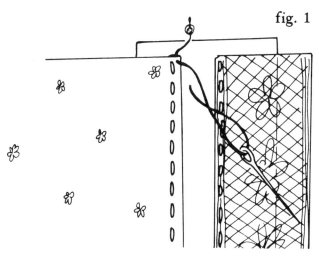

fig. 1

3. The needle will travel to the right to the lace heading and will catch the entire lace heading. The thread is held below the needle. The needle enters the lace heading and points to the left. **fig. 2**.

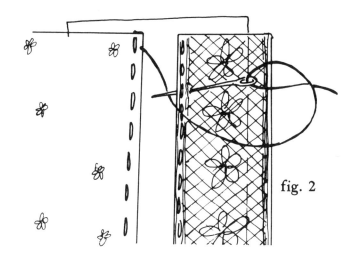

fig. 2

4. Again, back to the fabric edge and take a stitch. Catch only the edge of the fabric going all the way through the fold. The needle enters from the outside and goes to the right. **fig. 3**.

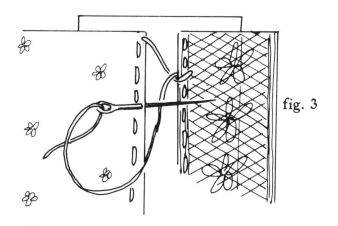

fig. 3

5. Continue to alternate these stitches until the lace and fabric are joined together. **fig. 4.**

6. Remove the basting threads and remove the fabric/lace from the guide. Press the seam to set the stitches.

fig. 4

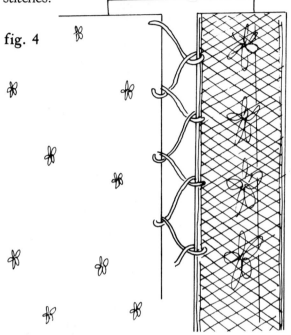

METHOD 5
PIN STITCH BY HAND (Point de Paris)

1. Tiny Baste the lace to the fabric. Press so that the lace will lie flat on the fabric. The use of spray starch lightly used on the fabric helps tremendously sometimes.

2. Begin stitching by securing the thread with a small Back Stitch.

Use a tapestry needle, # 24 is the one most commonly used, and lightweight thread.

a. Come up at point A. This stitch is in the lace heading. **fig. 1.**

fig. 1

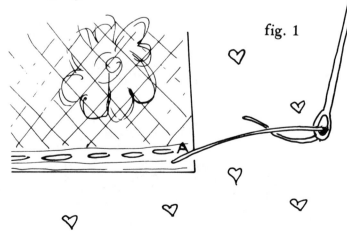

b. Insert the needle into the fabric directly below point A at point B, and move the needle to the left two or three threads in the fabric and come out at point C. **fig. 2.** Both point B and point C are below the lace and made in the fabric.

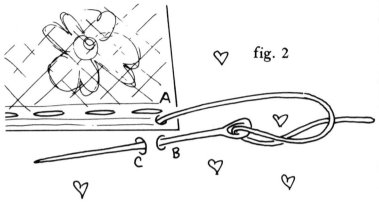

fig. 2

c. Take the needle back and insert at point B.

d. From point B, bring the needle forward and come up at point D, which is in the lace heading and just above point C. **fig. 3.**

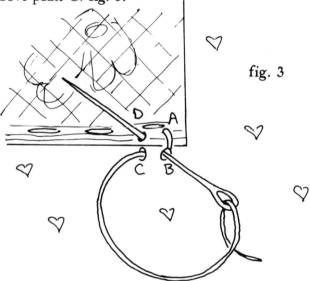

fig. 3

It is important to pull each stitch firmly in order to see the hole and be able to go back into the hole for the next stitch.

e. From point D, the needle will enter into the hole at point C and move to the left two or three threads and come out at a new point, which will be E. **fig. 4.**

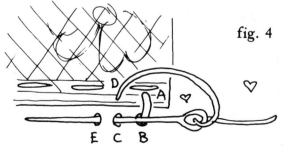

fig. 4

f. From point E, the needle will go back to the right and enter point C and move up and out at point F, which is in the lace heading. **fig. 5.**

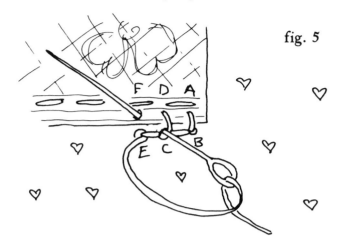

fig. 5

Continue this procedure until all the lace is attached. fig. 6.

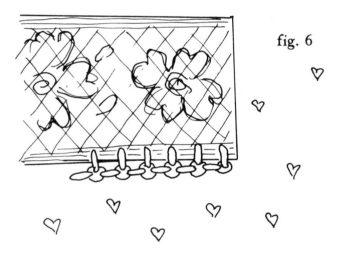

fig. 6

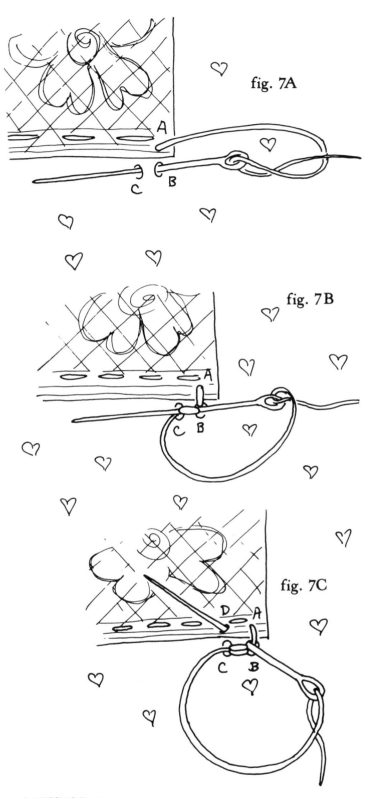

fig. 7A

fig. 7B

fig. 7C

OPTION:

Note: If working with some poly-cotton fabrics or heavier fabrics such as broadcloth, it may be more satisfactory to stitch from B to C two times. **fig. 7A and 7B**, ending with the needle entering B to point D. **fig. 7C.** By adding the extra B to C, the holes become more visible.

When ending a thread, take the needle to the back side and weave the thread through several of the stitches. Then to begin again, start from the back and weave the new thread through some of the diagonal stitches again.

METHOD 6 _____
PIN STITCH BY MACHINE

On the Elna 7000, select stitch # 746. Set the machine for 1.8 width, or a width that will just go into the lace heading. The length is 3.7, but if you prefer for it to be a little bit longer stitch, then you may select a longer or shorter stitch length.

GATHERED LACE TO FLAT FABRIC

1. Gather the lace by pulling the very top thread in the lace heading and distribute the gathers evenly.

2. Place the lace edge ⅛" to ¼" from the raw edge of the fabric. The right side of the lace will be to the right side of the fabric.

Pin and Baste to hold in place. **fig. 1.**

3. Set the width of the Zigzag so that it goes off the edge of the fabric on the right and into the lace heading on the left. The edge of the fabric will roll up and over the edge of the lace. **fig. 2.**

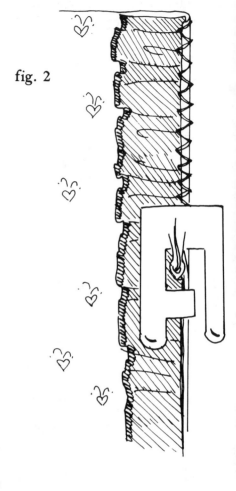

fig. 2

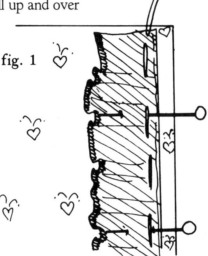

fig. 1

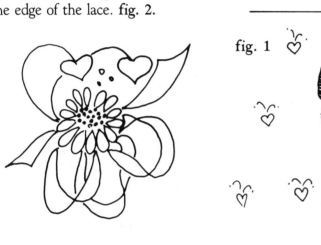

ENTREDEUX TO STRAIGHT EDGE FABRIC

METHOD # 1

1. Do not trim entredeux.

2. Spray starch and press entredeux.

3. Place the entredeux and fabric rights sides together. Straight Stitch close to the entredeux holes. **fig. 1.**

4. Trim the edge of the entredeux batiste and the fabric edge to about ⅛". **fig. 2.**

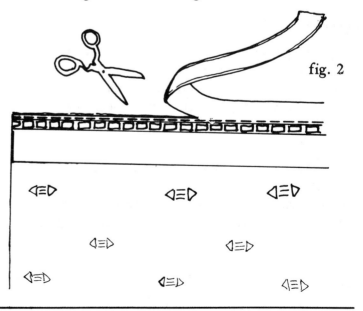

fig. 1

fig. 2

5. Set the machine to Zigzag into each hole of the entredeux and off. **Note:** The holes of the entredeux are facing up so that you can see where the needle is going. **fig. 3.**

6. The fabric edge and the batiste edge of the entredeux will roll together.

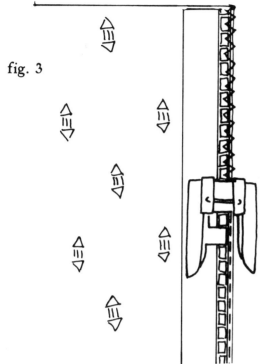

fig. 3

Follow the steps above 1 through 4

5. Set the machine to Zigzag so that it will zig *up to the* entredeux. DO NOT GO INTO THE HOLES. And, will clear the *edge as it* zags to the right. **fig. 4.**

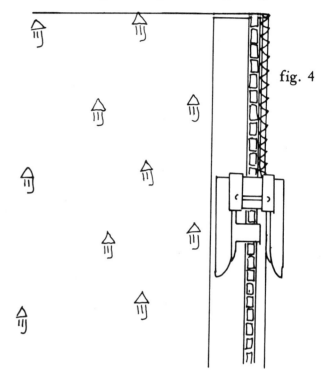

fig. 4

METHOD # 3 _____

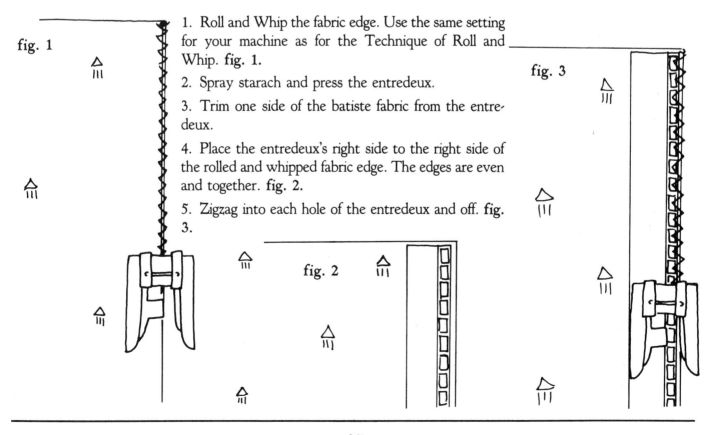

fig. 1

1. Roll and Whip the fabric edge. Use the same setting for your machine as for the Technique of Roll and Whip. **fig. 1.**

2. Spray starach and press the entredeux.

3. Trim one side of the batiste fabric from the entredeux.

4. Place the entredeux's right side to the right side of the rolled and whipped fabric edge. The edges are even and together. **fig. 2.**

5. Zigzag into each hole of the entredeux and off. **fig. 3.**

fig. 2

fig. 3

ENTREDEUX TO GATHERED FABRIC

METHOD 1 _____

1. Roll, Whip and Gather the fabric edge.

2. Trim one side of the entredeux. Press.

3. Place the right side of the gathered fabric edge to the trimmed edge of the entredeux. Edges even. Entredeux on top. **fig. 1.**

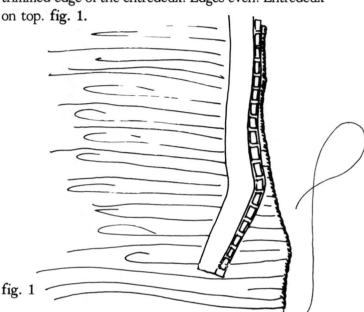

fig. 1

4. Zigzag going into each hole of the entredeux and off, making sure that the needle clears the edge as it zags. **fig. 2.**

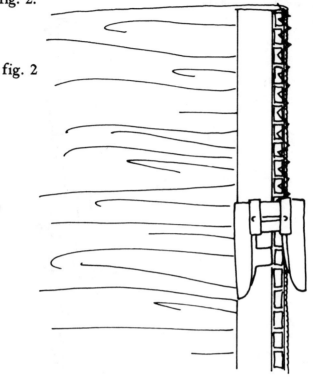

fig. 2

METHOD 2 _____

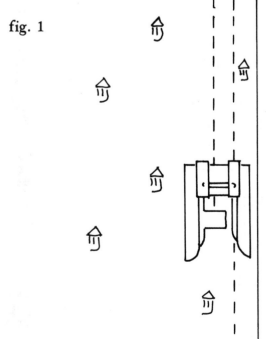

fig. 1

1. Run two rows of long machine stitching at the edge of the fabric, with the first row being about ¼" from the raw edge. Pull the bobbin thread and gather the fabric the correct amount. **fig. 1 and 2.**

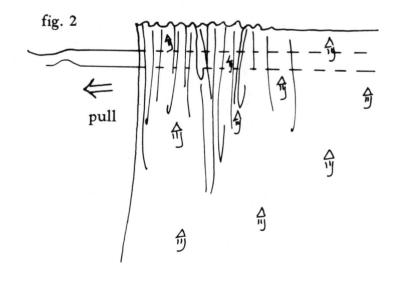

fig. 2

pull

2. Place the right side of a piece of untrimmed entredeux to the right side of the gathered fabric. The raw fabric edge and the edge of the entredeux will be about even.

3. Straight Stitch at the edge of the "row of holes" – DO NOT STITCH INTO THE HOLES OF THE ENTREDEUX. **fig. 3.**

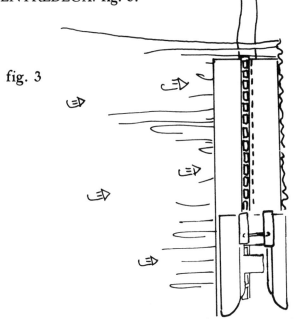

fig. 3

4. Trim the excess fabric . . . both from the entredeux's edge and the fabric edge. Leave about ⅛". **fig. 4.**

fig. 4

5. Zigzag over the edge, letting the needle zig into each and every hole of the entredeux and zag off to clear the fabric edge. **fig. 5.** This is a very strong method of attaching entredeux to gathered fabric and is excellent for use where there is a lot of stress.

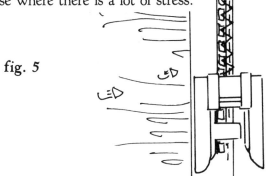

fig. 5

OPTIONAL: Zigzag up to the holes of the entredeux and clear the fabric edge as the needle zags. **fig. 5.**

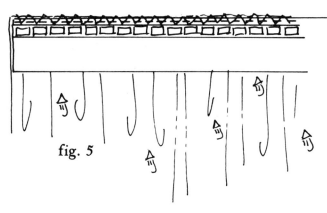

fig. 5

CUTTING AWAY FROM BEHIND LACE

1. Use a pair of blunt scissors and make a cut in the center of the fabric behind the lace. **fig. 1.**

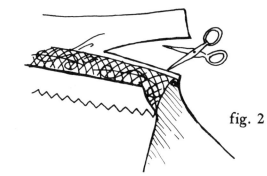

fig. 1

2. Fold the lace back toward you, letting the fabric which will be cut off extend away from you. Cut. **fig. 2.**

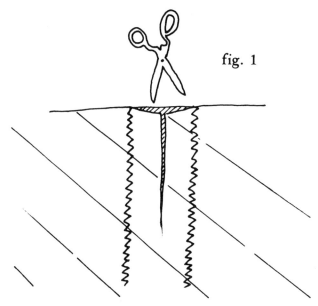

fig. 2

3. When trimming, excess fabric away from a lace edge. Hold the lace to you. Again, the fabric which will be cut away is extended away from you. **fig. 3.**

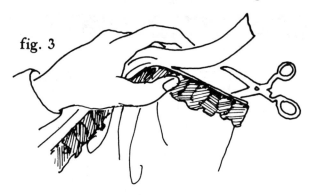

fig. 3

PULL A THREAD TO CUT OR STRAIGHTEN FABRIC

1. Clip at the appropriate place. **fig. A.**

2. Take hold of a thread running in the direction which you wish to cut. **fig. B.**

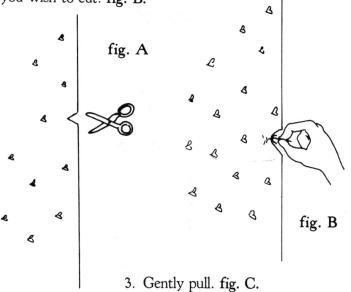

fig. A

fig. B

3. Gently pull. **fig. C.**

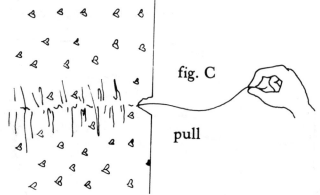

fig. C

pull

4. When the thread breaks, **fig. D**

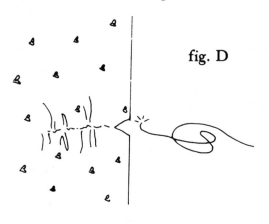

fig. D

5. Cut on the pulled thread line to the point where the thread broke. **fig. E.**

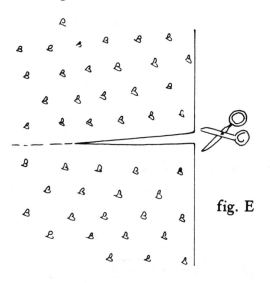

fig. E

6. Pick up another thread and pull and cut until the length/width to be straightened and cut has been obtained. **fig. F.**

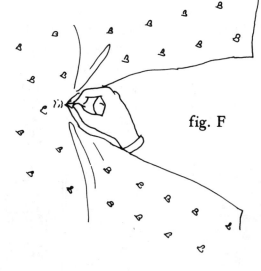

fig. F

TECHNIQUES WITH CHURCH DOLLS

AN OLD FASHION CHURCH DOLL

A long, long time ago, I am told,
Dolls like me were the thing of the day
Because little people went to church with mom and dad,
They had no other place to stay.

And, now that we are thinking so much of what used to be
I am very glad, you see.
For children can take along a doll like me,
And, I'll keep them quiet as can be.

Author Unknown

DIRECTIONS FOR THE BASIC CHURCH DOLL

Here are the Church Dolls in all their glory! Enjoy them! They are fun to do and a great teaching project to use when you need something small. Depending upon which one you choose to make will decide which techniques you will stitch. For example, there's the Fancy Band Doll which is ideal for the beginner. The Diamond Doll is great for learning how to miter lace and entredeux. The Heart Doll teaches how to miter and curve lace, as does the Tear Drop Doll. The Puffing Doll is perfect for learning how to do Puffing and the Scalloped Hem Doll will help you to master how to do the Scallop Hem. So, try one or try all . . . they're fun!

1. CUT ONE PIECE OF FABRIC 16" x 18". The choice of fabric is up to the individual – Swiss Batiste, Imperial Batiste, Broadcloth, etc.

2. Trace the face features which you desire onto the fabric. **fig. 1**. The eyes will be placed in the center about 3¾" from the top raw edge of the fabric. **fig. 2**.

The mouth will be centered slightly below the eyes. The mouth is very pretty to do using Shadow Embroidery. You may be just as creative as you like, stitching with as much or as little detail as you like.

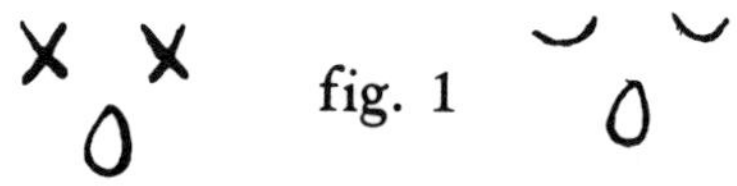

3. Choose the hemline finish you desire and complete the design.

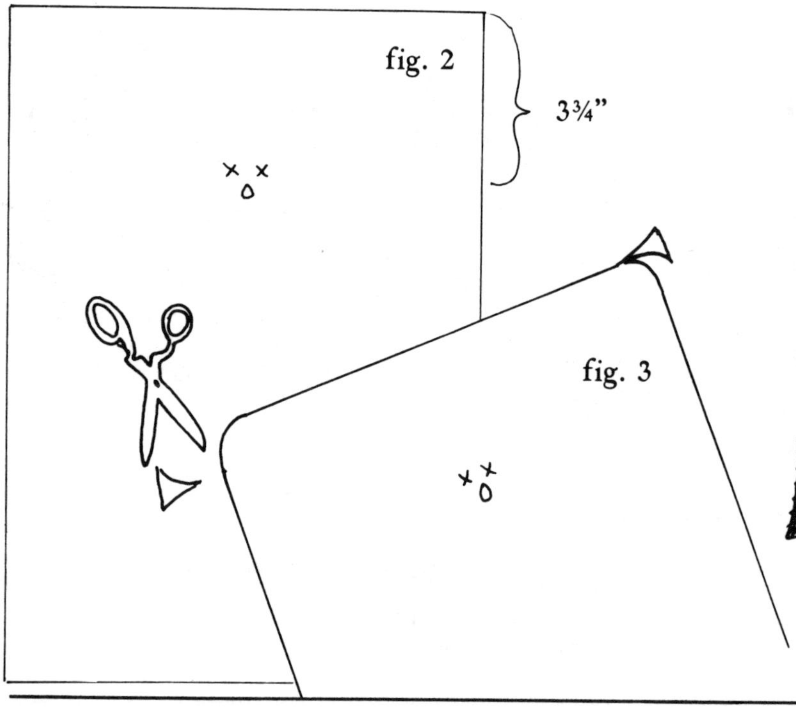

Just a few suggestions for hemlines for the Church Doll:

   a. Diamond
   b. Tear drop
   c. Heart
   d. Lace loops
   e. Fancy band
   f. Scalloped hem
   g. Continuous ovals
   h. Puffing
   i. Any combination your choice

4. After you have completed the hemline of your doll, round the two top corners. **fig. 3**. Roll and Whip the three unfinished sides. **fig. 4**.

fig. 1

fig. 2

3¾"

fig. 3

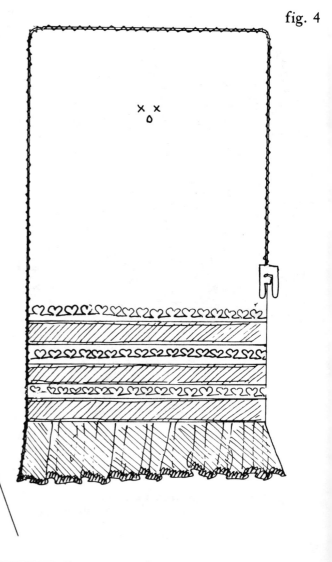

fig. 4

5. Fold the top edge back about 3", or to the point that the face will be on the front. **fig. 5**. Place about 1¾" to 2" ball of fiber-fill or cotton behind the face. **fig. 6**.

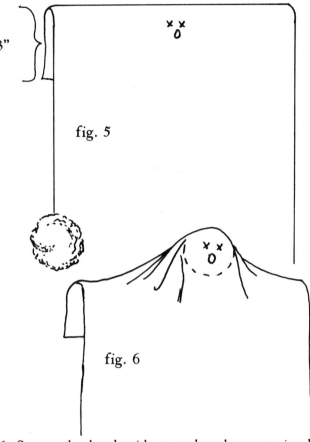

3"

fig. 5

fig. 6

6. Secure the head with a cord or heavy twine by wrapping and forming a neck. I like to secure the cord by tying it off and pushing the ends of the cord under the wraps which form the neck. This way, the cord can be taken loose and the doll washed and ironed as a flat piece of fabric. **fig. 7**. You are the judge as to how fat or skinny you make the neck of your doll.

Smooth the head (especially the face) by pulling the fabric down from the cord (neck). The doll is now ready to have the hair made if you choose to have hair.

If you choose to make hair using French Knots, bullion or any embroidery of your choice, choose the color of thread and type of thread to be used to suit you and your doll. I like using the Six-strand Embroidery Floss. Use six strands of floss if making French Knots for the hair. If making Bullion ropes, use about 3 strands and wrap about 30 to 40 times, as this will give you a curl with the rope.

Make a knot in your thread and bring the needle (milliners) up at the point where you want the first curl to be. **fig. A**.

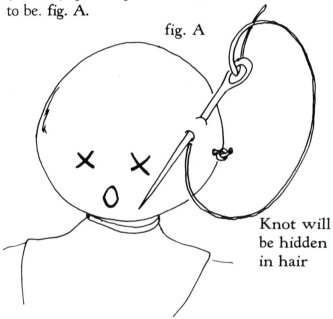

fig. A

Knot will be hidden in hair

Wrap the needle 30 to 40 times with the thread which you are holding with your left hand. **fig. B**.

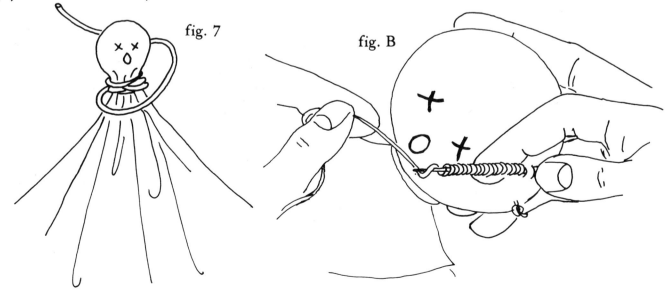

fig. 7

fig. B

Make sure that you hold the wraps with both your index finger and thumb when you start to pull. The wraps will be on the needle and as you pull the needle out, the wraps will be held between your index finger and thumb. Hold until you have pulled the thread to the end. The thumb was left out of the illustration in order for you to see what the wraps look like on the needle. **fig. C.**

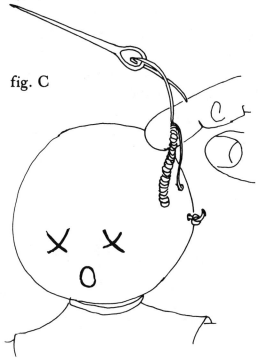

fig. C

Since you are wanting the Bullion ropes to look like hair, place them randomly on the head **fig. D** and continue to make them to cover as much or as little of the head as you prefer. **fig. E.**

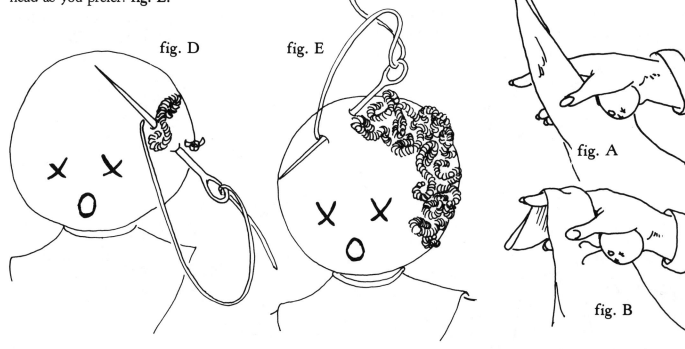

fig. D   fig. E

fig. A

fig. B

TYING THE ARMS

7. Fold the two sides back until they meet. **fig. 8.**

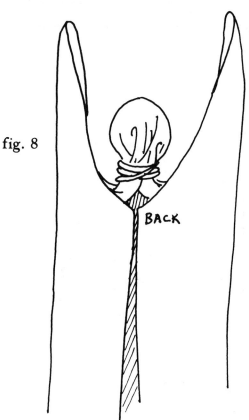

fig. 8

BACK

8. Follow the diagrams for tying the arms.

a. Hold the doll in your right hand with the left side of the doll's arm up. **fig. A.**

b. Let the upper left corner fold over the index finger to the back. **fig. B.**

c. Bring the corner under and up to the front. **fig. C.**

fig. C

d. Remove your index finger and as you do so, slip your left thumb into the opening. **fig. D.**

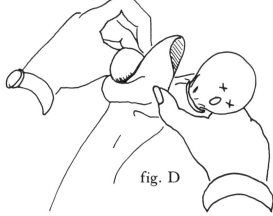

fig. D

Push the corner into the space which was left by the right index finger. Use your left index finger and thumb to guide the corner through the opening. **fig. E.**

e. Hold the corner with your left thumb and index finger and pull the corner through.

Pull and adjust the fabric until the fold looks like an arm — the point or corner of the fabric which has been pulled through becomes the hand. **fig. F.**

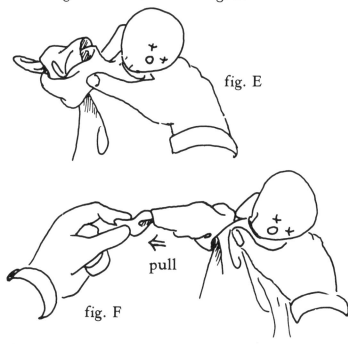

fig. E

pull

fig. F

f. For the right side, follow the diagrams as shown, and this time the doll will be held in your left hand with the fabric folded over the left index finger. Begin with **fig. A** and continue as you did for the left arm. **figs. G-J.**

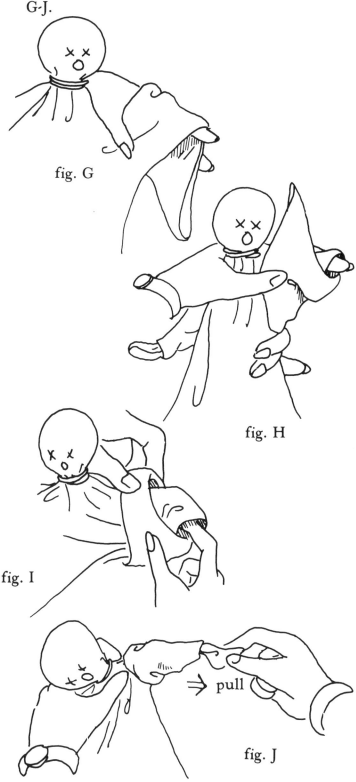

fig. G

fig. H

fig. I

pull

fig. J

The doll is now ready for you to make a bonnet and collar of your choosing. And, when all the little "things" are finished, you have a Church Doll.

THE DIAMOND

1. Using the lace guide, measure and mark a piece of Lace Insertion. Fold the piece of lace and place on the guide. Mark. Your lace will look like **fig. 1** after it has been marked and opened out flat.

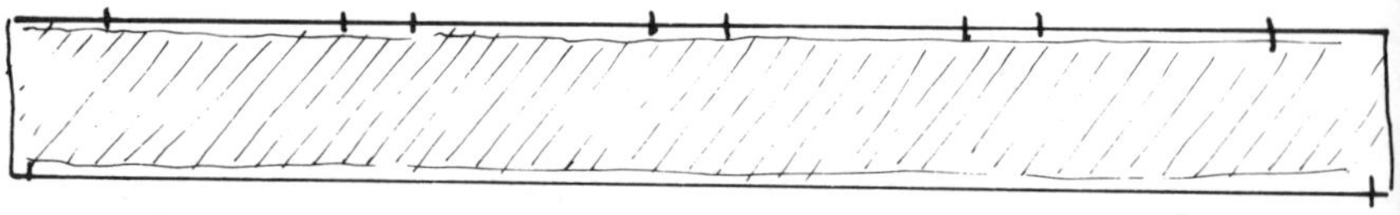

fig. 1

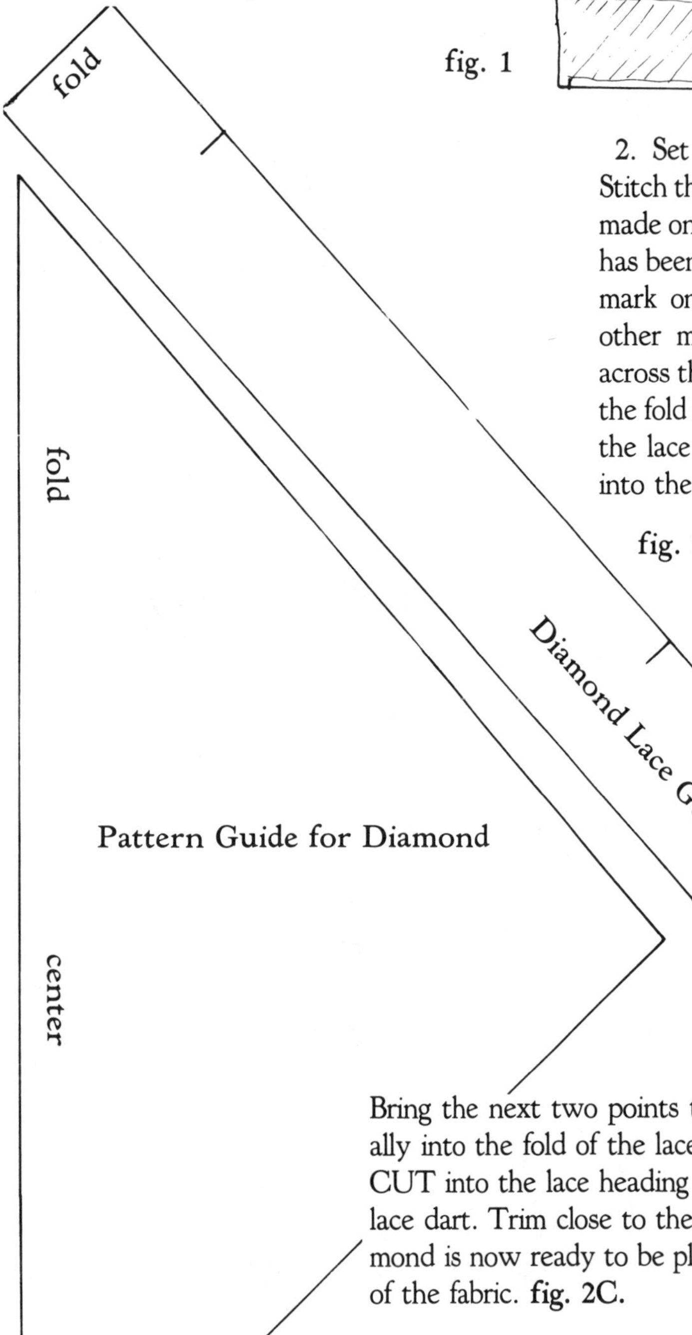

fold

fold

Pattern Guide for Diamond

Diamond Lace Guide

center

2. Set your machine for a narrow Zigzag setting. Stitch the lace together at the markings which you have made on the lace. Example: Fold the piece of lace which has been marked with the right sides together. The first mark on each end of the lace will be together. The other marks will also be together. Stitch diagonally across the two cut ends of the lace first. **fig. 2A.** Stitch the fold end of the lace diagonally but DO NOT go into the lace heading at the narrow end of the dart. Stitch into the fold of the lace. **fig. 2B.**

fig. 2A

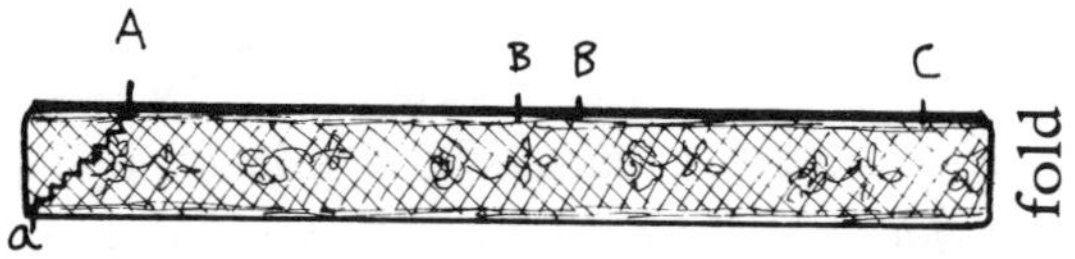

A   B B   C

fold

fig. 2B

A

fold

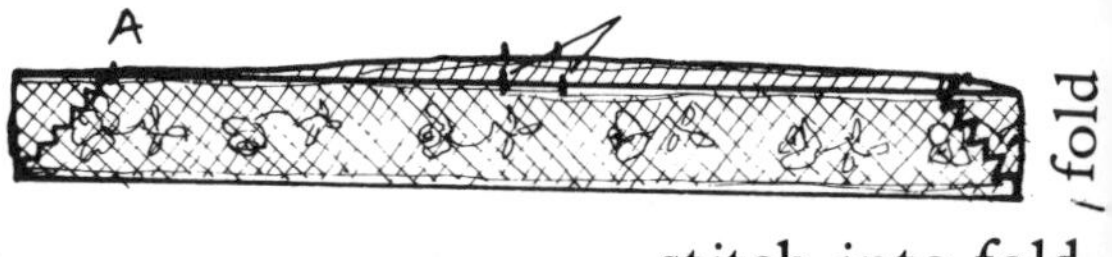

stitch into fold

Bring the next two points together and stitch diagonally into the fold of the lace. DO NOT STITCH OR CUT into the lace heading at the narrow point of the lace dart. Trim close to the Zigzag stitching. The Diamond is now ready to be placed onto the bottom edge of the fabric. **fig. 2C.**

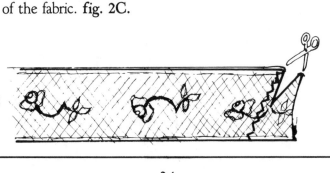

fig. 2C

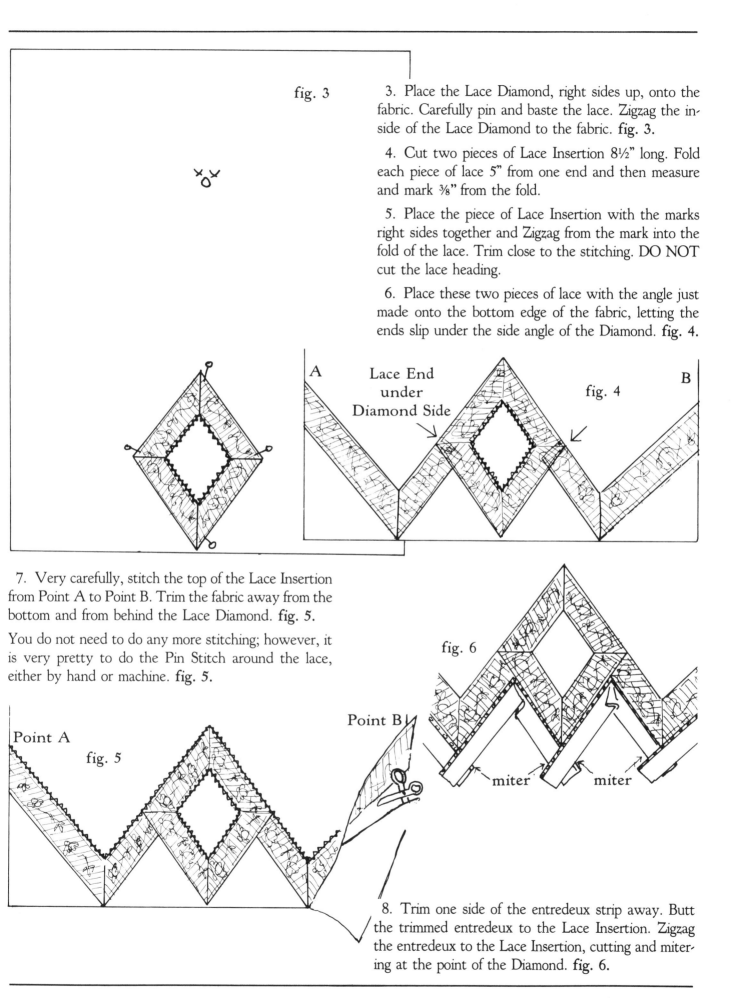

fig. 3

3. Place the Lace Diamond, right sides up, onto the fabric. Carefully pin and baste the lace. Zigzag the inside of the Lace Diamond to the fabric. **fig. 3.**

4. Cut two pieces of Lace Insertion 8½" long. Fold each piece of lace 5" from one end and then measure and mark ⅜" from the fold.

5. Place the piece of Lace Insertion with the marks right sides together and Zigzag from the mark into the fold of the lace. Trim close to the stitching. DO NOT cut the lace heading.

6. Place these two pieces of lace with the angle just made onto the bottom edge of the fabric, letting the ends slip under the side angle of the Diamond. **fig. 4.**

A Lace End under Diamond Side fig. 4 B

7. Very carefully, stitch the top of the Lace Insertion from Point A to Point B. Trim the fabric away from the bottom and from behind the Lace Diamond. **fig. 5.**

You do not need to do any more stitching; however, it is very pretty to do the Pin Stitch around the lace, either by hand or machine. **fig. 5.**

Point A   fig. 5

Point B

fig. 6

miter   miter

8. Trim one side of the entredeux strip away. Butt the trimmed entredeux to the Lace Insertion. Zigzag the entredeux to the Lace Insertion, cutting and mitering at the point of the Diamond. **fig. 6.**

MITERING THE ENTREDEUX

a. As you approach the end (at the corner or angle of the lace), continue stitching for a few more stitches. **fig. 6A.**

b. Cut the entredeux off leaving about ½" tail.

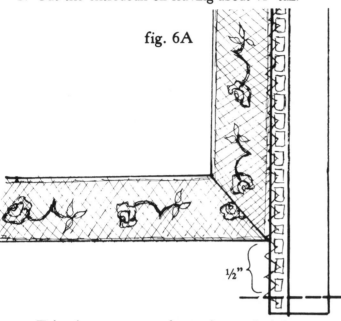

fig. 6A

½"

e. After the entredeux has been stitched to the lace, trim the remaining side of the entredeux away. **fig. 7**

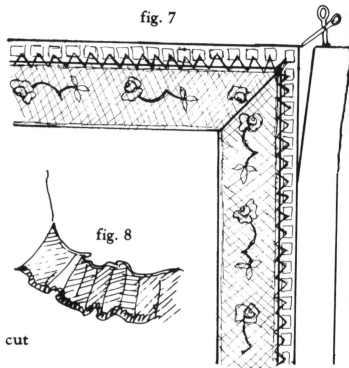

fig. 7

fig. 8

cut

c. Take the next piece of entredeux, which has one side trimmed away, and place the end over the end just stitched. Match up the hole at the corner so that one hole is on top of the other hole.

d. Begin stitching three or four holes before the corner where the holes of the entredeux have been matched up. **fig. 6B.**

9. Gather the lace edging by pulling the top thread of the heading to fit the entredeux. **fig. 8.**

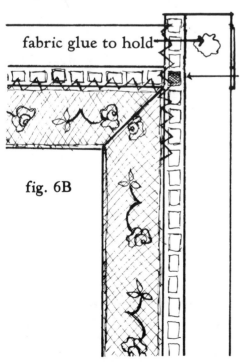

fabric glue to hold

one hole
on top
of the
other

fig. 6B

fig. 9

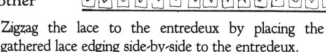

MITERING LACE EDGING

Zigzag the lace to the entredeux by placing the gathered lace edging side-by-side to the entredeux.

needle down

10. Miter the lace edging at the point.

a. As you arrive at the corner where the lace needs to be mitered, leave the needle in the down position in the hole of the entredeux at the corner. This is the hole with the two pieces of entredeux . . . one on top of the other where the entredeux was mitered. **fig. 9.** (DO NOT HAVE GATHERS right at the point. Leave about ½" free without gathers.)

b. Leave the needle in the down position in the hole of the entredeux, raise the presser foot of the machine, and fold the lace to the right so that the fold of the lace is lying along side the edge of the lace.

c. Hold the lace in this position **fig. 10** . . . and turn the lace so that the next side to have lace edging attached is in front of you.

fig. 10

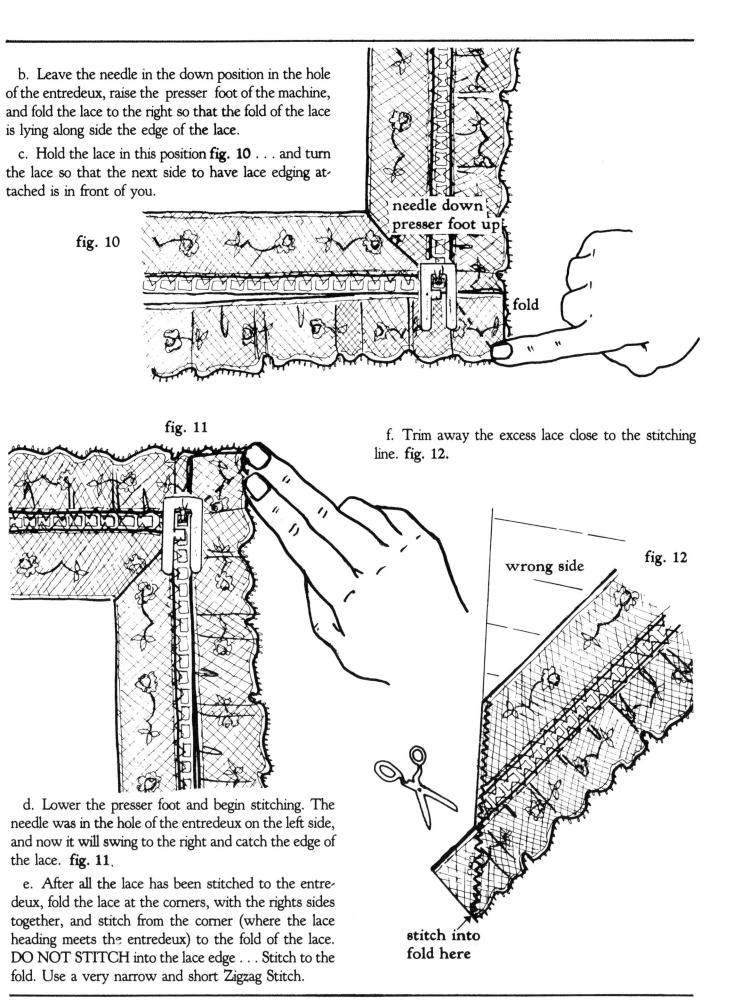

needle down
presser foot up

fold

fig. 11

f. Trim away the excess lace close to the stitching line. **fig. 12.**

wrong side

fig. 12

d. Lower the presser foot and begin stitching. The needle was in the hole of the entredeux on the left side, and now it will swing to the right and catch the edge of the lace. **fig. 11**.

e. After all the lace has been stitched to the entredeux, fold the lace at the corners, with the rights sides together, and stitch from the corner (where the lace heading meets the entredeux) to the fold of the lace. DO NOT STITCH into the lace edge . . . Stitch to the fold. Use a very narrow and short Zigzag Stitch.

stitch into
fold here

11. The bottom of the doll is now finished and ready for the sides to be finished, etc. fig. 13.

fig. 13

1. Use the guide and mark a piece of Lace Insertion by folding the piece of lace in half and placing onto the guide. Note that the guide shows only one half of the guide. Fold and place the 22" piece of lace on the fold of the lace guide and transfer the marking to the lace. **fig. 1. (LACE GUIDE)**

2. With the lace folded in half, stitch from one dot to the other at the cut ends. To simplify, you will stitch from dot "A" to dot "B." Then stitch from dot "C" to the fold. Do NOT stitch into the lace heading. Stitch into the fold. **fig. 2.** Stitch using a very short and narrow Zigzag setting. Using the Elna # 7000, set the machine for a Zigzag width 1.2 and stitch length .6. For the Bernina # 1130, set the Zigzag stitch width to 1 and the stitch length to 1.

Trim the seams close to the stitching.

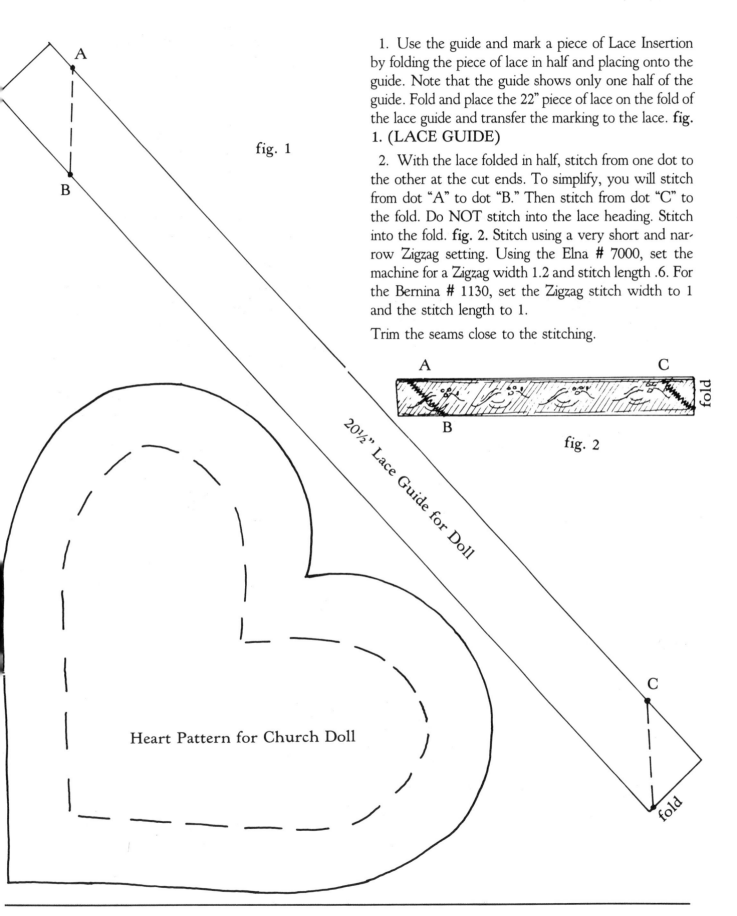

fig. 1

A

B

20½" Lace Guide for Doll

C

fold

A   C

B

fold

fig. 2

Heart Pattern for Church Doll

3. Trace the outline of the heart onto the bottom of the church doll fabric. **fig. 3**.

4. Place the lace onto the fabric which has the outline of the heart drawn onto it. **fig. 4**.

fig. 3

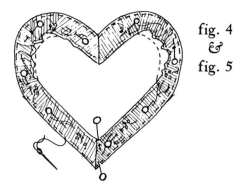

fig. 4
&
fig. 5

5. Baste the lace to the fabric. Baste the outside lace heading. **fig. 5**. Very gently pull the very top thread of the inside lace heading until the lace is perfectly flat. **fig. 6**.

Stitch the inside of the lace heart using a very narrow and short Zigzag Stitch. **fig. 7**.

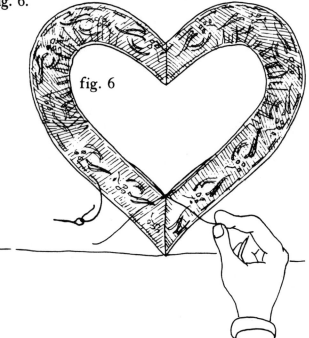

fig. 6

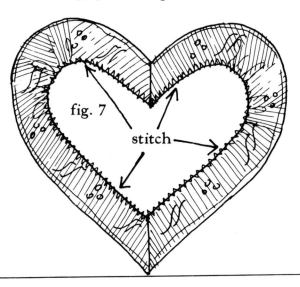

fig. 7

stitch

6. Cut two pieces of Lace Insertion 8½" long. Pull the top thread to curve the lace slightly. Pin the ends of the lace under the heart side. Baste on the outside edge. **fig. 8**.

fig. 8

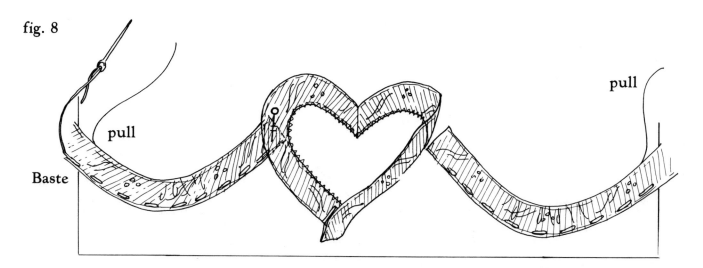

pull

pull

Baste

7. Stitch using a very narrow Zigzag Stitch width and short stitch length on the top lace heading and across the top of the heart. **fig. 9.**

Trim excess fabric from behind the lace.

8. Trim one side of a piece of entredeux 24" long.

9. Butt the trimmed edge of the entredeux to the Lace Insertion and stitch. Zigzag into each hole and onto the Lace Insertion encompassing the lace heading. **fig. 10.** Be sure to miter the entredeux at the bottom point of heart. Refer to the Diamond Doll for Mitering Lace and Entredeux.

10. Gather a piece of lace edging 36" long by pulling the top thread in the lace heading to fit the entredeux.

11. Place the lace edging side-by-side to the trimmed entredeux and attach. Zigzag into each hole of the entredeux and encompass the lace heading. **fig. 11.**

fig. 9

fig. 10

fig. 11

Doll with heart.

THE SCALLOP HEM

1. Make a cardboard template using the pattern given. fig. A.

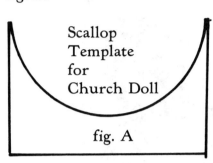

Scallop
Template
for
Church Doll

fig. A

2. Space the scallops evenly across the hemline. If they do not fit perfectly, adjust one or two scallops.

3. Be sure the points are facing down toward the cut edge of the hem. Lightly mark with a pencil. fig. 1.

4. Cut fabric ¼" away from the pencil marking. Trim the points off ¼". fig. 1.

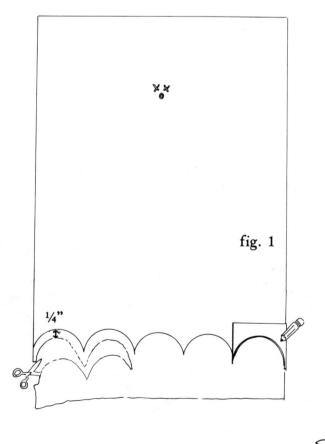

fig. 1

¼"

5. Fold the hem up to the desired depth. Baste the hem near the fold at the bottom. fig. 2.

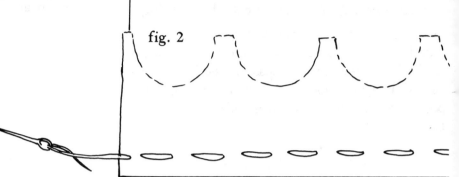

fig. 2

6. Turn under the ¼" allowance and baste in place. fig. 3.

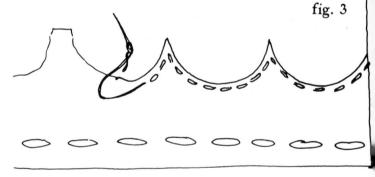

fig. 3

7. On the front side, use one strand of embroidery floss and work a small Feather Stitch around. When making the Feather Stitch, make one stitch on the hem and one on the garment fabric. fig. 4.

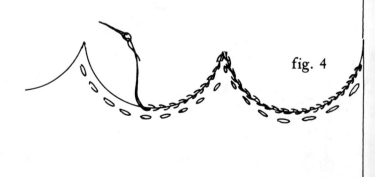

fig. 4

8. At each of the points, work a cluster of little Bullion roses. **fig. 5**.

fig. 5

FANCY BAND

1. Cut one 15" piece of a Swiss Embroidery, a Handloom, or you can make a tucked strip.

2. Cut four strips of Entredeux 15".

3. Cut 2 pieces of Beading 15" long.

4. Cut 4 pieces of Lace Insertion 15" long.

5. Cut 26" of Lace Edging about 2" wide.

6. Cut one piece of fabric 15" wide x 18" long.

7. Roll and Whip both long edges of the Swiss Embroidery. **fig. 1A.**

8. Trim one side of the two pieces of entredeux. **fig. 1B.** Butt entredeux and join to each long side of the Swiss Embroidery. **fig. 1C.**

9. Trim the remaining side of the entredeux batiste away. **fig. 2.**

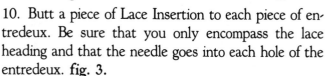

fig. 1B

fig. 1A

fig. 1C

fig. 2

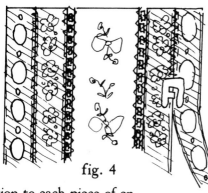
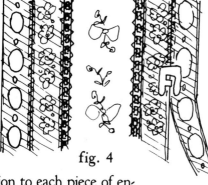
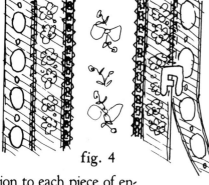
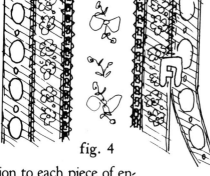
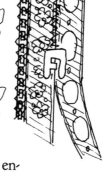
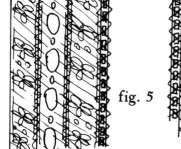

fig. 3

fig. 4

fig. 5

10. Butt a piece of Lace Insertion to each piece of entredeux. Be sure that you only encompass the lace heading and that the needle goes into each hole of the entredeux. **fig. 3.**

11. Butt a piece of Lace Beading to each side of the Lace Insertion. **fig. 4.**

12. Stitch a piece of Lace Insertion to each side of the lace beading. **fig. 5.**

13. Trim one side of the two remaining pieces of entredeux. Butt one to each side of the band. **fig. 6.**

14. Trim the batiste fabric from one side of one piece of entredeux. **fig. 7.**

15. Pull the top thread in the piece of Lace Edging to fit the 15" band which you have just stitched. **fig. 8.**

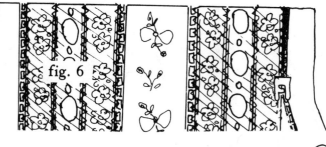

fig. 6

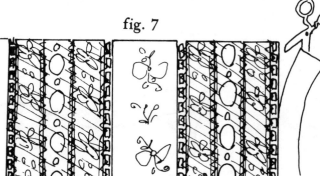

fig. 7

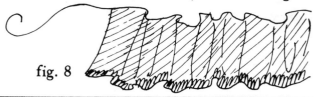

fig. 8

16. Place the trimmed entredeux on top (right sides together) of the gathered lace. Stitch into each hole of the entredeux as you zig and clear the edge as the needle zags to the right. **fig. 9.**

Fancy Band Church Doll.

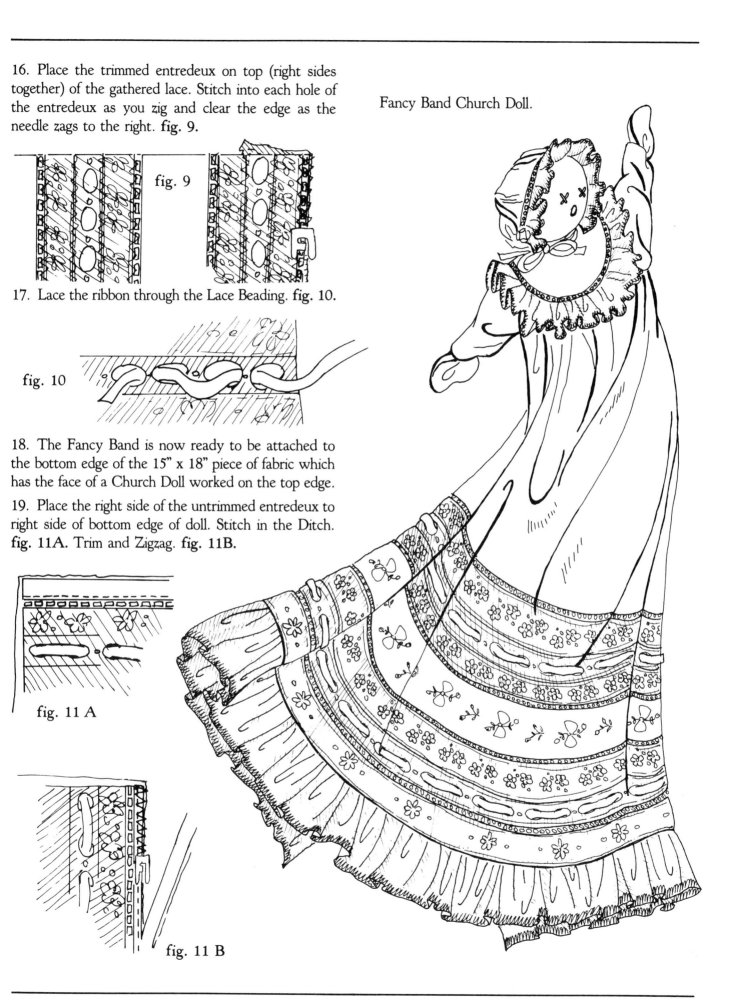

fig. 9

17. Lace the ribbon through the Lace Beading. **fig. 10.**

fig. 10

18. The Fancy Band is now ready to be attached to the bottom edge of the 15" x 18" piece of fabric which has the face of a Church Doll worked on the top edge.

19. Place the right side of the untrimmed entredeux to right side of bottom edge of doll. Stitch in the Ditch. **fig. 11A.** Trim and Zigzag. **fig. 11B.**

fig. 11 A

fig. 11 B

THE PUFFING DOLL

1. Cut one piece of fabric 2" x 30" from selvage to selvage.

2. Roll, Whip and Gather both long sides of this strip of fabric by using the Quilting Thread method.

3. Pull up the gathering thread on both sides until the piece measures 15".

4. After the puffing strip has been pulled up the desired length, place the strip of fabric onto your ironing board. **fig. 1**

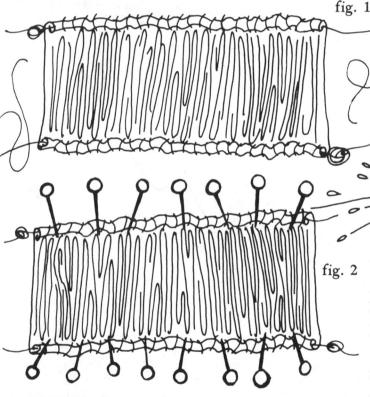

fig. 1

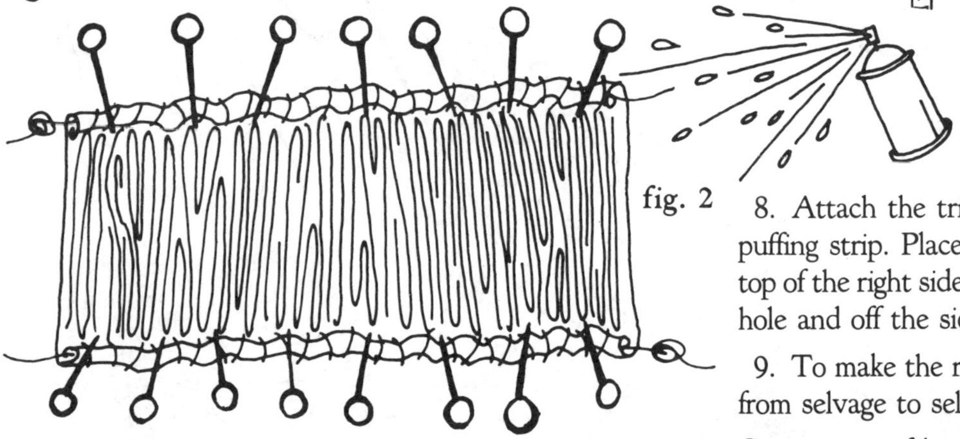

fig. 2

BLOCKING:

a. Pin both edges of the fabric strip down.

b. Make sure that the gathers have been evenly distributed and that they are straight.

Steam press by holding the iron above the fabric. *Do not* touch the iron to the fabric. You may choose to lightly spray starch the fabric and just leave to dry. **fig. 2.**

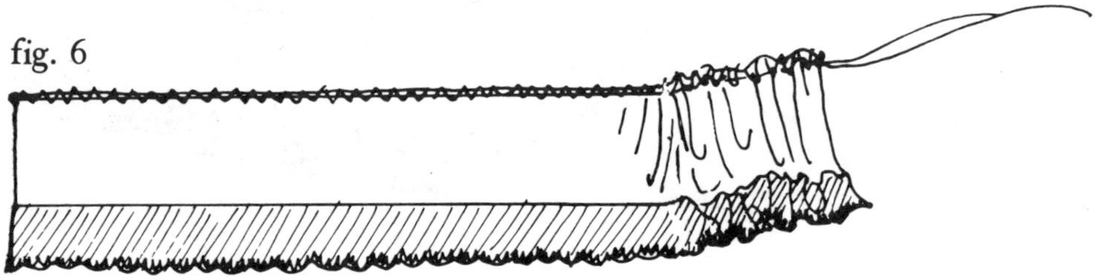

5. Cut four pieces of entredeux 15" long.

Cut two pieces of lace insertion 15" long.

6. Trim one side of the batiste fabric from entredeux. Attach a piece of entredeux to both sides of the Lace Insertion. **fig. 3.**

7. Trim the batiste from *one side* of the two strips. **fig. 4.**

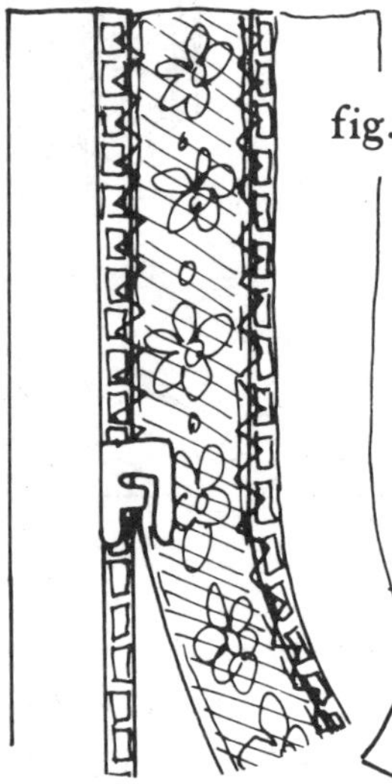

fig. 3

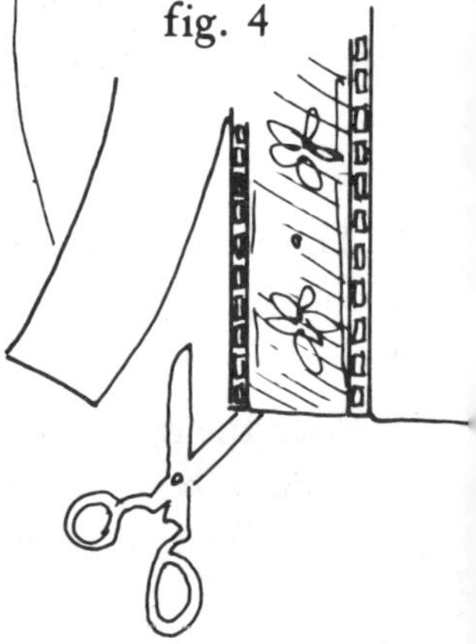

fig. 4

8. Attach the trimmed side of the entredeux to the puffing strip. Place the right side of the entredeux on top of the right side of the puffing strip. Zigzag into each hole and off the side edge of the puffing. **fig. 5.**

9. To make the ruffle, cut a piece of fabric 2½" x 30" from selvage to selvage.

Cut a piece of lace edging 30" long and attach to one side of the fabric strip using the method of Lace to Flat Fabric.

10. Roll, Whip and Gather the remaining side of the strip. Pull up the fabric until measures 15". **fig. 6.**

fig. 6

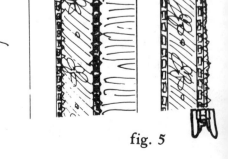

fig. 5

11. Trim one side of the batiste from the entredeux fancy band. Place the trimmed edge of the entredeux, right side down, on top of the right side of the ruffle. The edges should be together. Attach the ruffle to the puffing strip using a Zigzag Stitch wide enough to go into each hole of the entredeux and clear the fabric edge as it zags to the right. **fig. 7**.

12. Using the Method of Stitch in the Ditch for attaching fabric to entredeux, attach the Fancy Puffing Strip to the 15" bottom edge of the doll. **fig. 8**.

fig. 7

fig. 8

TEAR DROP
How to Make a Lace Guide

fig. 1

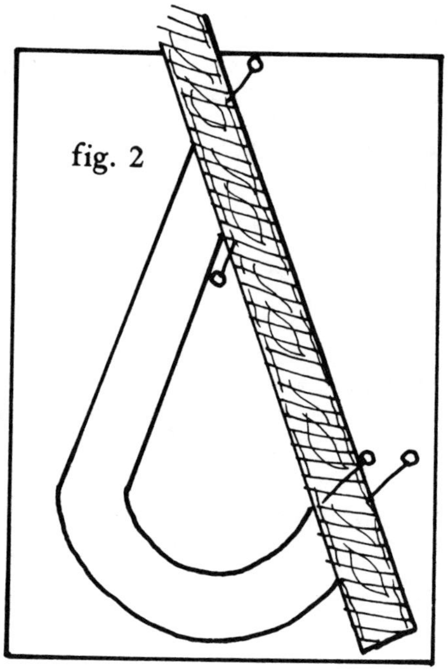

fig. 2

(These directions will direct you as to how to make a lace guide. The same principle applies for any shape you would like to make.)

Trace the Tear Drop onto a piece of paper.

1. Pin the Tear Drop pattern to a board – the ironing board will do, or any type board you can jab pins into.

Measure width of Lace Insertion to be used. Mark the width from the pattern line to the inside. Let the lines cross. **fig. 1.**

2. Start at a side point where the curve and the straight line meets and pin the end of the lace between the lines. The right side of the lace should be facing down. **fig. 2.**

3. Keep the lace edge on the line and pin the lace heading at the next point/angle. As you take the lace from one point to the next point, keep the OUTSIDE lace edge smooth. **fig. 3.**

4. Continue around to the second side point. **fig. 4.**

Pattern Guide for Tear Drop

fig. 3

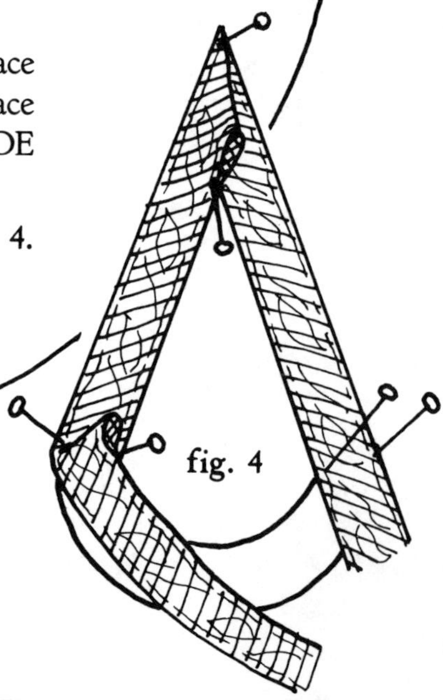

fig. 4

5. Pin only on the outside edge of the lace curve.

6. Leave about a ¼" tail where you begin and where you cut the lace after pinning.

7. Pull the very top thread until the inside edge of lace is lying flat and smooth. **fig. 5.**

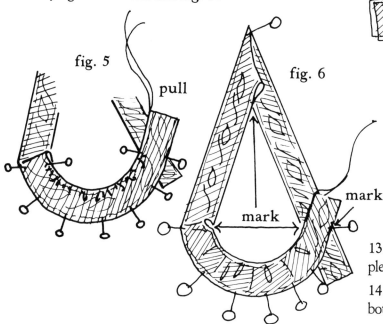

fig. 5

pull

fig. 6

mark

mark

8. With a marking pencil MARK the angles where the lace meets on the INSIDE points. Mark both edges at the two ends where they overlap. **fig. 6.**

9. Remove the lace from the board.

Note: This can become a permanent guide for making many more shapes the same size by transferring the markings now to paper. This enables you to transfer the same markings to as many pieces of lace as will be needed.

Use the lace which was marked when Making a Lace Guide, (using the Tear Drop shape) to make a Church Doll with a Tear Drop lace shape.

10. Using a narrow Zigzag setting, stitch the lace together at the markings which you have made on the lace strip. Example: Fold the piece of lace, right sides together, with the markings together. The first mark on each end of the lace will be together.

11. Stitch diagonally to the edge of the lace. **fig. 7.**

12. Bring the next two marks together. Stitch diagonally to the edge of the lace onto the FOLD SIDE. **fig. 8.**

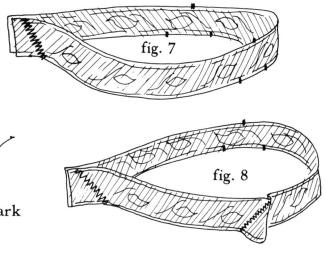

fig. 7

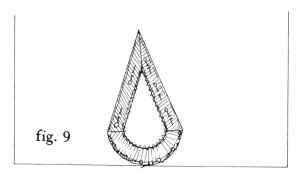

fig. 8

13. Continue stitching the lace until you have completed stitching all the darts.

14. Place the Lace Tear Drop, right side up, onto the bottom edge of the 16" x 18" fabric piece.

15. Carefully pin the lace into place. Pin the lace curve, making sure that the outside of the lace is flat to the fabric. Zigzag the inside of the Tear Drop only. **fig. 9.**

fig. 9

16. Cut two pieces of lace about 8" long. Lift up the edge of the lace on the side dart of the Tear Drop and place the end of the lace strip under. **fig. 10.**

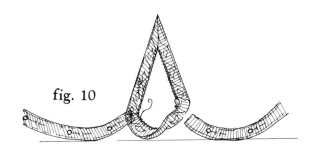

fig. 10

17. Stitch all the way around the top edge of the Lace Insertion and the top edge of the Tear Drop shape. **fig. 11.**

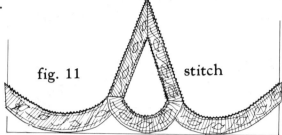

fig. 11   stitch

18. Trim very carefully from behind the Lace Insertion. **fig. 12.**

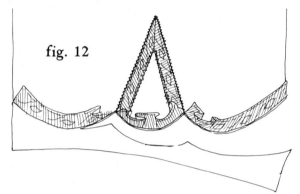

fig. 12

19. Trim one side of the entredeux off. Butt the trimmed side of the entredeux to the Lace Insertion. Zigzag the entredeux to the bottom edge of the Tear Drop lace. After the entredeux has been stitched all the way around, trim the other side of the entredeux batiste away. **fig. 13.**

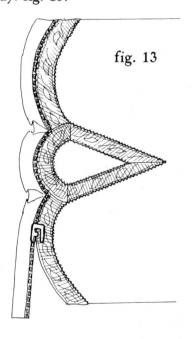

fig. 13

20. Gather the lace edging and, with right sides together, stitch going into each hole of the entredeux and off the entredeux/lace edge. Allow enough fullness at the bottom curve so that the lace will not cup, or use the Butt Method, **fig. 14.**

fig. 14

Doll with Tear Drop.

You will use the same directions for this doll as are given for the Christmas Stocking, so please refer to those directions if you would like to make this doll.

LOOPS OF LACE

1. Trace the loop onto the fabric. **fig. 1**. (Pattern guide included)

2. Pin and then tiny baste the outside edge of the lace to the fabric. **fig. 2**.

3. Pull the top thread at the inside curve of the lace to make it lie flat. **fig. 3**. And, I quote Kathy McMakin when I say, "Pull the very, very, very top thread."

Spray starch and then press on the wrong side.

4. Using a Zigzag Stitch wide enough to encompass the lace heading and very short, Zigzag over the lace heading of the top of the loop. Then, Zigzag inside the lace loop. Remember, DO NOT stitch at the lower edge of the lace when the loops are at the bottom of a garment. **fig. 4**.

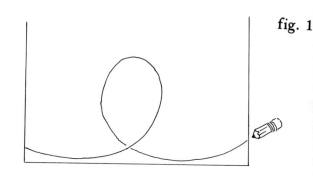

fig. 1

fig. 2

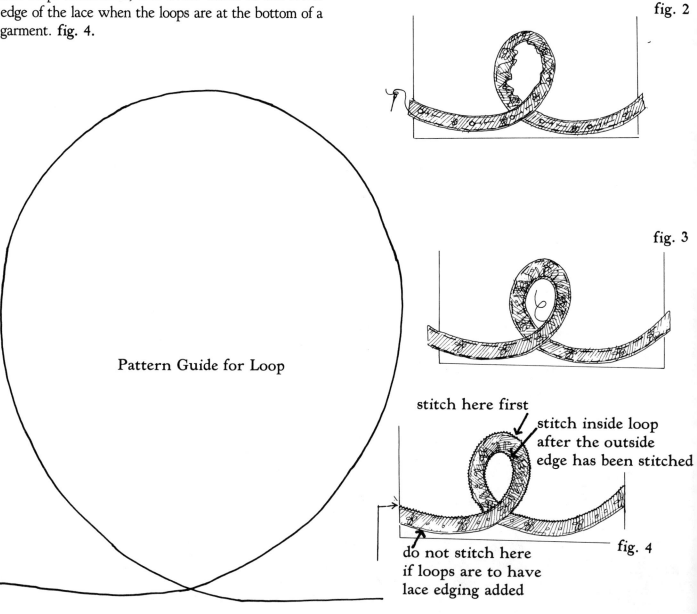

Pattern Guide for Loop

fig. 3

stitch here first

stitch inside loop after the outside edge has been stitched

do not stitch here if loops are to have lace edging added

fig. 4

5. Carefully trim the fabric from behind the lace – between the two rows of Zigzagged stitching to expose the lace. **fig. 5.**

7. Pull the top thread in the piece of lace edging to gather. Trim the remaining side of the entredeux. Place the trimmed edge of the entredeux to the edge of the gathered lace edging. Zigzag into each and every hole and on to the lace edge. **fig. 7.** (Doll with Loop of Lace)

fig. 5

6. Trim one side of the entredeux. Butt it to the bottom edge of the Lace Insertion. As you come to the point where the lace crosses, just straighten the lace out. **fig. 6.**

fig. 7

fig. 6

CONTINUOUS OVAL LOOPS

Trace the Continuous Ovals (pattern guide given, if needed) onto the bottom of the 16" x 18" piece of fabric. Use a marking pen which will disappear or will wash out. **fig. 1.** Baste the lace beginning at one side and taking it to the other edge. The *center of the lace* will be on the line for the ovals. Let the *basting remain* on the outside edge of the lace. Even as the lace crosses over and the inside of the lace edge becomes the outside, let the basting thread just go to the outer edge. **fig. 2.**

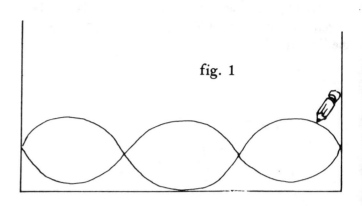

fig. 1

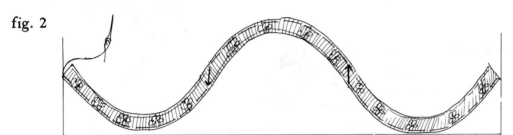

fig. 2

Baste the second piece of lace and where the laces cross, just let the second piece lie on top. **fig. 3.**

fig. 3

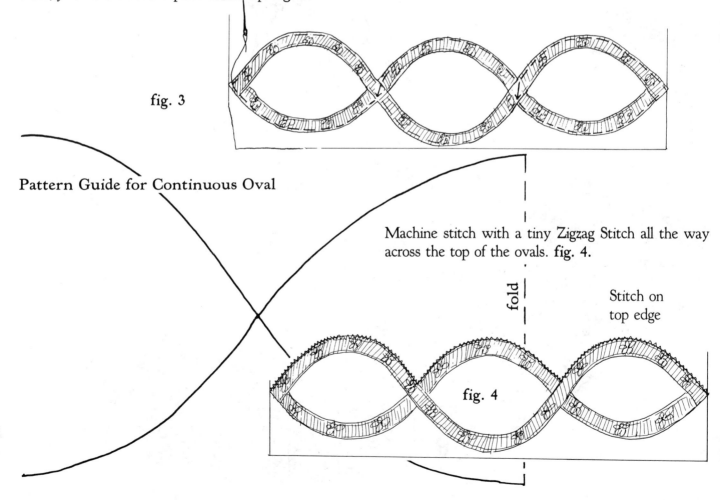

Pattern Guide for Continuous Oval

Machine stitch with a tiny Zigzag Stitch all the way across the top of the ovals. **fig. 4.**

fold

Stitch on top edge

fig. 4

Machine stitch inside the ovals. **fig. 5.**

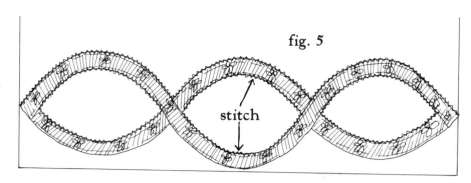

fig. 5

stitch

Trim away the excess fabric. **fig. 6.**

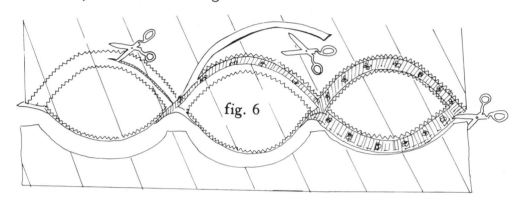

fig. 6

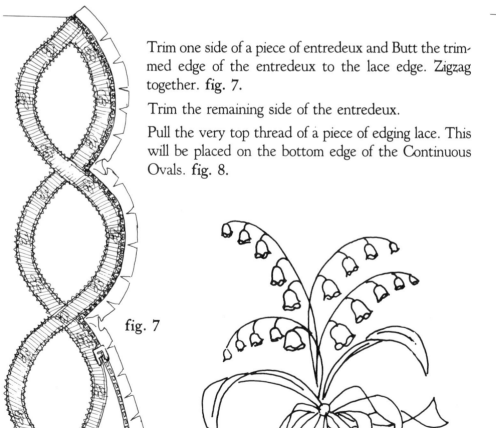

fig. 7

Trim one side of a piece of entredeux and Butt the trimmed edge of the entredeux to the lace edge. Zigzag together. **fig. 7.**

Trim the remaining side of the entredeux.

Pull the very top thread of a piece of edging lace. This will be placed on the bottom edge of the Continuous Ovals. **fig. 8.**

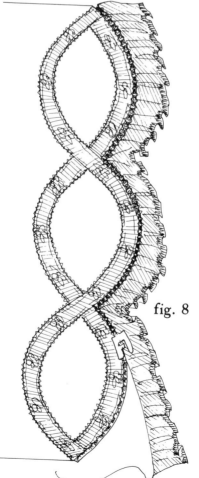

fig. 8

Doll with Continuous Loops.

BONNET **Lace Brim**

1. Cut a piece of entredeux 4½" long and trim one side of the batiste fabric away.

2. Cut a piece of Lace Edging 8" long. Pull the top thread to gather the lace to fit the entredeux strip. **fig. 1.** Note the dotted lines for placing the entredeux. Zigzag into each hole of the entredeux and as you approach the place where the entredeux and the gathered edge of the lace meets, let the needle go into each hole of the entredeux on the left and clear the edge on the right. **fig. 2.**

5. Run two rows of lengthened machine stitching on the long side without the curve. **fig. 4.**

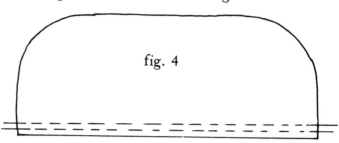

fig. 4

6. Roll, Whip and Gather the other side using the Quilting Thread method. **fig. 5.**

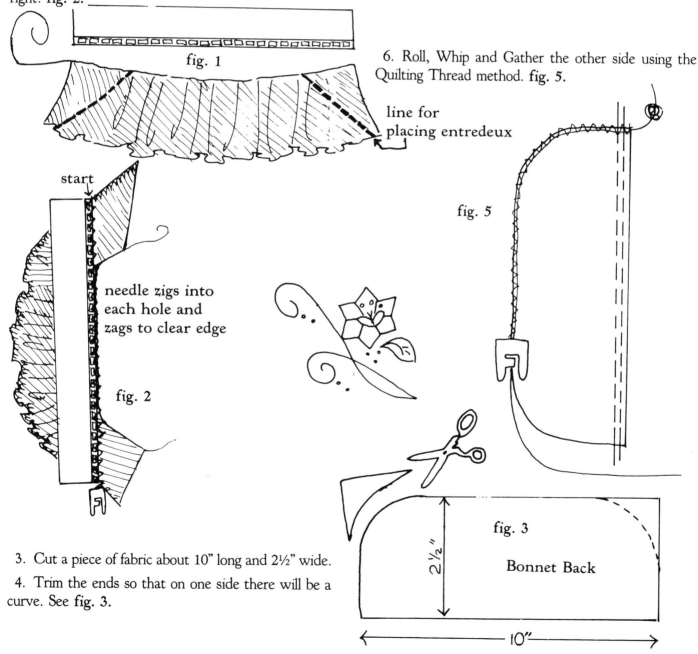

line for placing entredeux

fig. 5

fig. 1

start

needle zigs into each hole and zags to clear edge

fig. 2

3. Cut a piece of fabric about 10" long and 2½" wide.

4. Trim the ends so that on one side there will be a curve. See **fig. 3.**

fig. 3

Bonnet Back

2½"

10"

7. Pull the two rows of lengthened machine stitch up to fit the untrimmed edge of the entredeux. Place the entredeux on top, right sides together, to the two rows of machine stitching. Stitch in the Ditch. **fig. 6.**

Trim to ⅛". Zigzag to finish the edge. The needle should NOT go into the holes of the entredeux – just to the edge and then clear the fabric on the other side. **fig. 7.**

8. Pull the quilting thread up as tight as you can pull it. Thread a needle with the quilting thread and anchor the gathers. **fig. 8.**

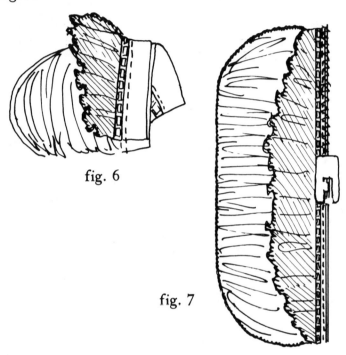

fig. 6

fig. 7

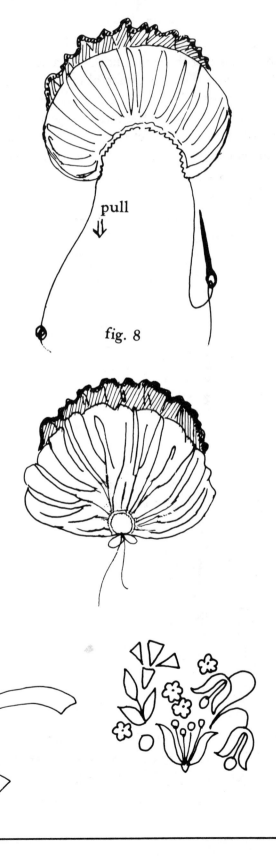

pull

fig. 8

9. Cut a piece of ⅛" ribbon 12" long. Make a flower or ribbon rose for both sides. **fig. 9.**

fig. 9

The band of this bonnet is made using only a very narrow piece of Lace Insertion with entredeux attached to both sides of the insertion.

1. Cut a piece of Lace Insertion 4½" long. Cut two 4½" pieces of entredeux and trim one side of the batiste fabric away.

Place the trimmed side of the entredeux side-by-side to the piece of Lace Insertion and Zigzag together. Make sure that the needle is going into each and every hole of the entredeux and then zags to encompass the lace heading. **fig. 1.**

2. Cut a piece of lace edging (⅜" to ⅝" wide is a good width) 8" long. Pull the very top thread of the lace heading to fit the 4½" piece of entredeux.

Do not have gathers at the very ends of the lace edging. **fig. 2.**

3. Trim one side of the entredeux/insertion strip. Place the right side of the entredeux edge on top of the right side of the gathered lace edging. Note the broken lines in **fig. 2.** Let the entredeux just lie on top following the lines. Zigzag into each and every hole. When the entredeux comes to the edge of the gathered lace edging, let the needle continue to go into each hole, and as the needle swings to the right to clear the edge. **fig. 3.**

Trim the remaining side of the entredeux.

4. Cut a piece of fabric about 6" x 2½". Roll, Whip and Gather one of the long edges. **fig. 4.**

5. Place the right side of the fancy ruffle band to the right side of the Rolled, Whipped and Gathered edge of the fabric. With the entredeux even with and on top of the rolled and whipped edge, Zigzag into each and every hole of the entredeux, and as the needle swings to the right let the needle clear the edge. **fig. 5.**

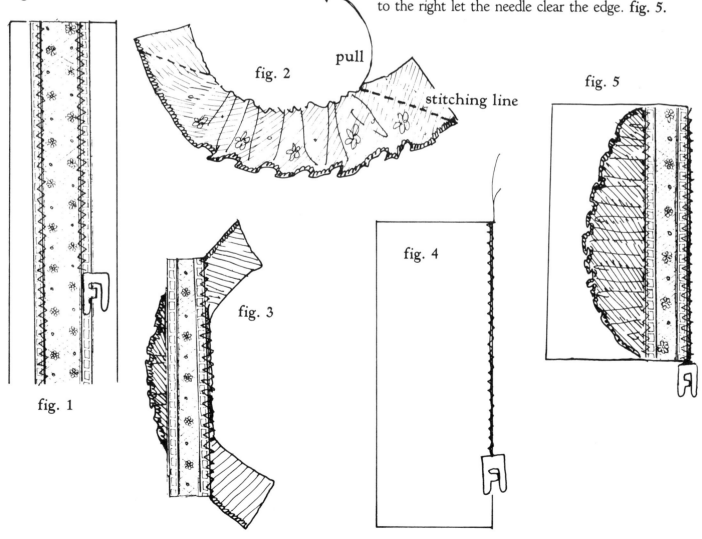

fig. 2

pull

stitching line

fig. 5

fig. 1

fig. 3

fig. 4

6. Finish both short ends of the fabric strip with a Mock French Roll. Make a small casing in the remaining long side by turning under the raw edge ⅛" and then turning again. Machine stitch to hem, or you may prefer to Hand Whip the hem. **fig. 6.**

7. Run a ribbon through the casing (1/16" ribbon is best) and pull up and tie in the back. **fig. 7.**

8. Attach a ribbon to both sides of the front to tie. **fig. 8.**

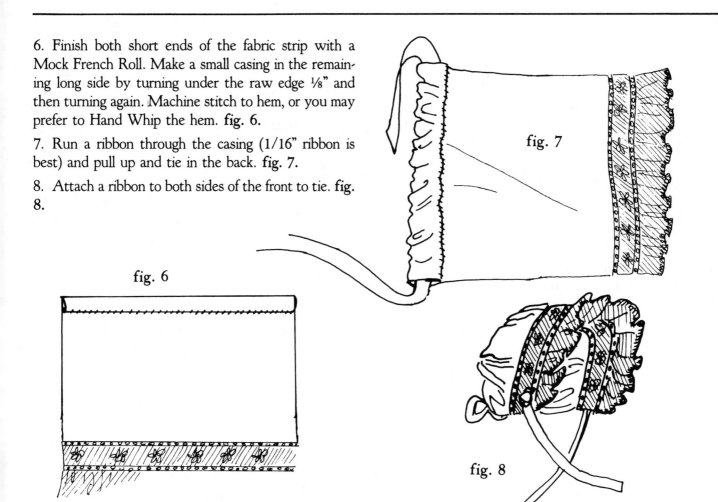

fig. 7

fig. 6

fig. 8

SMOCKED BONNET FOR CHURCH DOLL

Cut a piece of fabric 12" x 3". Pleat 5 rows using the one half spaces. You will only Smock on the three in the middle. **fig. 1.** After you have pleated the strip of fabric, pull fabric flat and attach Lace Edging before Smocking. **fig. 2.**

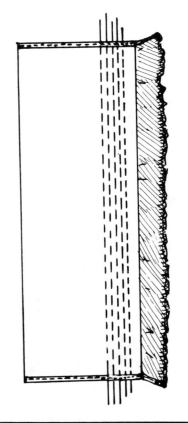

fig. 2

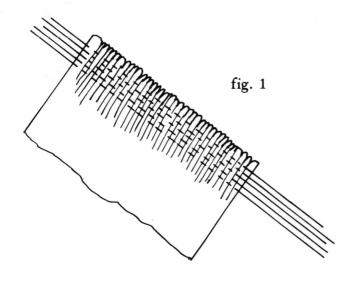

fig. 1

If you do not wish to use Lace Edging and would like to have a self fabric ruffle, press under ½" and baste into place *before* Pleating. **fig. 3**.

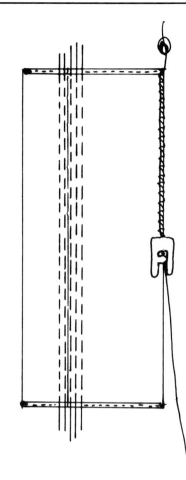

fig. 4

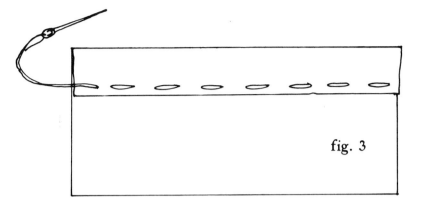

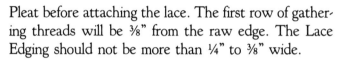

fig. 3

Pleat before attaching the lace. The first row of gathering threads will be ⅜" from the raw edge. The Lace Edging should not be more than ¼" to ⅜" wide.

For the self ruffle bonnet, the first gathering row will be ¼" to ⅜" from the folded edge.

With the bonnet still flat, finish both short ends of fabric and/or lace with a narrow hem. This hem can be the Mock French Hem or a machine hem.

Make a casing in the back by turning under ¼" and machine stitching; or, if you prefer, you may Roll, Whip and Gather using the Quilting Thread method and pull the back of the bonnet up. **fig. 4**. Then, to keep the gathers in place, Roll and Whip over the gathered edge. **fig. 5**.

fig. 5

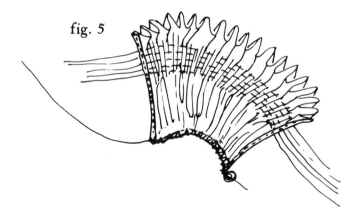

Smock the bonnet using the design provided or one of your choice. I prefer to use only 2 strands of floss for this, as it is so tiny.

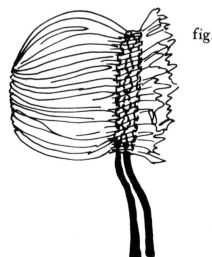

fig. 6

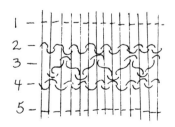

Trace the outline onto a piece of fabric. It will be easier for you to work if the collar shape is traced onto a larger piece of fabric, and after you have embellished it to trim away the excess fabric. **fig. 1.**

Trim a piece of entredeux leaving the batiste fabric about ¼". **fig. 2.** Place the right side of the entredeux to the right side of the collar neck edge. **fig. 3.** Stitch in the Ditch. **fig. A.** Trim the raw edges until they are about ⅛". **fig. B.** Roll and Whip the raw edges, letting the stitching go only to the edge of the entredeux. Do not go into the holes. **fig. C.**

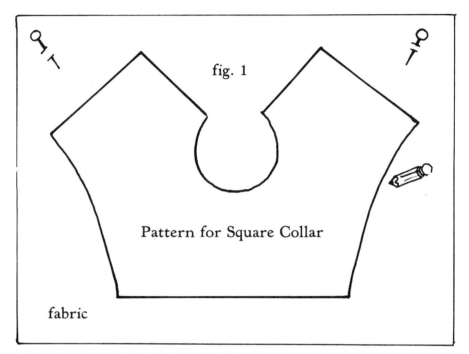

fig. 1

Pattern for Square Collar

fabric

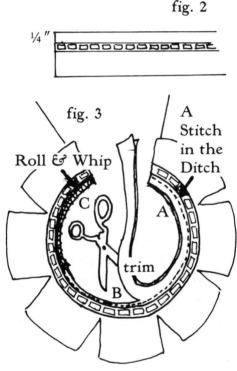

fig. 2

¼"

fig. 3

Roll & Whip

A
Stitch
in the
Ditch

C

A

B

trim

Some suggestions for the Square Collar:

  a. Tucks
  b. Shadow embroidery
  c. Lace insertions (entredeux is very pretty to use with 1/16" ribbon laced through for beading).

Place a narrow piece of lace insertion to the collar placing the edge of the lace on the collar line. You may prefer to use the Pin Stitch to secure the lace in place, or the Feather Stitch. You also may choose to use a tiny Zigzag Stitch, or a pretty machine Hem Stitch on the sewing machine. For the Elna # 7000, the Stitch Selector is # 746 and is ever so lovely if you reduce the stitch width so that the machine only encompasses the lace heading.

Use a piece of 1/16" ribbon and thread through the holes of the entredeux, leaving the ends about 6" long to tie in the back to close the collar. **fig. 4.**

fig. 4

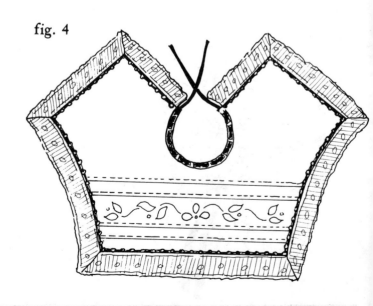

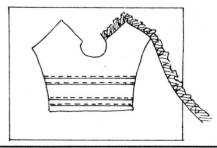

POINTED COLLAR

Draw the collar shape onto a piece of fabric. Do not cut at this time. It's easier to to work with the fabric if you have a larger amount. **fig. 1.**

1. Place lace edging on the seam line of the collar. Baste and then Zigzag the lace along the drawn collar edge. Miter the lace at this point. (Directions for mitering lace is illustrated in the techniqies section of The Diamond Church Doll.) **fig. 2.**

You may also choose to use the Pin Stitch, the Feather Stitch, or Hem Stitching to give the collar a finished look.

2. Trim away the excess fabric. **fig. 3.**

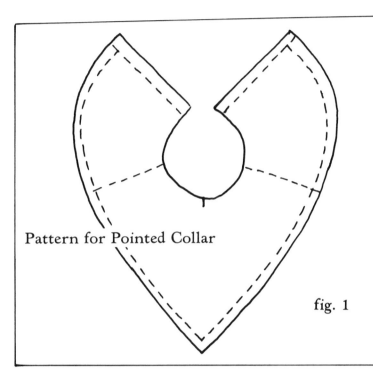

Pattern for Pointed Collar

fig. 1

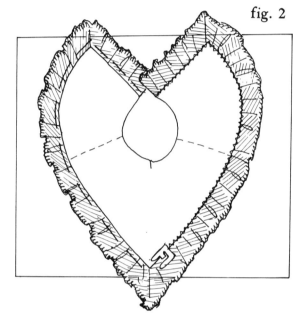

fig. 2

Some suggestions for the Pointed Collar:

  a. Embroidery at the point.
  b. Tucks
  c. Lace insertion
  d. Plain

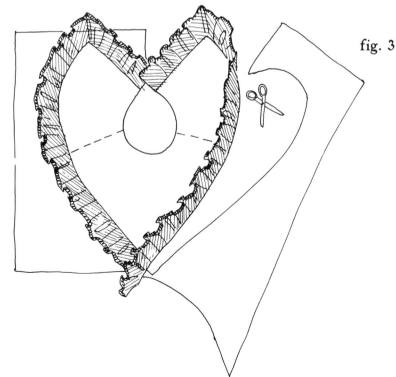

fig. 3

3. Finish the neck edge with the use of entredeux as for the Square Collar, or Roll and Whip the edge using the technique for Rolling and Whipping a Bias Curve. figs. A, B, C and D.

fig. A   Straight stitch

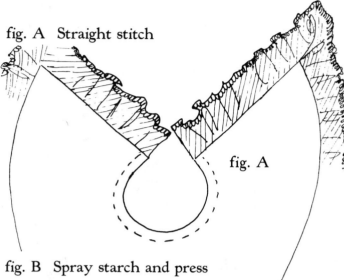

fig. A

fig. B   Spray starch and press

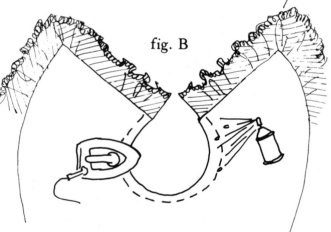

fig. B

fig. C   Trim to stitching

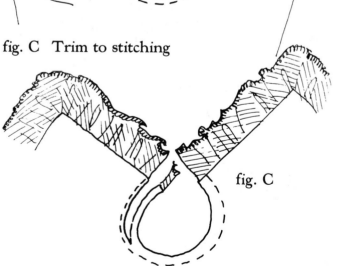

fig. C

fig. D   Roll and Whip

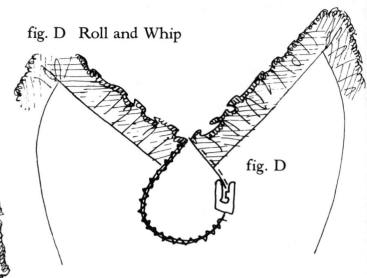

fig. D

Close using a plastic snap or if entredeux was used, close with a ribbon run through the holes. fig. 4.

fig. 4

BERTHA COLLAR

Trace the shape of the collar onto the fabric. **fig. 1.**

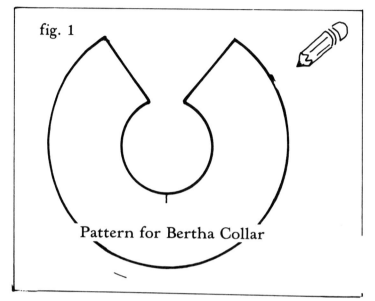

fig. 1

Pattern for Bertha Collar

Select a decorative stitch and stitch around the inside edge. **fig. 2.**

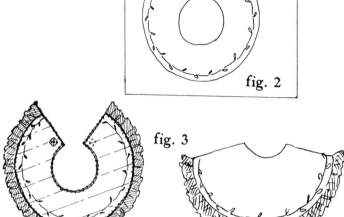

fig. 2

fig. 3

Cut the collar out on the line and finish the edge of the collar and the neck edge with a Roll and Whip. Use the technique of Roll and Whip for a Bias Edge.

Apply a narrow lace edging to the outside edge.

Use a snap to close the collar. **fig. 3.**

ROUND LACE COLLAR

Cut a piece of wide lace insertion about 1¾" to 2" wide.

Finish both ends by turning under and stitching into place. **fig. 1.**

Pull the very top thread to pull the gathers up to fit around the neck. **fig. 2.**

Once you have pulled the gathers to fit, hold in place and machine stitch. Try a tiny Zigzag at the neck edge (the edge of the lace) to give a more complete look.

Close the back with a tiny button, a snap, or attach ribbon to both sides and tie. **fig. 3.**

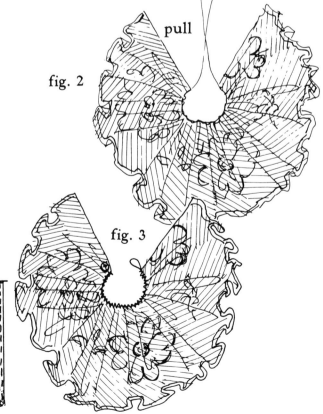

pull

fig. 2

fig. 3

fig. 1

SMOCKED COLLAR FOR CHURCH DOLL

Cut a strip of Swiss Edging which is about 1¾" to 2" wide and 25" long.

Pleat as many rows as you can using the half spaces. Smock using the simple smocking design below.

Pull out about ¼" from each end. **fig. 1.** Fold and Whip down so that snap can be attached to close the collar. **fig. 2.**

Cut a piece of bias ½" x 2". Fold in half and attach to the neck edge. **fig. 3.** You may wish to stitch two times, as you will need to trim very close to the stitching line. Turn the bias to the inside and whip down. **fig. 4.** This will be about ⅛" wide when finished. The seam allowance at the neck edge should be no more than ¼".

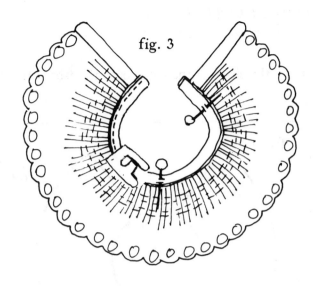
fig. 3

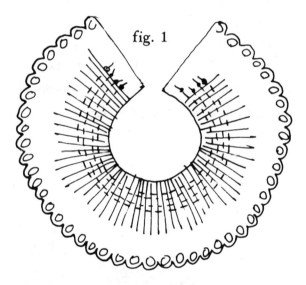
fig. 1

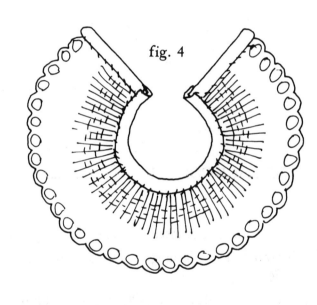
fig. 4

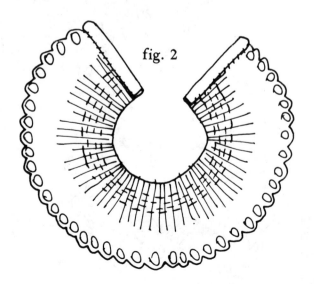
fig. 2

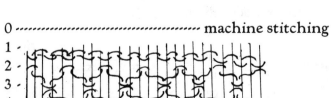

66

HEMS AND HEMLINES

One can be as creative as you like when dealing with hemlines. And, most of these techniques can be applied to old hemlines to hide the crease or faded line or to a new garment. So, for the sake of simplicity, directions will be written to include both situations.

Great care should be taken to *turn a hem*.

Of course, one of the most important steps to all hem finishes is the marking of the hemline. With the exception of the pleated garment and children's styles, marking is done after the construction has been completed. A fairly good rule to follow is that when marking a hem above the hipline, use a flat surface for marking and a hem below the hip line should be marked on the wearer.

However, for us grandmothers who sew for our grandchildren that do not live in the same country, we must mark the hemline by carefully cutting and measuring the garment. When turning a hemline for my own grandchildren, I hang the dress on a hanger which I have padded to resemble their little shoulders, and check to see if the dress is going to hang properly. If it is in line, then the hemline is marked on a flat surface.

Before turning up the hem, press the seams well. You may need to trim the seam allowances or clip the seam allowance to reduce bulk with the hem allowance.

TURNING UP A HEM

1. Turn a narrow edge under, basting or pressing the edge in place. This step can be performed after the hem has been turned up, or you may finish the bottom edge first. When working with fine 100% Swiss Batiste, you can almost finger press the raw edge under. However, if you are using a heavier weight fabric, you will need to press and baste. **fig. 1.**

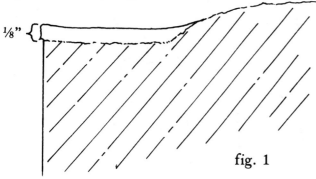

fig. 1

2. You may prefer to use an Over Lock to finish the raw edge of the hem. The Elna Lock sews and cuts simultaneously at great speed and will adapt to the lightest of fabrics. When using the Over Lock Machine (or Serger, as sometimes called) I prefer to use thread the same color as the fabric. **fig. 2.**

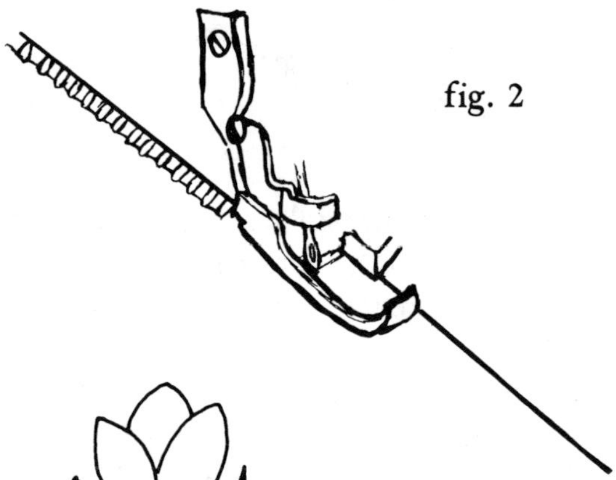

fig. 2

3. From this narrow turned edge, measure with a ruler from the first turning to the depth the finished hem is desired. (**Note:** a gauge for measuring the hem depth can be made by taking a straight piece of cardboard and cutting a notch at the exact width the finished hem is to be. **fig. A and B.**) Mark by placing a pin where the hem will be turned, or you may use chalk or a basting thread. **fig. 3.**

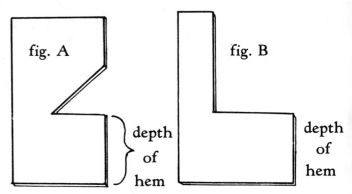

fig. A
fig. B
depth of hem
depth of hem

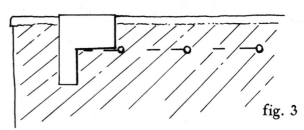

fig. 3

4. Remove the pins and make the second turning by turning the fabric up where the pins were. **fig. 4.**

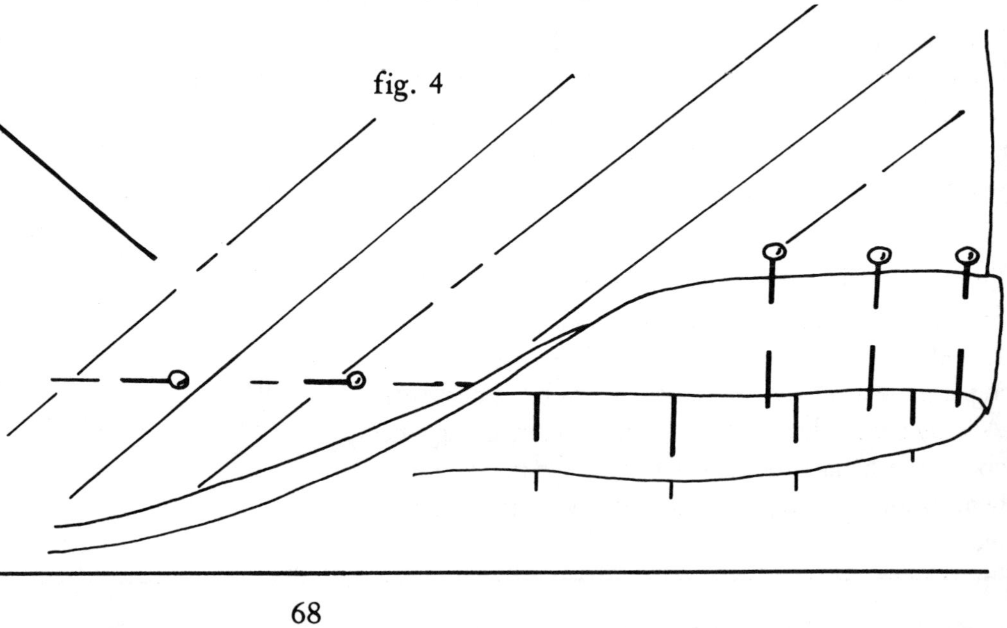

fig. 4

TEMPLATE FOR A SCALLOPED HEM

1. Measure the circumference of the garment or the length of the material in which the Scallop Hem will be used. If all the seams have been made and you are working with a definite measurement (a measurement which CAN NOT be altered), then take that measurement and divide by the width you desire your scallop to be. Example: the width of the garment is 72" and you would like for the scallop to be 4½" wide. Divide 72" by 4.5 and you will have 16 scallops. If the garment is 84" and you would like the scallop to be 6" wide, divide six into 84 and you will find that you will need to have 14 scallops.

On the other hand, let's assume you know how many scallops you desire. Divide the number of scallops into the circumference measurement of the garment. That will tell you the width of the scallop. Example: You want 14 scallops. The width of the garment is 84". 84" ÷ 14 will give you 6" wide scallops.

2. Place the width of the scallop measurement onto a piece of cardboard. **fig. 1**.

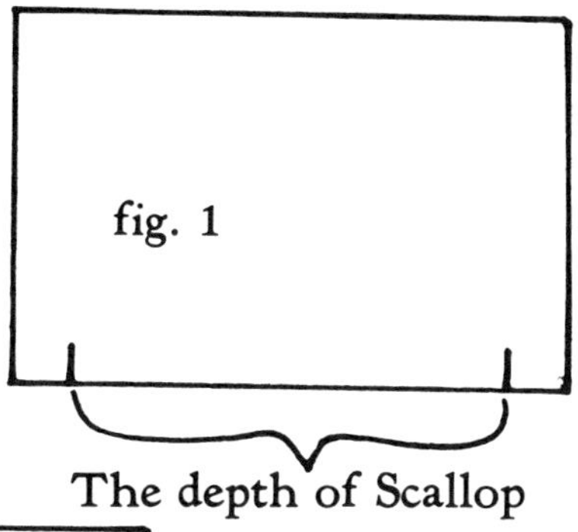

fig. 1

The depth of Scallop

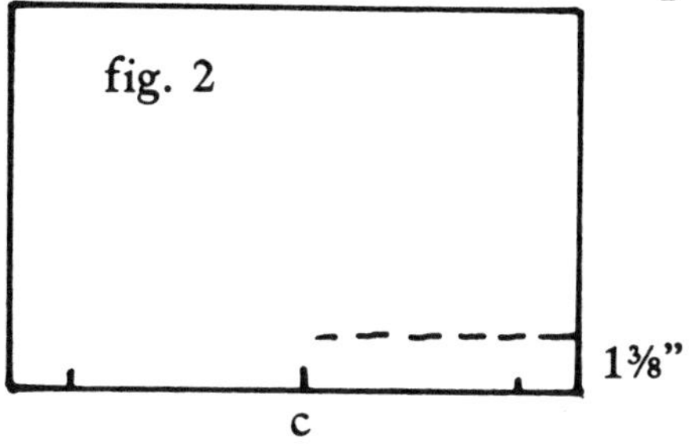

fig. 2

1⅜"

c

3. The depth you would like the scallop to be is personal; however, if you make the scallop too deep, it is much harder to turn and make a pretty hem. A depth of 1⅜" is very pretty for a 6" wide scallop. Place this mark on your cardboard measuring from the previous dots. **fig. 2**.

4. Use the memory curve (this tool will bend to your desired shape), and draw your scallop/curve onto the cardboard. **fig. 3**. There are other methods of making your scallop/curve onto the cardboard. Some will find that a kitchen plate will make the exact curve, or the protractor will work nicely for some. Whatever you choose, make the drawing onto a piece of cardboard as the template. This will make doing the scallop hem so much easier.

5. After you have drawn the curve onto the cardboard, cut away the excess. This way, you can trace the outline. **fig. 3**.

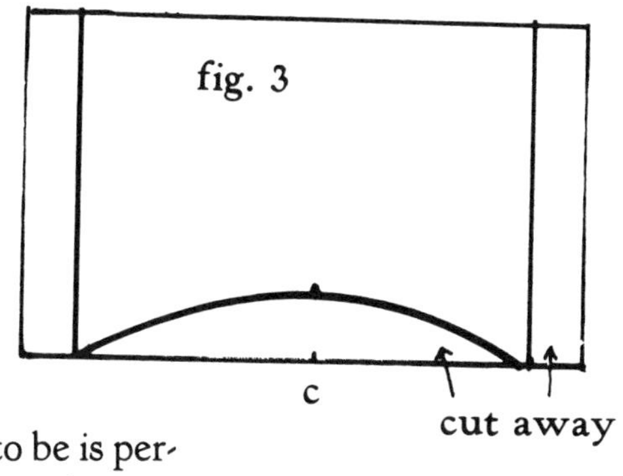

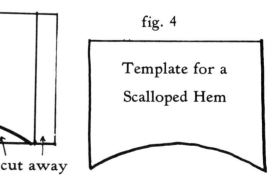

fig. 3

c

cut away

fig. 4

Template for a Scalloped Hem

6. **Figure 4** shows the scalloped hem template ready to be used.

It is much easier to measure and draw the placement of the scallops if you are able to keep the fabric flat. Leave one seam open until the scallops have been drawn onto the bottom edge.

1. Using the template just made (or whatever tool you chose), draw the scallops onto the fabric. I prefer beginning in the center and working to the sides. **fig. 1.**

4. Cut ½" of each of the points away. **fig. 4.**

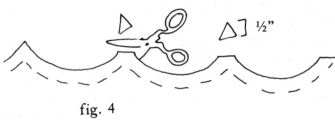

fig. 4

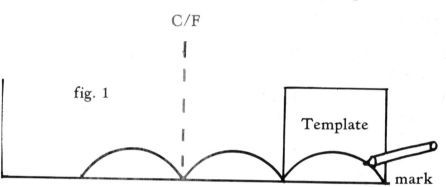

C/F

fig. 1

Template

mark

2. Very carefully, measure and mark a ½" seam allowance. **fig. 2.**

5. Turn the hem up to the correct length (finished) and baste at the bottom edge. **fig. 5.**

3. Trim the fabric away on the first line drawn to make the scallop shape. **fig. 3.**

6. Baste on the second drawn line (seam allowance). **fig. 6.**

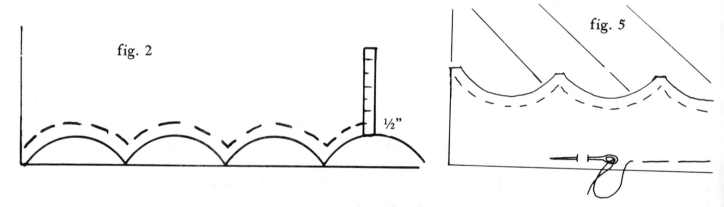

fig. 2

½"

fig. 5

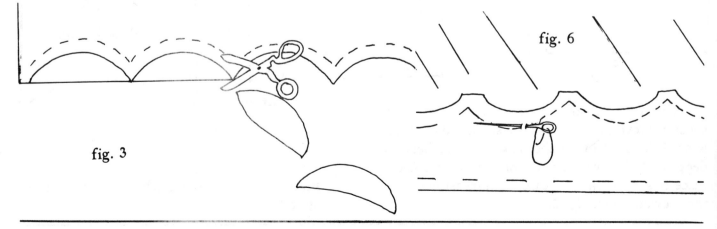

fig. 3

fig. 6

7. Turn raw edge under ¼" and blind hem or slip stitch. The basting thread will keep the turned under edge the same depth. **fig. 7.** You may wish to do a Feather Stitch on the right side of the garment, which would hold the hem in place as well as being decorative. **fig. 8.**

The Point de Paris Stitch is perfect for making the dress into a very special heirloom. If you prefer, the Point de Paris Stitch can be done on the machine, also. Check with your sewing machine dealer about the possibilities of your machine's stitching the pin stitch. On the Elna # 7000, you would use the Stitch Selector # 746 and the width setting would be changed to 1.8.

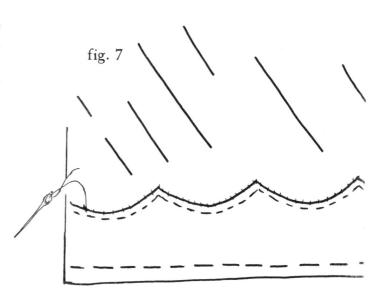

fig. 7

fig. 8

THE FRENCH HEM

The French Hem is a flat uniform hem made on the right side of the garment.

This hem is especially pretty when it is finished with the Feather Stitch, Pin Stitch or Briar Stitch. You would NOT want to use this hem if the fabric of the garment showed a true wrong side.

However, this is a good way to lengthen a dress which a child has outgrown, if you have fabric that will match or contrast with the existing fabric. The fabric must then be attached to the bottom edge. The extension would be stitched with the seam on the outside, so that it would be encased in the hem fold. In other words, the wrong side of the skirt to the right side of the extension.

The French Hem With Seams ALREADY Constructed

When the seams of the garment have already been constructed, then it is necessary to take out a portion of the seam that will be in the hem allowance.

1. Working on the wrong side of the garment, measure the exact depth you wish for the hem to be. Mark. **fig. 1.**

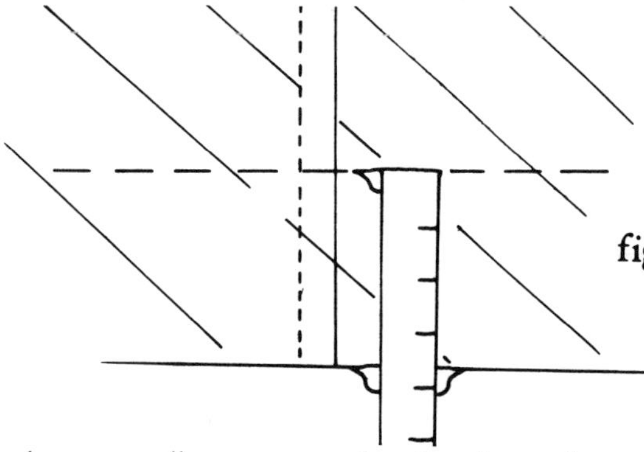

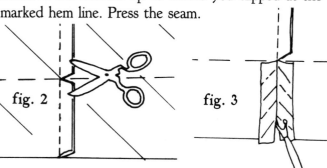

fig. 1

2. Clip the seam allowance to the already made seam. **fig. 2.** It is safer and easier at this time to clip the threads of the already existing seam by running the seam ripper under the thread at your mark. **fig. 3.** Remove the threads up to where you clipped at the marked hem line. Press the seam.

fig. 2

fig. 3

3. Place the wrong side of the fabric together with the raw edges of the seams together. Make a new seam. This time, the seam allowance will be seen on the right side of the garment.

4. Make absolutely sure that the new seam begins where you clipped and marked the old seam. **fig. 4.**

Press the seam open.

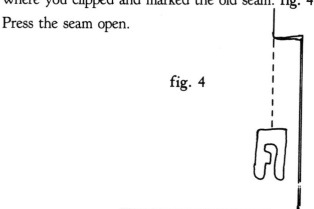

fig. 4

5. Turn the raw edge under about ¼" press and baste if necessary to hold the edge under nicely. **fig. 5**

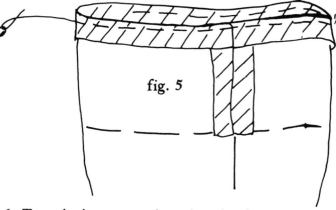

fig. 5

6. Turn the hem up to the right side of the garment. Baste about ½" from the bottom fold. **fig. 6.**

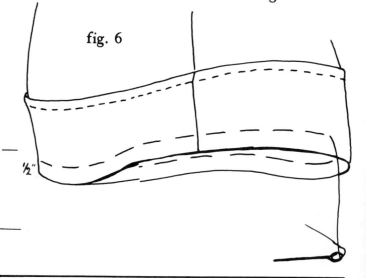

fig. 6

7. The Pin Stitch is lovely if working with the sheer fabrics such as a Swiss batiste. If using a heavier fabric, I prefer the Feather Stitch. **fig. 7.**

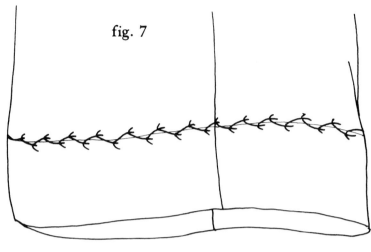

fig. 7

The French Hem With Seams NOT YET Constructed

If the garment seams have NOT yet been stitched (you are just now making the garment, for instance), tie off the seam before completing it to the end.

1. At the point where the hem is to be turned up, tie off the seam. **fig. 1.** DO NOT complete the seam at this time of stitching.

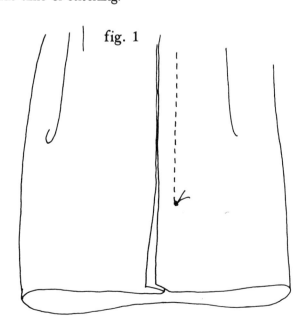

fig. 1

2. Clip into the seam. **fig. 2.**

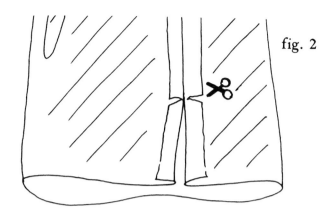

fig. 2

3. Treat each seam of the garment in this same manner.

4. Turn the garment so that the right side of the garment is on the outside and complete making the seam by placing the wrong side of the garment/seam edges together. **fig. 3.**

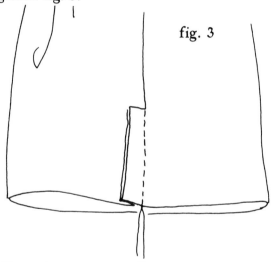

fig. 3

5. Press the seam open. **fig. 4.**

6. The hem is now ready to be turned up and hemmed either with a decorative hem, such as the Feather Stitch . . . or you may wish to use the Invisible Whip Stitch and add some Tatting.

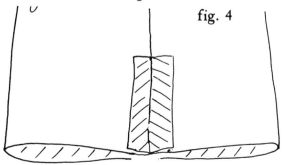

fig. 4

BLIND HEM · BY MACHINE

Using the sewing machine to place a Blind Hem saves time and adds extra sturdiness. There are some garments that can take the Blind Hem by machine nicely; however, the machine hem is more casual than a hem by hand and I do not feel that the Blind Hem by Machine should be used on garments made of the really fine fabrics, such as Swiss Batiste. The Blind Hem by Machine is used mainly for children's clothing and very full skirts.

1. Mark the exact hemline. **fig. 1**. Measure the *depth* of the hemline to make sure that it is the same depth all the way around. **fig. 2.**

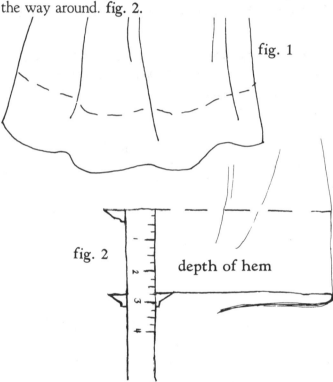

fig. 1

fig. 2

depth of hem

2. Turn under about ⅜" at the bottom edge and press. **fig. 3.**

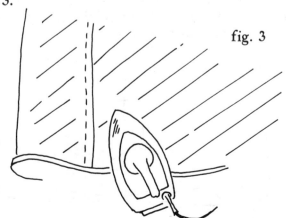

fig. 3

3. Fold the hem up on the fold line and baste into place. This line of basting can be made using the machine also. **fig. 4.**

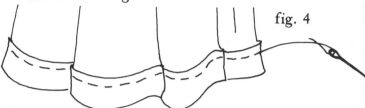

fig. 4

4. Adjust the machine for blind hemming. The Elna 7000 would use the E Foot and your Stitch Program # 5. W/5.0 L 2.5 will vary as to the depth and length of stitch desired.

5. Place the hem allowance face down. Fold the garment back to reveal the hem edge where the ⅜" edge has been turned.

Stitch. The machine, if adjusted properly, will catch only a couple of threads in the garment. If the machine is catching more than just one or two threads, the width of the zigzag stitch is too wide. You will need to move the adjustable guide. **fig. 5.**

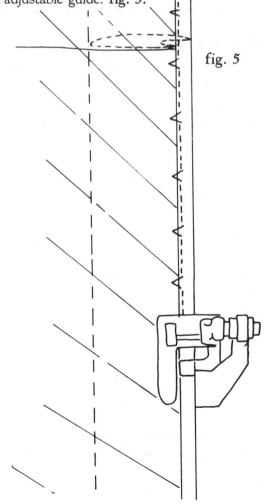

fig. 5

The ruffle may be made of matching fabric, the use of eyelet, or a contrasting fabric could be attractive and appropriate.

1. Cut strips of fabric on the straight edge of grain and join together. Here again, with children's clothing, we are in the habit of using tiny French seams; however, if you prefer, you may use the Over Lock and seam the strips of fabric together. You will need to determine the fullness by multiplying 1½ to 2 times the bottom edge of dress.

2. Finish one edge of the strip of fabric. You may choose to add a piece of lace edging to the edge or use just a tiny rolled hem. **fig. 1.**

fig. 1

3. Gather the strip of fabric with two rows of machine stitching on the opposite side from the finished edge or you may use the gathering foot with your machine. **fig. 2.**

fig. 2

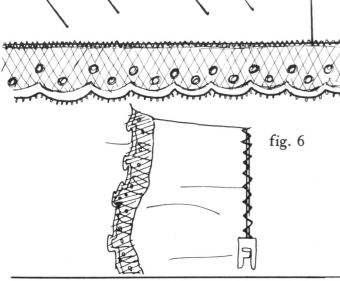

fig. 6

Another way to gather the ruffle, especially if you are going to make it extra full, is to use the Pleater. Put in 4 half rows and pleat. Pull the pleats up to fit the bottom of the skirt and stitch in place. This method gives the appearance of very small pleats.

Pull the gathers to fit the bottom hem line. **fig. 3.**

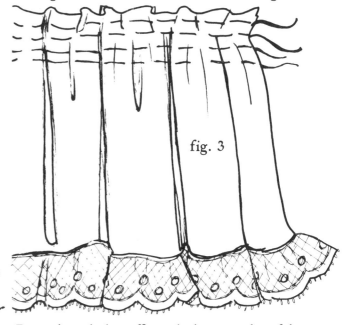

fig. 3

4. Pin and stitch the ruffle to the bottom edge of dress. **fig. 4.** Trim. **fig. 5.** Zigzag to finish the seam. **fig. 6.**

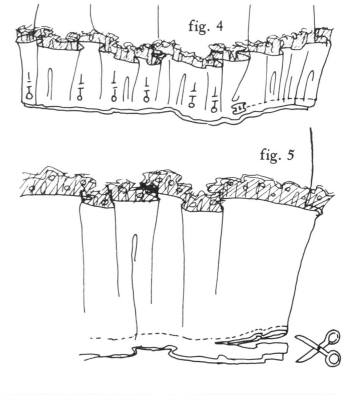

fig. 4

fig. 5

ADDING LENGTH WITH A RUFFLE

Another dress with teardrops or hearts on the bottom! This dress had length added by simply removing the lace edging from the bottom, adding a fabric ruffle with the lace edging added to it. A row of Feather Stitching was used to add a special touch.

1. Roll, whip and gather one long edge of the ruffle to be attached to the bottom edge of the dress. **fig. 1.**

fig. 1

fig. 2

2. Attach the lace edging, which you removed from the bottom edge of the hearts, to the other long edge of the ruffle. **fig. 2.**

3. Very carefully with the right sides together, attach the entredeux on the bottom of the hearts to the ruffle by going into each and every hole. **fig. 3.**

fig. 3

ADDING LENGTH WITH EYELET TRIM

When this dress was constructed, it certainly did not need any additional trim. The use of the smocking with the eyelet trim was sufficient! **fig. 1**. It was comfortable to wear and was still like new when it was passed on to another child that was tall. At first, the dress appeared to be hopeless without destroying the lines of the dress. Sometimes, dresses can have just too much added and it ruins the beauty of the dress!

However, after finding just the right eyelet trim and attaching the ruffle made out of the eyelet to the bottom of the dress, it was apparent that adding a ruffle to this dress would not ruin the dress and would add to it. **fig. 2**.

Don't be timid about trying something new to make the dress wearable!

Follow the directions for a ruffle hem to attach the eyelet ruffle.

fig. 2

fig. 1

78

ADDING LENGTH TO A GARMENT WITH LACE INSERTION

This is one of the prettiest ways of adding length to a dress . . . especially if the dress fabric and style can take the treatment.

First, let's explore the possibilities of adding insertions when the dress has already been constructed, worn and loved by the wearer . . . or, you have accidently cut the skirt too short when making the dress . . . or, something happened and you didn't get the dress completed when you had planned and the child grew . . .

There are so many different combinations one can use! Laces, beading with ribbon, handlooms, tucked fabric inserted, embroideries, lace insertions with different combinations of treatment, puffing, etc. The width of the insertions you chose to use will depend on the length needed or design of the dress and how much the skirt can take before the line of the dress is spoiled with too much.

A few examples of what you may choose to use and how:
Dress "A" began with a plain hemline. **fig. 1.**

fig. 2

fig. 1

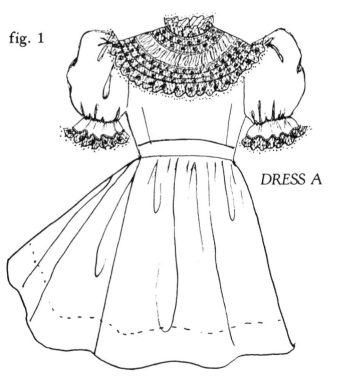

DRESS A

Near the end of the first season of wear, the dress only needed to be lengthened about 1½". The top two rows of lace insertion was added, which added just the right length to the dress. **fig. 2.**

TO ADD THE LACE INSERTION:

1. Carefully measure from the bottom edge of the hem and mark the location where the lace insertion is to be added. Make sure that you measure and mark on both placements for the insertion before cutting. **fig. 3.**

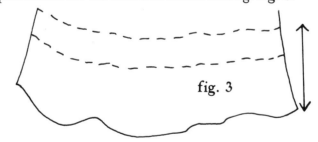

fig. 3

2. Cut on the marking line. One row at a time is easier for me. **fig. 4.**

3. You may use the technique of joining flat edge lace to fabric or the technique of placing the lace on top of the fabric using the zigzag stitch. You may also use entredeux to join the lace insertion to the fabric. Whichever method you choose is a personal choice.

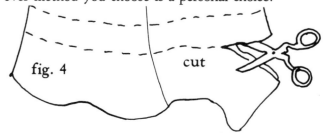

fig. 4   cut

The child loved the dress and when the second season of wear arrived, fashionable hemlines had dropped. Additional length needed to be added to the dress again.

1. Release the hem. Measure and mark from the bottom edge of the lace insertion. **fig. 5**.

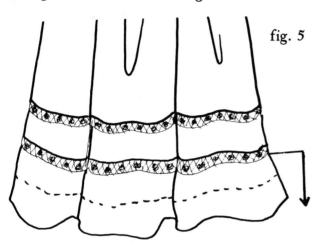

fig. 5

2. Cut on the mark. **fig. 6**. Add another row of lace insertion to the bottom edge. **fig. 7**.

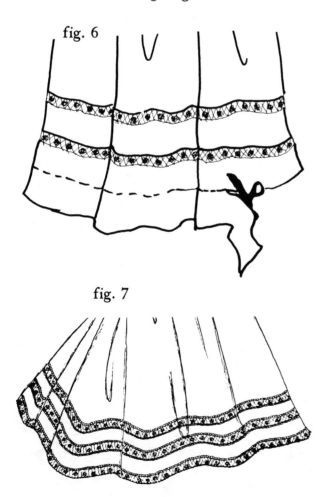

fig. 6

fig. 7

3. Take the fabric which has been cut away from the hemline and fold and press in half. **fig. 8**. **fig. 9**

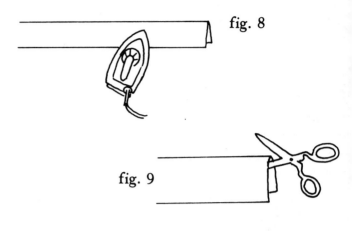

fig. 8

fig. 9

4. Join the two ends together. **fig. 10**.

fig. 10

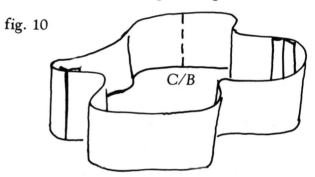

C/B

5. Add a rather wide lace insertion to one side. You may use the technique of joining flat lace to fabric or use entredeux to join the lace to fabric. If you use the flat lace to flat fabric technique, it's especially pretty to Hem Stitch using the **#746** stitch for the Elna. A Pin Stitch is also pretty if using a sheer Swiss Fabric. **fig. 11**.

fig. 11

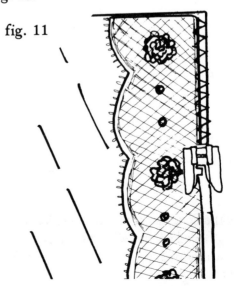

6. Roll, whip and gather the remaining side. **fig. 12.**

fig. 12

8. Trim the remaining side of the entredeux batiste away. Attach to the bottom of the lace insertion, either by the Butt Method or Right Sides Together. **fig. 14**

fig. 14

7. Attach to a piece of entredeux which has been trimmed on one side using the method of right sides together. **fig. 13.**

fig. 13

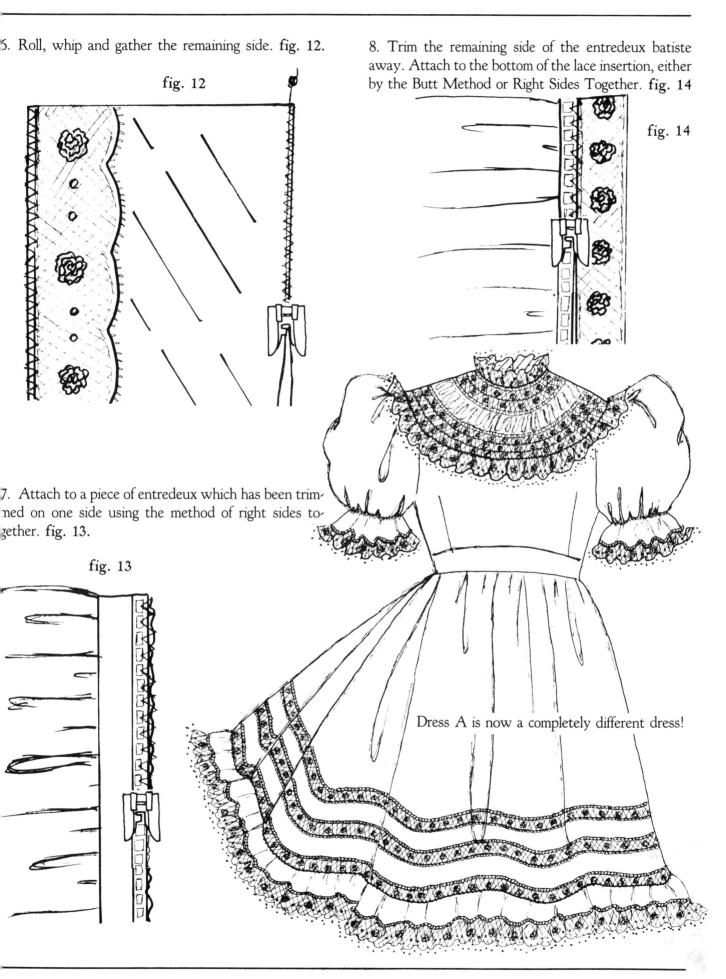

Dress A is now a completely different dress!

ADDING LENGTH WITH TUCKS AND LACE

With fashion trends changing the hemlines so rapidly, it is very possible that your child has a favorite dress which still fits perfectly, except for the length. This dress is a good place to use tucks and lace.

1. Let the old hemline down. If there is a faded crease line where the old hem was turned up and you need that fabric for making the dress the correct length, then incorporate that line into the underside of one of the tucks. **fig. 1.**

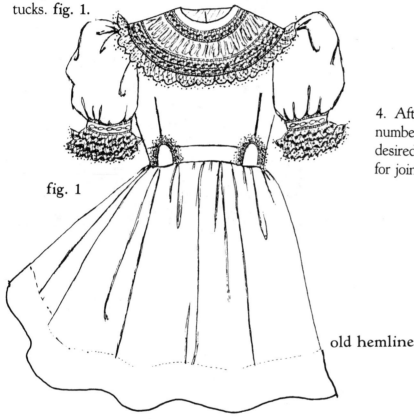

fig. 1

old hemline

The width of your tuck can vary from ¼" to 1" or more if you desire. I prefer to use odd numbers of tucks at the hemline, but that is not always what I need. So, use the number of tucks which you need and desire to make the dress pretty.

2. Mark the position of tucks. Fold on the mark and crease the edge with the iron. **fig. 2.**

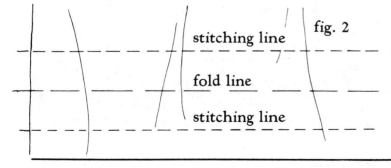

stitching line

fold line

stitching line

fig. 2

3. Stitch the desired width tuck using the guide to make sure that the width of your tuck is even. This can be a line added to your sewing maching table with a piece of tape or, as with the Elna 7000 and a lot of the newer machines, you can use the Adjustable Fabric Guide. **fig. 3.**

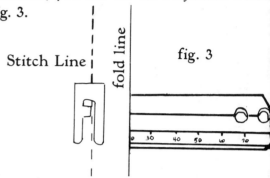

Stitch Line

fold line

fig. 3

4. After you have the tucks completed, add the number of rows of lace insertion needed to give you the desired length. See the techniques for help, if needed, for joining lace to fabric, lace to lace, etc.

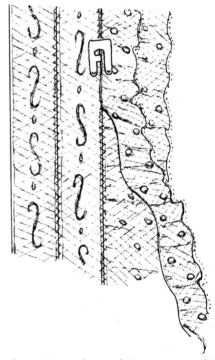

fig. 4

When doing this dress, I ran short of the amount of lace edging I needed to go around the bottom of the dress. I attached the first lace edging to the insertion without the use of gathers. I had plenty of the lace edging which was much narrower than previously used. I gathered it and placed it on top of the first lace edging and stitched it into place. It's different and made a pretty finish. **fig. 4.** It has been copied to make an original dress using the lace edging on top of lace edging.

MAKING YOUR OWN TEMPLATE

Note: You may prefer to use a template when marking the placement of the tucks. Directions for making a template and for marking the placement of the tucks is given at the end of these directions.

Note: This is the device I use when marking tucks — especially in a dress which has already been sewn up.

1. Use a piece of cardboard which has a straight edge. The bottom of the straight edge will be the first stitching line. fig. A.

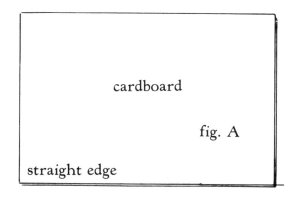

cardboard

fig. A

straight edge

2. Draw a line above the edge of the cardboard the depth you want the tuck to be. This will be the fold line. fig. B.

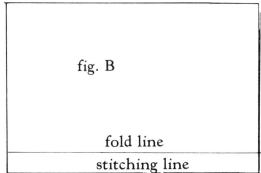

fig. B

fold line
stitching line

3. Draw another line above the fold line the same distance as the bottom edge of the cardboard is to the fold line. fig. C.

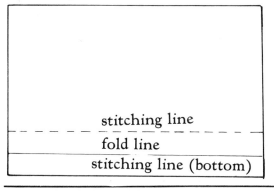

fig. C

stitching line
fold line
stitching line (bottom)

Completed dress!

4. Draw another line above the stitching line the distance which you want the tucks to be apart. This line will also become the new stitching line. fig. D.

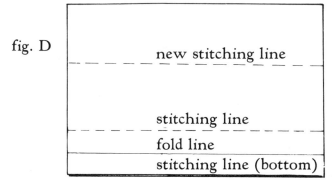

fig. D

new stitching line

stitching line
fold line
stitching line (bottom)

5. Cut the cardboard off at this line. This will become an edge for marking a new stitching line.

Cut the cardboard away on the fold line and stitching line as shown in fig. E, leaving one end not cut!

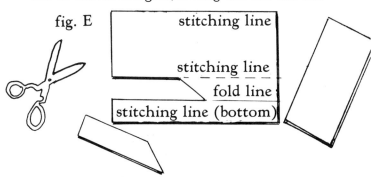

fig. E

stitching line

stitching line
fold line
stitching line (bottom)

Using the Template for Marking Tucks

1. Place the bottom of the template on the line drawn for the placement of the first tuck. **fig. 1.**

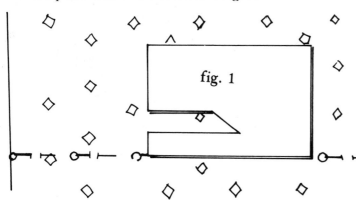

fig. 1

2. Mark at the stitching line with broken lines. **fig. 2.**

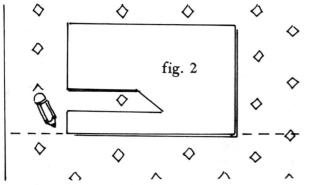

fig. 2

3. Mark at the fold line with a longer line. **fig. 3.**

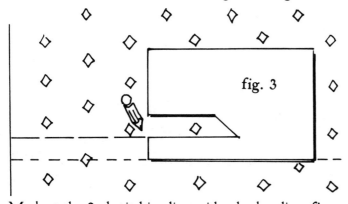

fig. 3

Mark at the 2nd stitching line with a broken line. **fig. 4.**

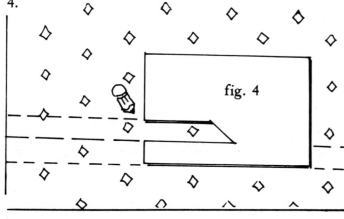

fig. 4

4. Mark at the top edge of the template (this will be stitching line also). **fig. 5.**

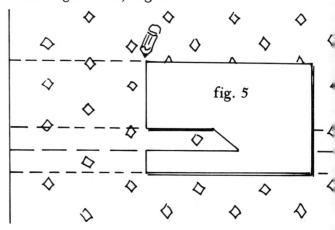

fig. 5

5. Move the template so that the bottom of the template is on the line just drawn. **fig. 6.**

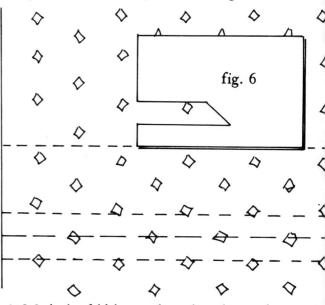

fig. 6

6. Mark the fold line and stitching line and continue for as many tucks as needed moving the template up. **fig. 7.**

fig. 7

fig. 1

This dress is a favorite with a lot of little girls; however, all little girls who can wear this dress are not all the same height. **fig. 1.**

The dress was made for one little girl . . . the length was perfect. She grew, dress lengths changed, and it was passed down to a little cousin. However, the little cousin was tall for her age and needed more length added to be able to wear the dress. What to do? It was much too complicated and time consuming to make another dress, plus the additional expense.

Solution: A petticoat **fig. 2** was designed to go with the dress! The ruffle of the petticoat with the same lace which was used on the bottom edge of the hearts was used. I think it really enhanced the dress and made the hearts stand out.

The dress was of Swiss Batiste, so to cut the expense of the petticoat only the ruffle was of the same color and fabric as the dress. **fig. 3.**

There are so many different ways in which you can finish off the bottom edge of a dress . . . and sometimes it's the hemline of a dress which will make the dress!

fig. 2

fig. 3

ADDING LENGTH WITH PUFFING

Another dress! This time, there was no way in which to match the embroidered insertion which was used in the yoke. However, a piece of the batiste was located and another puffing strip was made.

fig. 1

measure

1. Measure very carefully from the edge of beading up the distance which you would like to have between the puffing strips.

2. Mark on this measurement and cut away. This is where the new puffing strip will be added. **fig. 1.**

4. Attach the Swiss beading using the Right Sides Together technique. **fig. 3.**

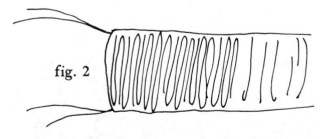

fig. 2

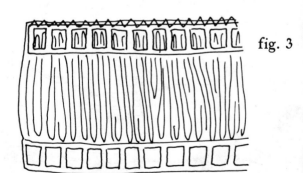

fig. 3

3. Make the new puffing strip to match the original one, resembling the original as much as possible. Use the Quilting Thread Method to Roll, Whip and Gather. **fig. 2.**

5. Attach this puffing strip with the beading attached to both sides to the top of the dress skirt which was cut off.

Roll and whip the fabric edge which was cut.

Additional length was added, as well as making the dress just a little bit more special.

It is very pretty to add pin tucks between the two puffing strips, if you desire to do so.

The pin tucks may be stitched onto the fabric above the puffing/ruffle strip cut from bottom of dress.

Add the new puffing and beading strip. **fig. 5**

6. Place the right side of the Swiss beading edge to the right side of the cut edge of the dress.

Stitch in the Ditch and finish the seam.

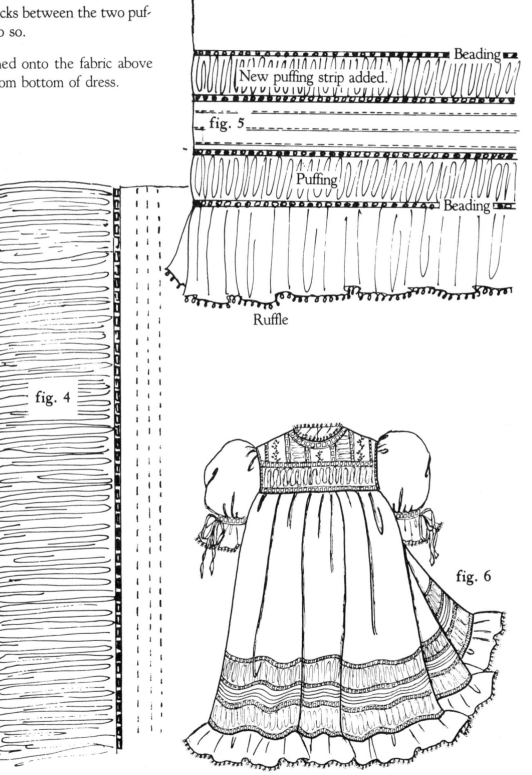

Beading

New puffing strip added.

fig. 5

Puffing

Beading

Ruffle

fig. 4

fig. 6

ADDING LENGTH TO A SMOCKED GARMENT

One of the quickest and least expensive ways of letting a dress down and hiding the old faded hemline is with the use of machine decorative stitching.

One of my granddaughters had a Bishop-style smocked dress that she loved wearing. With the Bishop-style, the child can wear the dress for several years if the length can be changed. This particular dress was a dark cotton print dress, and after the many washings there was a definite faded line so that the hem could not be lowered without the use of insertion, or something to hide the line. As the dress was for more casual wear than dress up, lace insertion was not a possibility, nor was the use of fabric, as the dress was several years old and the fabric no longer available.

Studying the smocking design, which was all smocked in white, and comparing the design of smocking to the decorative stitches on the sewing machine, the decision was made to use the machine and do a row of decorative stitching over the old hemline! Not only did the line of machine stitching hide the faded line, it changed the looks of the dress for the better! **fig. A.**

fig. A

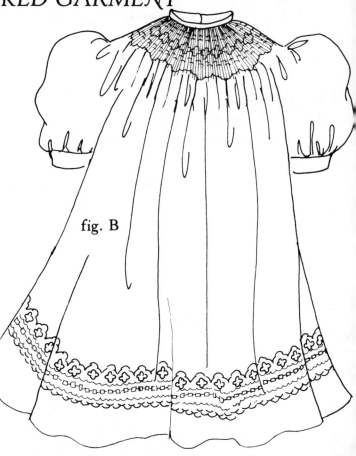

fig. B

This led to trying the same thing on another smocked dress, but this time there were more colors to choose from, as the smocking design was smocked using 3 colors of floss. With careful study of the smocking and comparing the sewing machine stitches, a whole band of machine decorative stitches was placed over the hemline and called attention to the bottom of the dress along with the beautiful smocking. **fig. B.**

Do try using some of the pretty stitches which you have available on your sewing machine. The Elna 7000 keeps coming out with new cassettes and the combination of stitches is unlimited.

If the dress which you are working with can take the use of an additional piece of fabric — for example, if the dress is of a print, the collar is a solid fabric, and you have fabric enough to make a solid color band to add in, by all means, use the sewing machine and create your own decorative band of stitches and insert the band into the dress. It would also be pretty to put piping on either side of the decorative stitched band.

The new sewing machines, such as the Elna 7000, make it possible for all kinds of pretty embroidered designs to be made and placed into the dress or directly onto the dress.

ADDING LENGTH WITH FANCY MACHINE STITCHING

OPTION # 1   *OPTION # 2*

1. Take out the old hem. It is sometimes good to wash and press to remove as much of the visible signs of the old hem as possible. **fig. 1.**

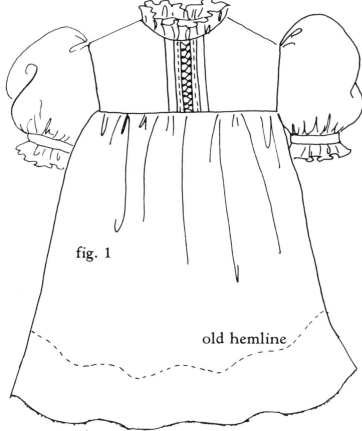

fig. 1

old hemline

2. Do several rows of fancy machine stitching, pin tucks, decorative stitches, etc. as desired to the bottom of the dress.

Turn up the hem and the old faded hem will be hidden with the use of the pretty machine stitches. You may or may not need to add a facing to give more depth to the hem. **fig. 2.**

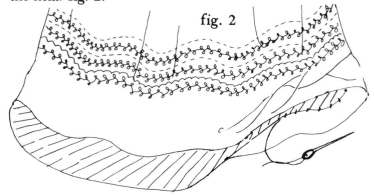

fig. 2

To add more length to the dress, if there is not enough fabric to turn up, you will need to do all of the stitching first, then add a new piece of fabric which will be turned up and hemmed. This piece of fabric could be a contrasting or blend to the dress.

However, it is especially pretty to make a band of decorative stitches using a new piece of fabric which blends or accents the fabric of the dress. For example, if the dress is a print, it would be pretty to find a solid color fabric which you could do fancy stitches on and insert it into the garment to add the additional length needed.

1. Cut the band the width you will need for the additional length needed.

2. Use decorative stitches, tucks or what is on your machine to make a fancy band. **fig. 1.**

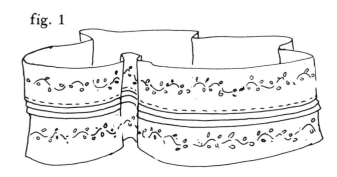

fig. 1

3. Add piping to both long sides of the band. **fig. 2.**

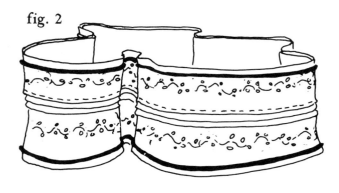

fig. 2

4. Measure carefully and mark on the bottom of the dress where the fancy band insert will go. Cut on this marking. **fig. 3.**

6. Place the right side of the cut off bottom edge of the skirt (the fabric which has the hem in it and which has been cut off) to the right side of the bottom edge of the band. **fig. 5**

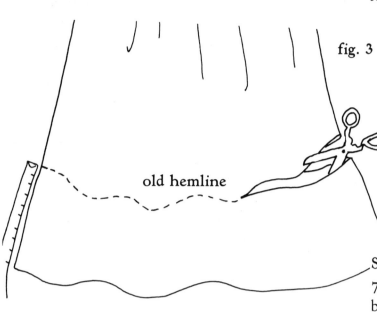

fig. 3

old hemline

fig. 5

Stitch into place. Turn up and hem.

7. Depending on where you cut the dress for the band to be inserted will determine whether you will need to re-do the hem.

5. Place the right side of the band to the right side of the dress, pin and stitch, making sure that you match up seams, etc. if necessary. **fig. 4.**

fig. 4

Finished dress.

**piping   tucks and fancy
machine stitching**

ADDING LENGTH WITH A CONTRASTING FABRIC

Choose a fabric which will complement the dress you are needing to give length to. If the dress is a print, check or stripe, choose a solid color to work with. A pretty finish is a dress with stripes going up and down and extra fabric added with the stripe going in the other direction.

1. Take the old hem out. I like to wash the garment at this time and press it well. If the old hem line remains visible, then you will be able to use that line for the seam allowance to add your new contrasting fabric.

2. Measure carefully the circumference of the bottom edge of the dress. **fig. 1.**

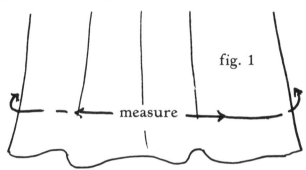

fig. 1

← measure →

Cut the fabric the length and depth needed.

If the dress has two side seams and a center back seam, it is permissible to have only a center back seam in the *new band* if you are using the fabric cross grain. If seams are needed to make the new strip long enough, make sure that the seams are joined so that they will match exactly the seams already in the garment.

Seam the new fabric together to form a tube. **fig. 2.**

C/B

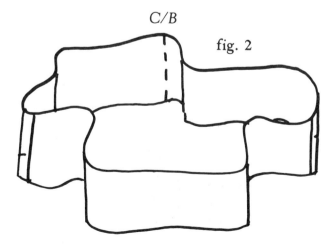

fig. 2

3. Place the right side of the fabric strip to the right side of the garment, matching the seams very carefully. Pin, baste and stitch into place. Press. **fig. 3 and fig. 4.**

4. Mark the desired finished hem line.

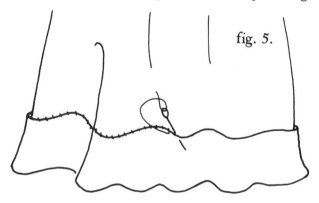

fig. 3

fig. 4

5. Turn the new hem up and hem into place. **fig. 5.**

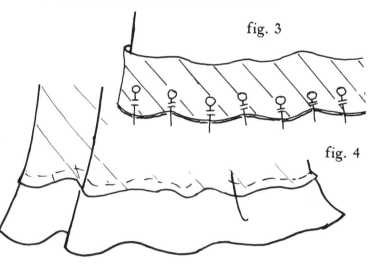

fig. 5.

ADDING LENGTH WITH A HANDLOOM AND LACE

It is so easy to insert lace and/or handlooms into the bottom of a dress to add length or just to make the dress special.

This dress was a smocked Bishop Collar dress and the use of a Swiss Eyelet Embroidery was used for the sleeve trim. The dress was lovely with the plain hemline; but, the child grew and the dress fit perfectly everywhere, except the length of the dress was much too short.

With some careful shopping, a handloom was found with the same colors as the dress was smocked with, and combining the handloom with beading/ribbon the length that was needed made the dress even prettier than the original.

1. The old hemline was removed, the dress washed and pressed. **fig. 1.**

2. The new fancy band and ruffle was constructed by joining the beading and handlooms together, along with the ruffle which had eyelet attached.

To make the new fancy band, the use of entredeux was applied to both long edges of the handloom. You may use the Stitch in the Ditch Method or Roll and Whip the handloom and then apply the entredeux by placing the right side of the entredeux to the right side of the handloom. Zigzag into and off of each hole of the entredeux. **fig. 2.**

fig. 2

Join a strip of beading to each side of the entredeux. First trim the batiste fabric from the entredeux, and butt the beading and entredeux together. **fig. 3.**

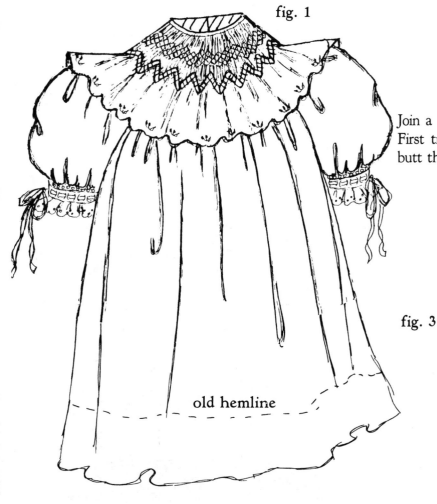

fig. 1

old hemline

fig. 3

Attach a piece of entredeux to the outer edges of the beading. One edge will be used to attach the band to the dress and the other will be used to attach the ruffle to the band. **fig. 4.**

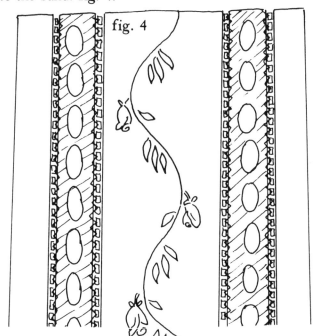

fig. 4

Place the rolled, whipped and gathered edge to the right side of the fancy band, and with the hole of the entredeux facing up so that you can see them, Zig Zag into each hole and off the fabric. **fig. 6.**

fig. 6

Skirt attached
to Band

Ruffle attached
to Band

Cut a strip of fabric the width planned for the additional length times 1½ times length.

Attach a piece of eyelet trim to one of the long sides of the fabric which has been measured and cut. Again, the method which you use will depend more on the method you like to do than that which is correct or incorrect. Or, you may have chosen to use one of the wider eyelets to make the ruffle, in which case nothing needs to be added before you Roll, Whip and Gather with the use of quilting thread. **fig. 5.**

fig. 5

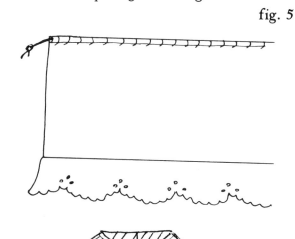

USING PINTUCKS

When using pintucks in the hemline of a garment, use the double needle. This will work on just about any fabric, as long as you use the appropriate size double needle and presser foot for the type of fabric. My fabric for this project was poly/cotton.

I have used the 2.0/70 double needle and the pintuck foot G for the Elna # 7000. This is a pintuck foot with five grooves. However, if you are using a Bernina # 930, use the 7 or 9 groove pintuck foot and a 1.6/70 needle will work. For the Bernina # 1130, I like the 7 groove and the 2.0/70 or 2.5/70 needle.

Mark the position of the first tuck. If using a pintuck foot, the foot itself will guide for even spacing. However, if you are using a machine which does not have a pintuck foot, use the edge of your presser foot as a guide.

Adjust tension if necessary and stitch tucks in the same directions. The Elna 7000 setting would be set automatically by touching the button on the selection keyboard for straight stitching.

You may or may not wish to insert pearl cotton or gimp for firmer tucks. This is especially pretty on the broadcloth and heavier fabrics, but I do not prefer to use it with batiste.

1. Remove the old hem. Press well. If you need to cut off any of the fabric to obtain the correct length for the dress, do so now. If the old hem line remains, do not despair. The hemline can be hidden with a tuck. **fig. 1**.

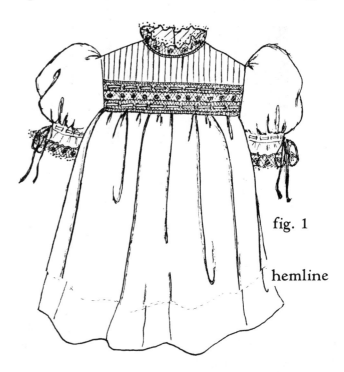

fig. 1

hemline

2. Decide how many tucks are needed. Begin the pin tucking at a side seam and follow the directions for your machine in making the pin tucks. Leave enough fabric from the first pin tuck at the bottom edge to attach your laces. **fig. 2**.

3. Once you have the tucks in place, you may wish to just add some lace edging, slightly gathered. **fig. 3**. Or you may add several strips of lace insertion and beading and then the lace edging. If you need the length, add the lace insertions, if you don't, then just add the lace edging.

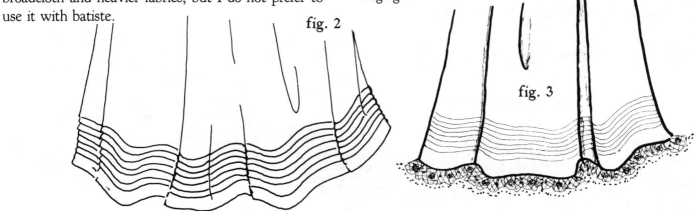

fig. 2

fig. 3

4. It is easier to completely make the band of lace to be added before it is placed onto the bottom edge of the dress. Stitch several rows of lace together, adding lace edging to the bottom of the lace band. **fig. 4.**

When adding the lace edging, you may choose to use entredeux to join the two, or you may join the lace edging directly to the lace insertion. **fig. 5.**

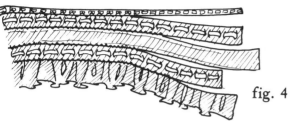

fig. 4

5. Attach to the bottom edge of the dress, with the new tucks already stitched. The dress is even prettier after altering the hem than it was before you began. **fig. 6.**

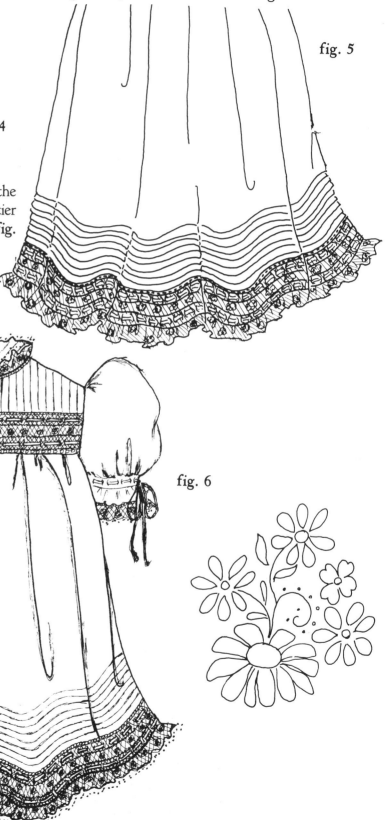

fig. 5

fig. 6

SOME PRETTY HEMLINES –

1.   A handloom and lace edging combination!

Find a pretty handloom, attach a piece of entredeux to both long sides, and add a ruffle with a pretty lace edging applied to the bottom. Choose the method you prefer to attach the entredeux to fabric and flat lace edging to entredeux. **fig. 1**

2.   Or use a handloom with a combination of lace, Swiss beading, and an eyelet embroidery for the ruffle. It's fun and pretty to combine the different trims together for use in the same garment. **fig. 2** .

3.   This is a lovely combination to use, particularly if you like to do Fagoting! The use of tucks, lace insertion, fagoting, and a narrow lace edging gives a pretty finish to the bottom of a dress. **fig. 3** .

4.   Another combination I like is the use of lace insertion with puffing. Puffing can add a lot of length to a garment with very little cost. **fig. 4   Dress A** ✤

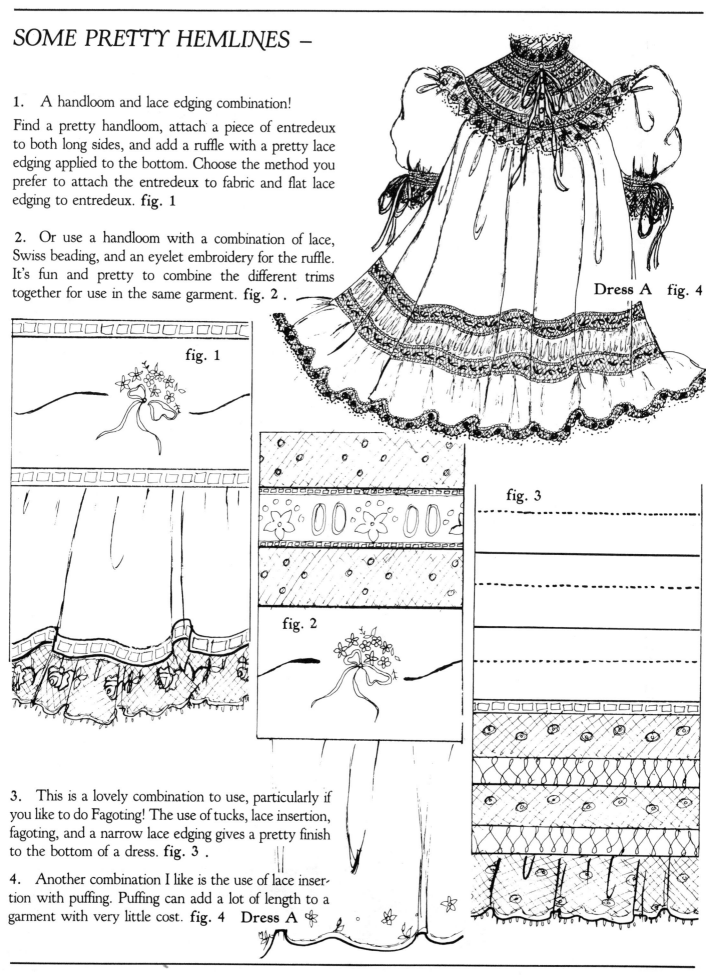

Dress A   fig. 4

fig. 1

fig. 2

fig. 3

5. Or, if you are making the dress for a really special occasion, you may want to add more laces to either side of the puffing strip. **fig. 5** .

6. To add something a little bit different, when using just lace insertions and lace edging to the bottom of a dress, try using a different width lace edging and place it on top of the wider lace edging. This gives the dress a certain flair at the bottom edge. **fig. 6 Dress B**

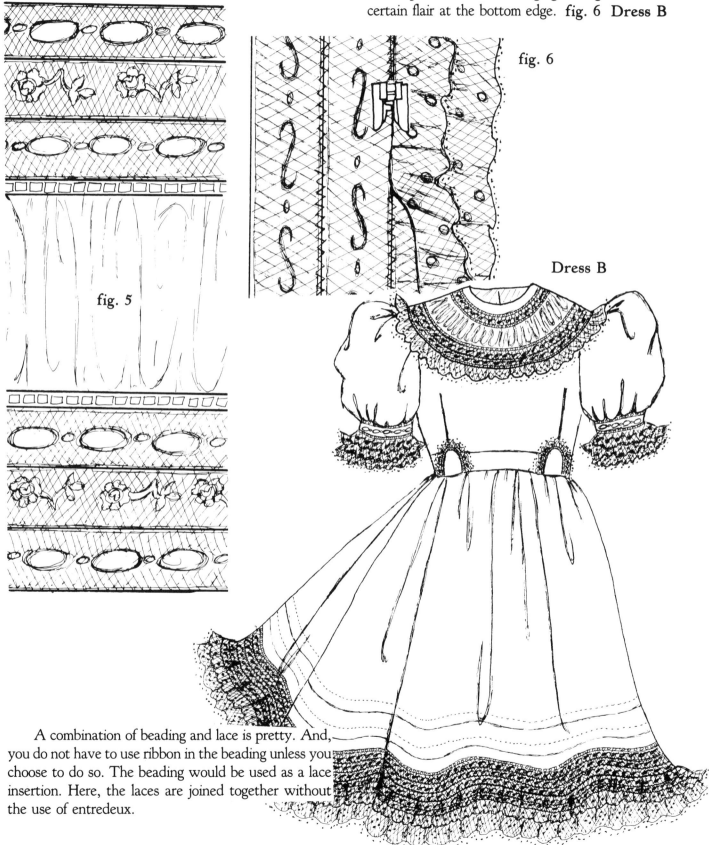

fig. 5

fig. 6

Dress B

A combination of beading and lace is pretty. And, you do not have to use ribbon in the beading unless you choose to do so. The beading would be used as a lace insertion. Here, the laces are joined together without the use of entredeux.

7. Making a strip of vertical tucks and adding lace insertion on both sides is so pretty to add as a fancy band. **fig. 7**

8. A fancy band with horizontal tucks are easy to do and makes a pretty showing. **fig. 8**

9. Fancy Bands on very small clothes can be very effective without adding a whole lot.

A little smocked Swiss batiste dress for an infant can be expecially pretty with just a simple little band of one piece of lace insertion added to the bottom with the narrow lace edging. **fig. 9 Dress C**

fig. 7

fig. 9

fig. 8

Dress C

10. This dress is pretty with Swiss Beading and an embroidery strip with a narrow eyelet ruffle! **Dress D**

Dress D

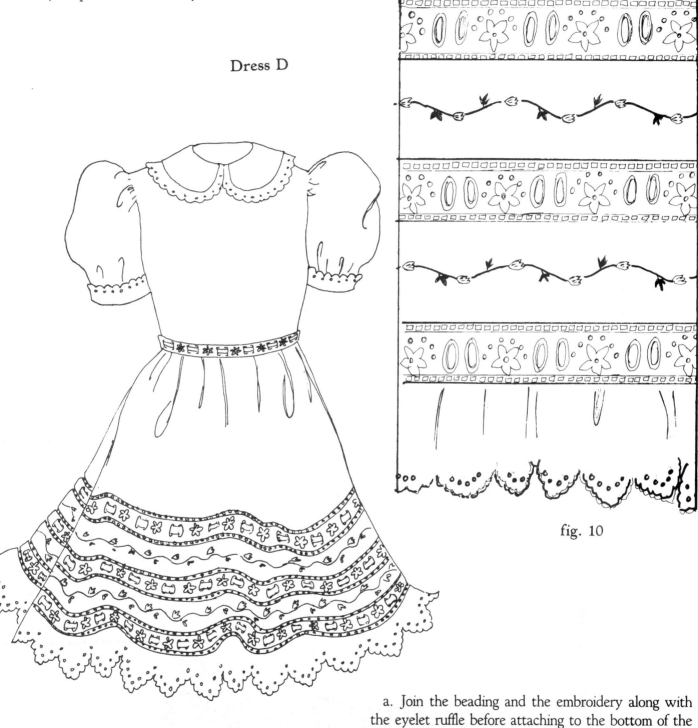

fig. 10

a. Join the beading and the embroidery along with the eyelet ruffle before attaching to the bottom of the dress. **fig. 10**

The Swiss Beading has the entredeux ready to be attached to the embroidery strip! This is a fairly quick way to make a dress really special without a lot of time involved.

SOME FANCY BAND SUGGESTIONS:

There are so many fancy band combinations which one can use in a dress, that I almost decided not to put any illustrations in, for fear that someone would think that they were limited by so few.

When planning a dress or making a fancy band, let your imagination and your creative juices flow! Some of the prettiest combinations I have seen have been created in just this way.

To help you get started, here's a few with some suggestions as to how to put them together.

1. The use of tucks, entredeux and beading.

The beading was applied to the tucked strip using the method of Right Sides Together.

Make two strips of pin tucks. Use the method of Tucking-in-the-Round for speed. **fig. 1.**

See *Mimi's Machine Heirloom Sewing Book* by Mildred Turner, (page 32) for Pintucking In The Round.

fig. 1

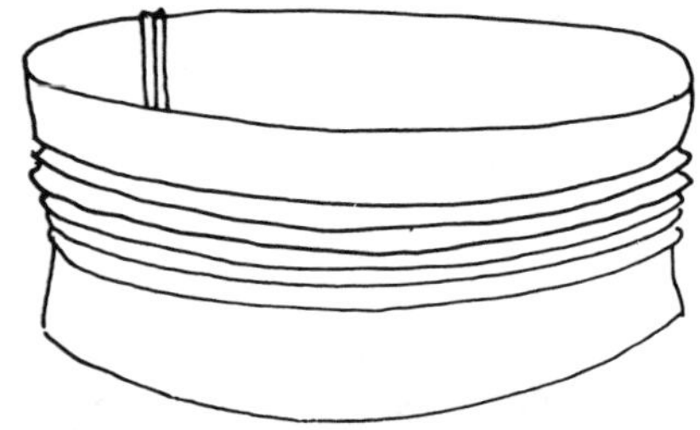

Attach entredeux to both sides of the tucked strip. **fig. 2.**

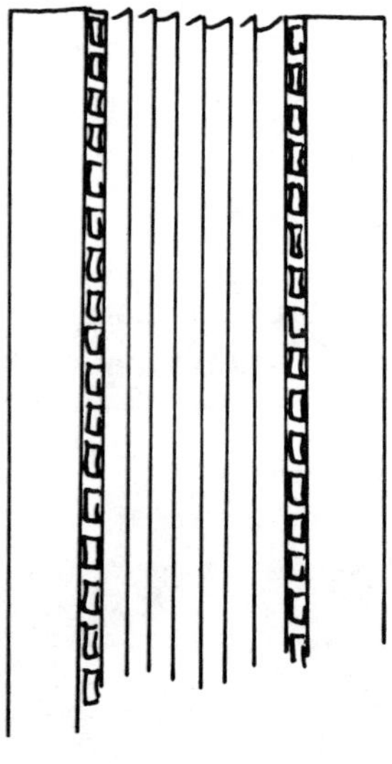

fig. 2

To attach the two tucked pieces together, use a strip of beading between the two.

The Fancy Band with the tucks is ready to be attached to your dress.

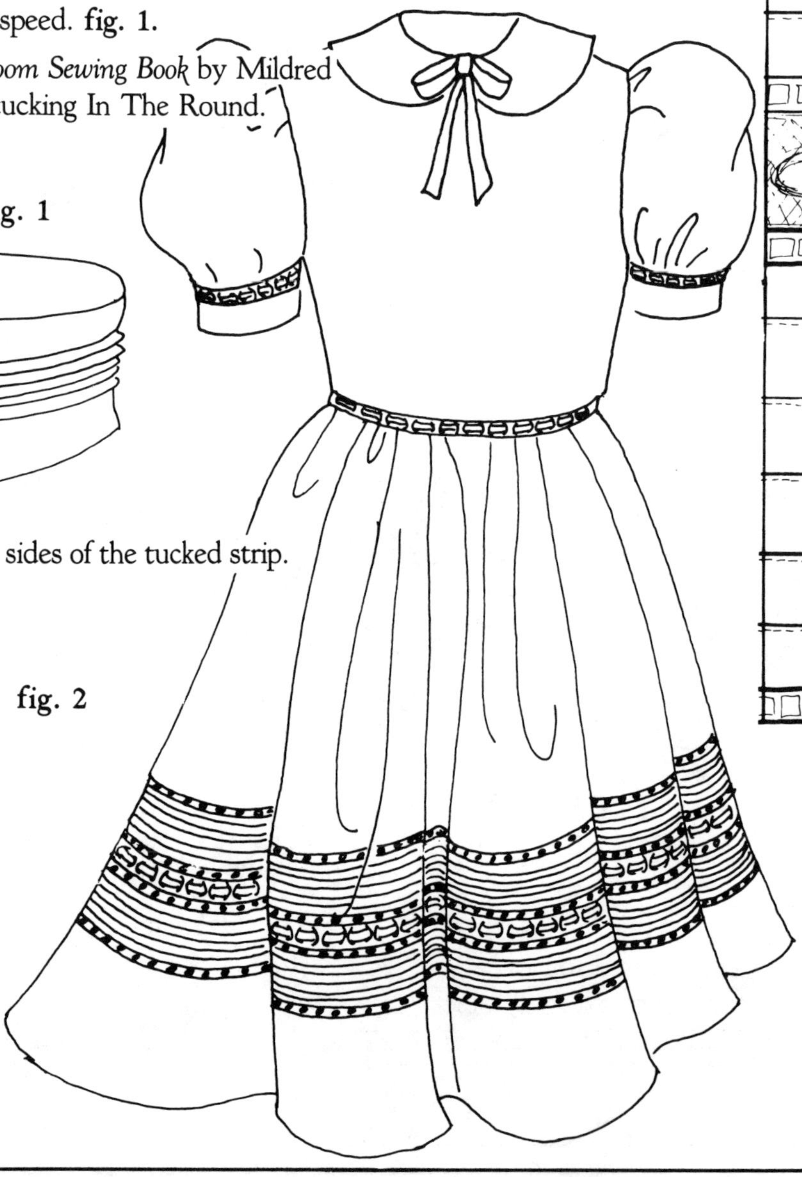

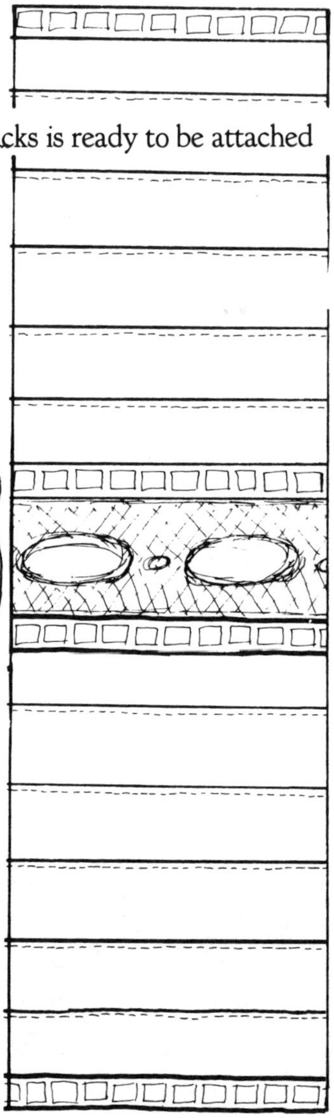

100

2. Vertical lace insertion with a piece of embroidered insertion added, as Janice Ferguson did with her Heirloom Dress, is so lovely. **Dress A.**

b. Apply entredeux to both sides of the tucked strip. You may choose the method of attaching entredeux to fabric that you prefer. **fig. 2.**

c. Join the lace insertions together. Be sure to remember to spray starch and press the laces before joining together. **fig. 3.**

Dress A

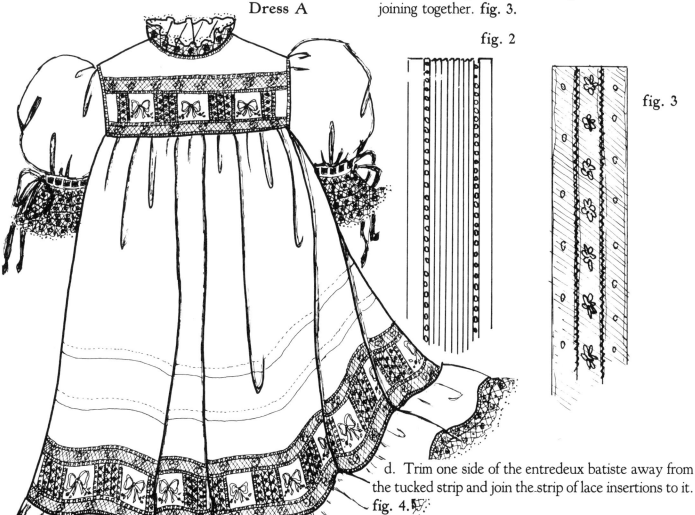

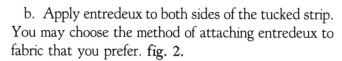

fig. 2

fig. 3

d. Trim one side of the entredeux batiste away from the tucked strip and join the strip of lace insertions to it. **fig. 4.**

e. Measure and cut this strip into pieces the length you desire the fancy band to be. Add about ½" to the length to allow for attaching the entredeux to the strip after it is joined together.

a. Tuck a long strip of fabric. **fig. 1.**

fig. 4

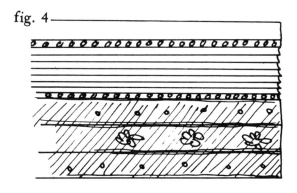

fig. 1

f. Join the side of the lace insertion to the trimmed entredeux side. This will go together rather quickly. **fig. 5.**

Once you have all the pieces put together, attach entredeux to both long edges by using the method of Right Sides Together and Stitch in the Ditch. **fig. 6.**

After this has been completed, you add a piece of insertion lace all the way across with a piece of entredeux placed on the other side of the lace insertion. **fig. 7.** This fancy band is now ready to be attached to the ruffle and then to the bottom edge of the dress.

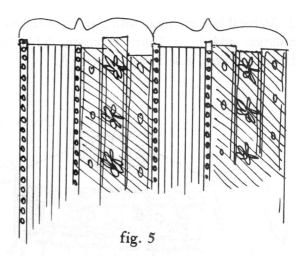

fig. 5

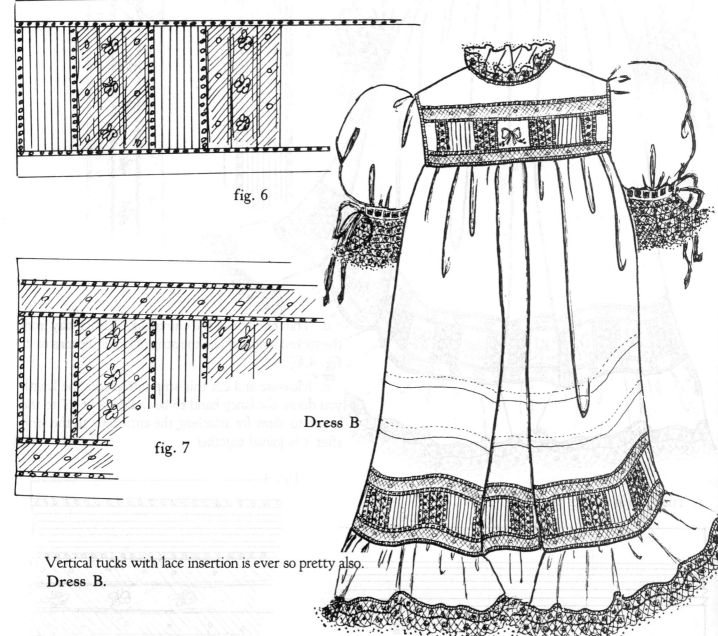

fig. 6

fig. 7

Dress B

Vertical tucks with lace insertion is ever so pretty also. **Dress B.**

YOKES

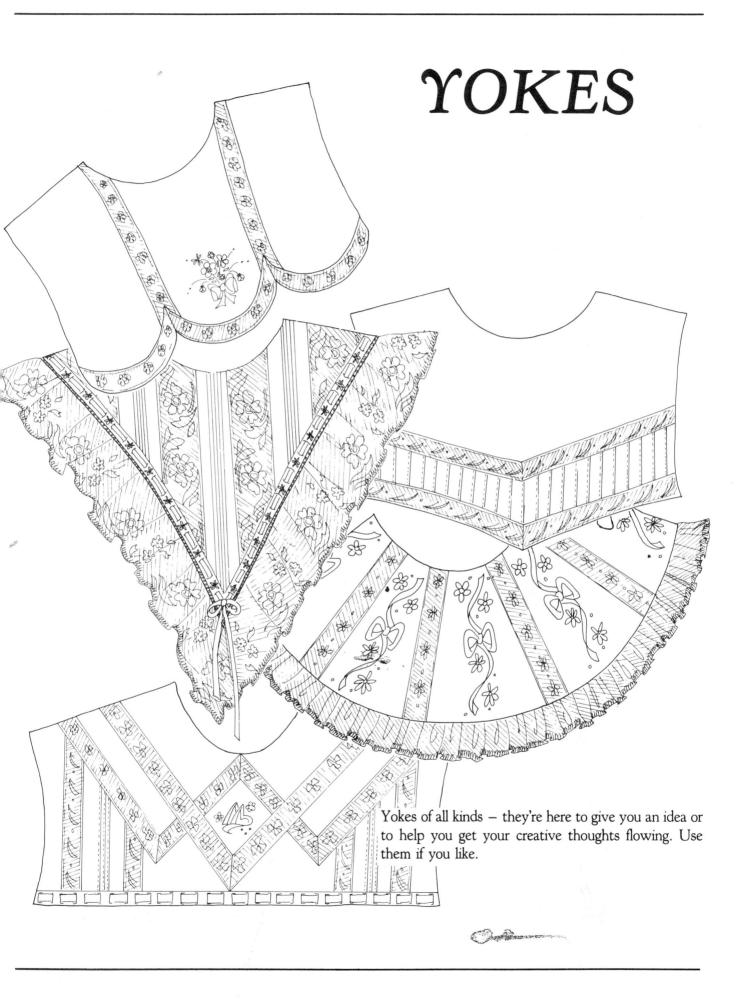

Yokes of all kinds – they're here to give you an idea or to help you get your creative thoughts flowing. Use them if you like.

THE BASIC YOKE

To plan a yoke with insertion (laces, beadings, handlooms, tucked strips, etc.), it is best to have a complete yoke for a guide. **fig. 1.**

When designing your own combination of insertions, experiment with laying the laces, entredeux, beading or any other insertions which you like on the yoke. Move the pieces around until the best combination or placement is found. I make a note on paper of the placement which I like so that I don't get confused, forget, etc. when I begin stitching the laces together.

When using a fabric insert (tucks, handlooms, etc.), allow at least ¼" overlap, as you will loose between ⅛" to ¼" on each side when rolling and whipping the edges.

I feel that it is best to start your pattern design in the center and continue outwards, placing the laces, etc. **fig. 2.**

Attach all insertion laces, handlooms, tucks, etc. together in a block form first, using the guide to keep the shape and size. **fig. 5.**

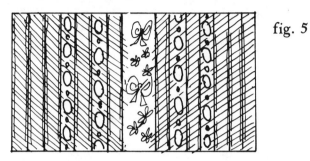

fig. 5

You may or may not choose to do a back lace yoke.

2. After all the laces have been attached, draw the yoke pattern onto the lace. **fig. 6.**

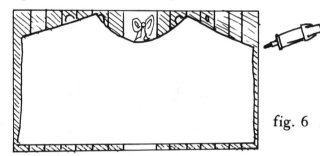

fig. 6

3. Machine stitch on the line drawn. Use a very narrow short Zigzag Stitch for this stitching. **fig. 7.**

4. Trim as close as you can without cutting into the line of stitching. **fig. 8.**

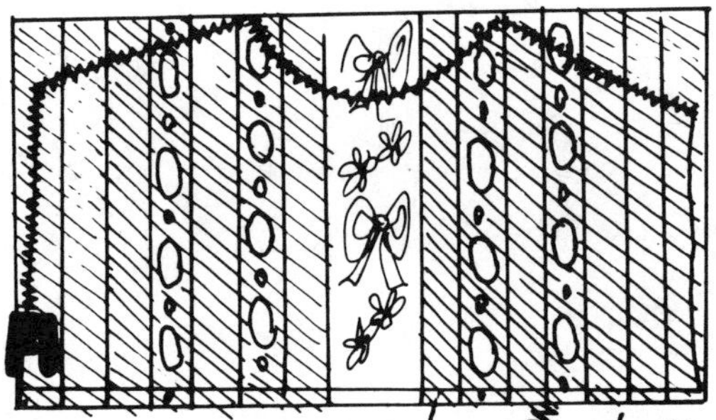

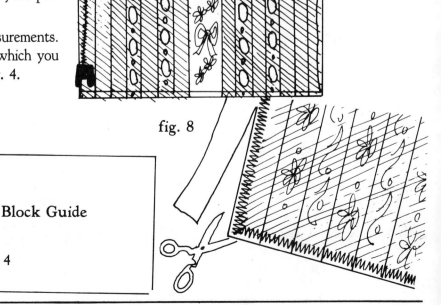

fig. 7

fig. 8

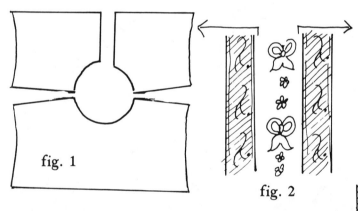

fig. 1

fig. 2

1. Measure the width and the depth of the yoke pattern of your choice. **fig. 3.**

Add 1" to both the width and length measurements. You will have a rectangle. This is a guide which you will use to make a block of laces to size. **fig. 4.**

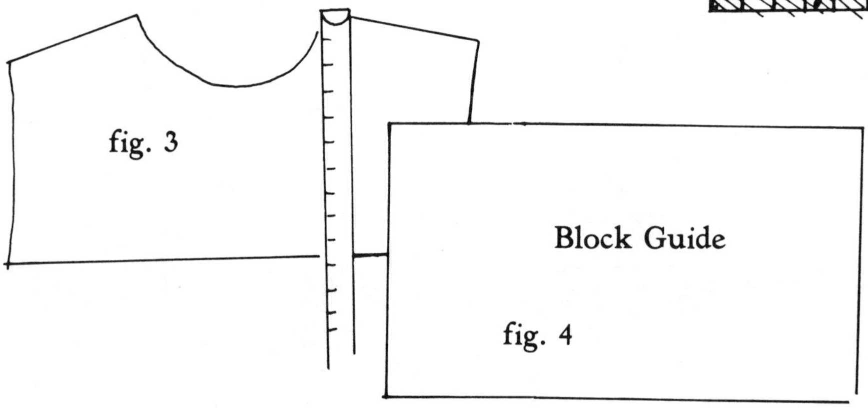

fig. 3

Block Guide

fig. 4

5. Straight stitch ⅛" outside the seam allowance. **fig. 9.**

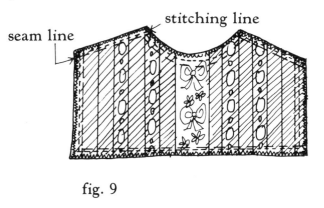

seam line

stitching line

fig. 9

6. Stitch the shoulder seams. You may use entredeux to join the front to the back, or very *carefully* match the laces (if laces were used to make the back yoke) and join together the front to the back using a French Seam. **fig. 10.**

Note: When doing an all lace yoke, you should use entredeux to join the skirt and set-in the sleeves. If the yoke has fabric at the armhole edge, then it's not a necessity to use entredeux.

fig. 10

7. Stitch entredeux to the bottom edge of the front and back yokes. DO NOT trim the entredeux edge. Place the entredeux right side to the right side of the yoke. Stitch in the Ditch. **fig. 11.**

fig. 11

Trim and zigzag to roll the raw edge. **fig. 12 & 13.**

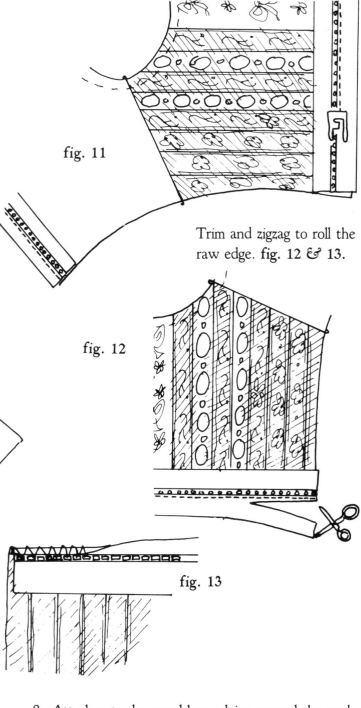

fig. 12

fig. 13

8. Attach entredeux and lace edging around the neck edge.

   a. Trim one side of a piece of entredeux.

   b. Gather a strip of lace edging and attach to the entredeux. If the lace is attached using the Butt Method the lace is more likely to stand up rather than flop over.

THE ALL LACE ROUND YOKE

1. Making or adjusting your pattern. If the pattern which you are using is not an entire yoke, make one by putting the front and back yoke together at the shoulder seams. **fig. 1. and fig. 2.**

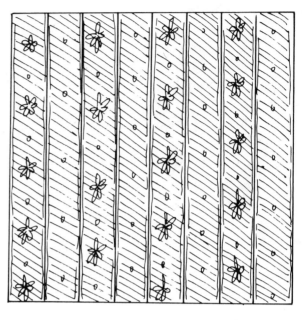

fig. 3

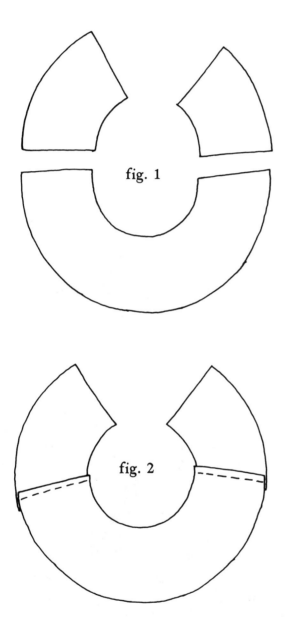

fig. 1

fig. 2

3. After you have stitched your block of laces together, I like to spray starch lightly and press, making sure that all the laces are straight, etc. Place the pattern onto the block of laces. Pin very carefully to make sure that the pattern has not caused the laces to shift. Trace around the pattern with a marking pen which does not require pressure to make it mark. **fig. 4.**

fig. 4

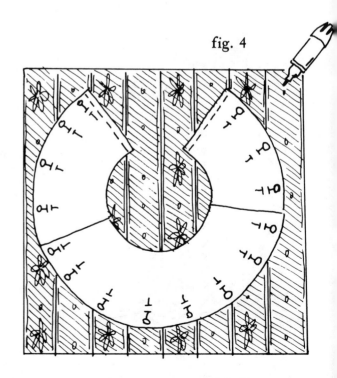

2. Make a block of your laces by stitching them together. **fig. 3.** Arrange the laces, beading, handloom or other trim which you have chosen, letting the block be at least ½" larger than the pattern.

4. Remove the paper pattern from the lace and machine stitch on the line drawn. Make one row of very tiny machine stitching first and then come back with a very narrow Zigzag Stitch, but do not make it a Satin Stitch. The length would be 1.2 using the Elna 7000, and 1½ with the Bernina # 930. With the 1130 Bernina, the setting would be just slightly above the one mark.

5. Trim away excess laces as close to the stitching as possible, but making sure that you do not cut into the stitching line. **fig. 5**.

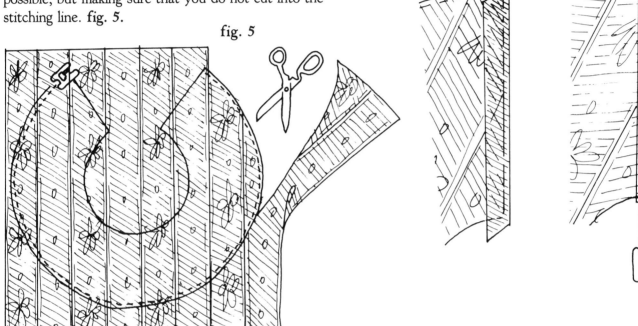

fig. 5

6. Complete the placket at this time. When using an all lace yoke, it is nice and I feel best to use lace in making this placket.

a. Measure two pieces of lace insertion the length of the back opening. Lay two pieces of lace insertion with the wrong sides together and zigzag one long side together. Make sure that you have just encased the lace heading. This will give you a nice finish. **fig. 6**.

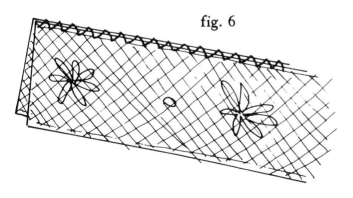

fig. 6

b. Place one of the long sides of the lace insertion on top and even with the seam allowance at center back with the top piece of insertion. Baste into place. Let the underneath lace edge be even with the top so that when you machine stitch the top piece, both edges will be stitched. **fig. 7 & 8.**

fig. 7   fig. 8

FINISHING THE NECK EDGE

1. Trim one side of the entredeux cut to the size of the neck measurement.

2. Attach gathered lace edging using the Butt Method of attaching gathered lace to entredeux. The right side of the lace and the right side of the entredeux will be facing up. **fig. 9**.

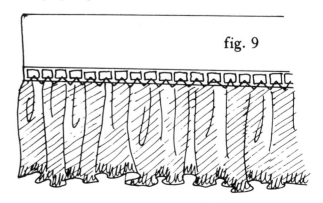

fig. 9

3. Place the raw edge of the entredeux batiste to the raw edge of the neck and Stitch in the Ditch. **fig. 10**.

Trim to within ⅛" and roll and whip the edge using a Zigzag Stitch just wide enough to touch the edge of the entredeux and off the edge. **fig. 11**.

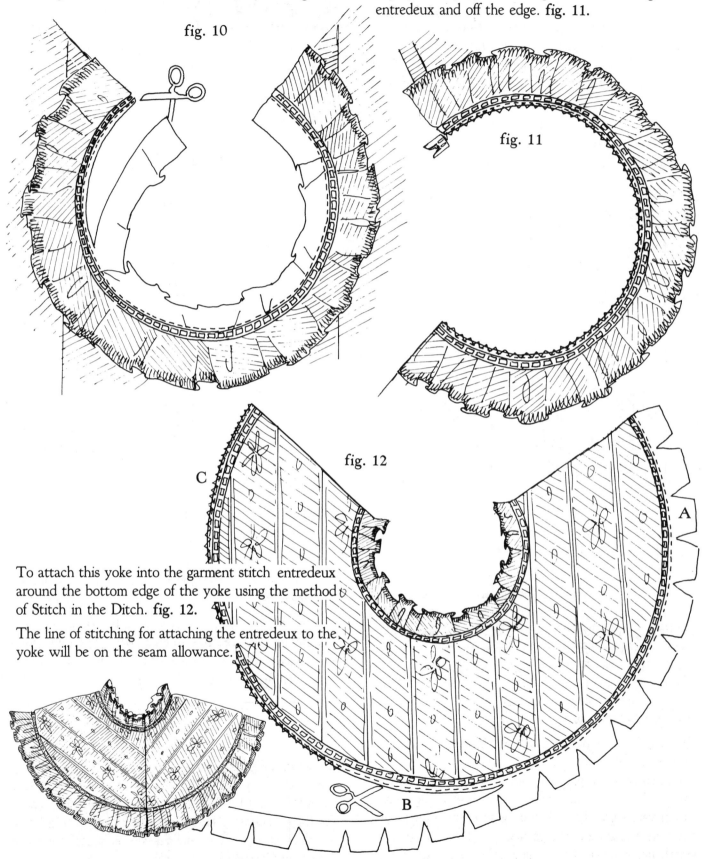

fig. 10

fig. 11

fig. 12

To attach this yoke into the garment stitch entredeux around the bottom edge of the yoke using the method of Stitch in the Ditch. **fig. 12**.

The line of stitching for attaching the entredeux to the yoke will be on the seam allowance.

PLACKETS

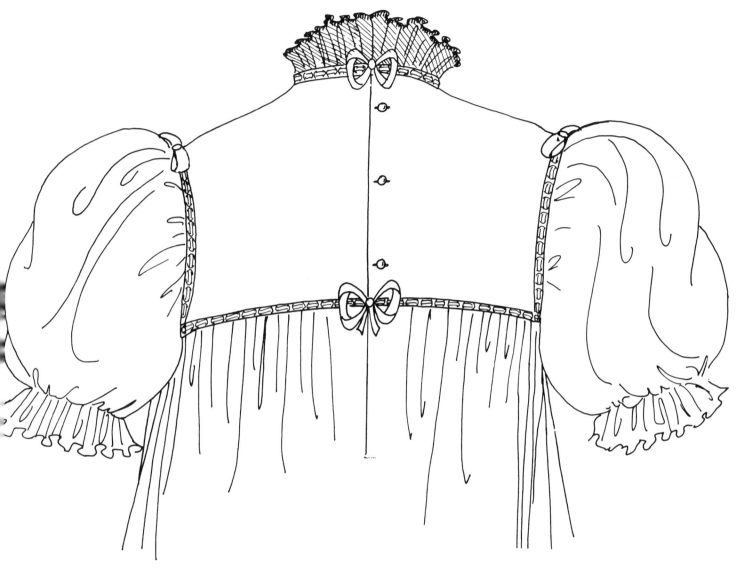

No part of a garment shows inexperienced or careless work to more disadvantage than the Placket! So, choose the placket which suits your garment best. There are so many ways to finish a closure that it would be impossible to illustrate them all. So, only the most popular ones will be discussed.

The length of the placket is usually marked on the pattern. When it is not marked, it should be of sufficient length so that the garment can be easily slipped over the head without tearing the placket opening. This length varies greatly with the figure of the individual, and with the style of the garment, that any set rule of length might make the opening either too long or too short.

Nearly all plackets are arranged so that the upper portion of the closing comes on the right-hand side, and the under closing on the left-hand side of the seam, which makes the placket fasten from right to left.

Snaps or fasteners should be sewed on before the placket is finished. This way, all your stitches are concealed.

Usually, the type of placket to be used will be dependent upon the width of the seam or for no seam. Most times, if you have a wide seam, the Lap Placket would be the one chosen. However, there have been a lot of changes in how the Lap Placket is made with the Smocked Garment.

CONTINUOUS LAP PLACKET WITHOUT A SEAM

1. Measure and cut the opening for the placket. **fig. 1.** Stay Stitch to add extra strength, if desired.

2. Beginning at the top edge, pin the right side of the placket to the right side of dress opening. **fig. 2.**

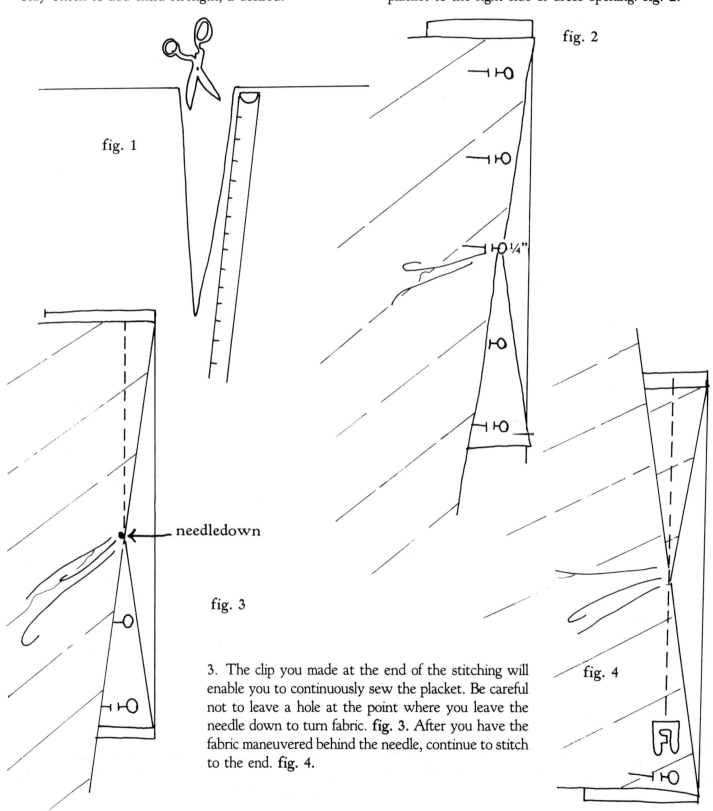

fig. 2

fig. 1

needledown

fig. 3

3. The clip you made at the end of the stitching will enable you to continuously sew the placket. Be careful not to leave a hole at the point where you leave the needle down to turn fabric. **fig. 3.** After you have the fabric maneuvered behind the needle, continue to stitch to the end. **fig. 4.**

fig. 4

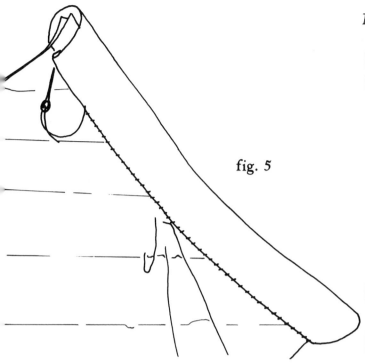

fig. 5

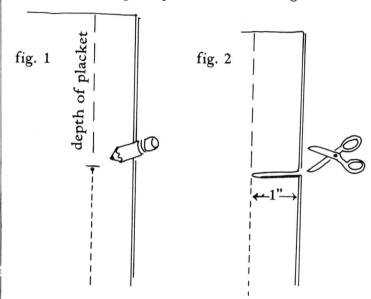

1. Mark the length of placket to be used. **fig. 1**.

fig. 1

depth of placket

fig. 2

←1"→

4. Trim the placket seam to ¼". Press seam toward placket strip.

5. Turn under the other side of the placket piece ½".

Baste the placket over the seam you have just stitched. Slip Stitch to hold into place. **fig. 5**.

6. Turn back the right side of the placket to the wrong side. Sew diagonally at the end of the placket to hold in place. **fig. 6**.

If your garment needs a back seam, you may French Seam and then use Lap Placket.

2. Clip into the seam allowance 1" at the *bottom edge* of the placket. **fig. 2**.

3. Trim ⅝" of an inch from the seam allowance from the bottom edge of the placket to the bottom edge of the garment. **fig. 3**.

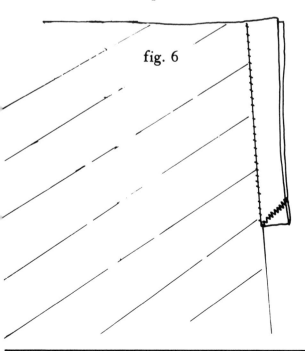

fig. 6

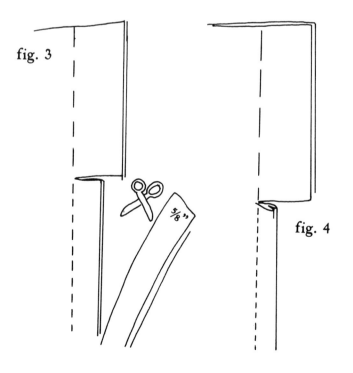

fig. 3

⅝"

fig. 4

4. Complete the French Seam. **fig. 4**.

CONTINUOUS BOUND PLACKET FOR THE
SMOCKED GARMENT WITH A FRENCH SEAM *(Back Opening)*

1. Measure the length of the placket opening. Clip the French Seam at end of placket opening. **fig. 1.**

4. Begin stitching at the top, keeping the same seam allowance all the way to the other end. **fig. 3.**

5. As you get to the very center, the needle will only catch 2 to 3 threads. Leave the needle in the down position and pivot the placket so that the excess will be behind the presser foot and flat in front. **fig. 4.**

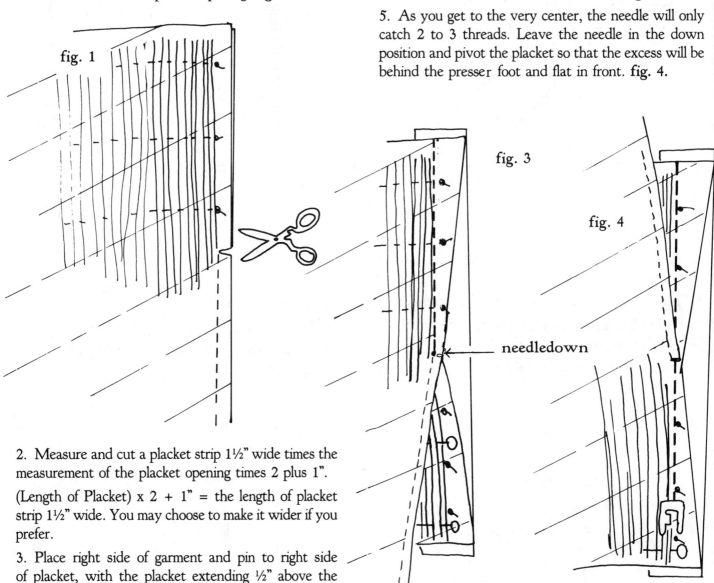

fig. 1

fig. 3

fig. 4

needledown

2. Measure and cut a placket strip 1½" wide times the measurement of the placket opening times 2 plus 1".

(Length of Placket) x 2 + 1" = the length of placket strip 1½" wide. You may choose to make it wider if you prefer.

3. Place right side of garment and pin to right side of placket, with the placket extending ½" above the garment. The placket will be on the under side of the garment. **fig. 2.**

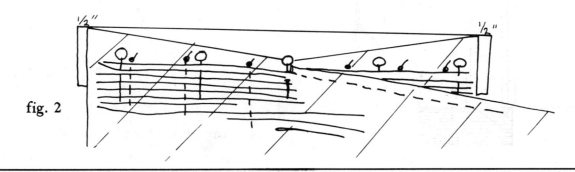

fig. 2

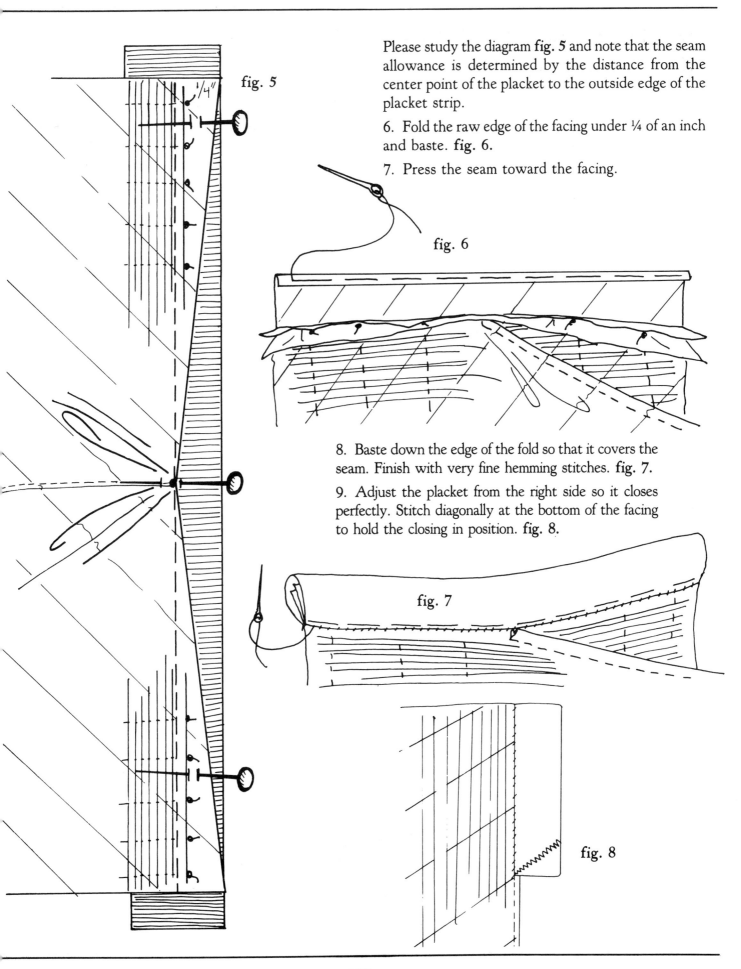

fig. 5

Please study the diagram **fig. 5** and note that the seam allowance is determined by the distance from the center point of the placket to the outside edge of the placket strip.

6. Fold the raw edge of the facing under ¼ of an inch and baste. **fig. 6.**

7. Press the seam toward the facing.

fig. 6

8. Baste down the edge of the fold so that it covers the seam. Finish with very fine hemming stitches. **fig. 7.**

9. Adjust the placket from the right side so it closes perfectly. Stitch diagonally at the bottom of the facing to hold the closing in position. **fig. 8.**

fig. 7

fig. 8

¼″

115

THE TRADITIONAL LAP PLACKET FOR THE WIDE SEAM

To make the Lap Placket:

1. The seam should be at least 1" wide. Leave the top portion of the seam open the length desired for the placket opening. **fig. 1.**

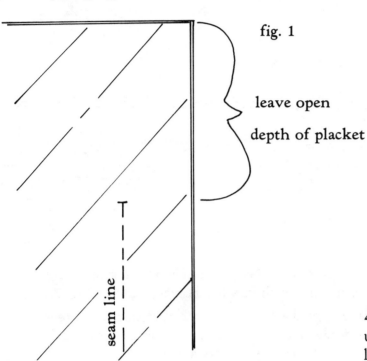

fig. 1

leave open

depth of placket

seam line

2. On the top portion of the lap placket, turn the raw edge under about ⅛" and machine stitch. **fig. 2.**

fig. 2

seam line

3. Turn under the top placket on the seam line and baste near the edge. **fig. 3.**

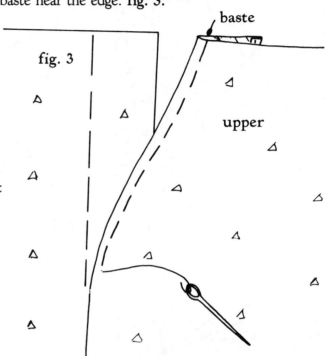

fig. 3

baste

upper

4. To finish the underneath portion of the lap placket, use a piece of the garment material and cut a straight lengthwise strip of material for the facing. It is good to cut with the selvage edge to sew to the seam edge of the placket.

5. Pin and baste the right side of the facing to the right side of the loose edge of the placket opening and stitch ⅛ of an inch from the edge. **fig. 4.**

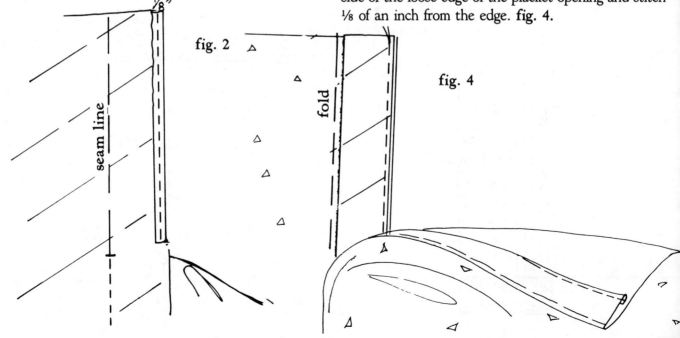

fold

fig. 4

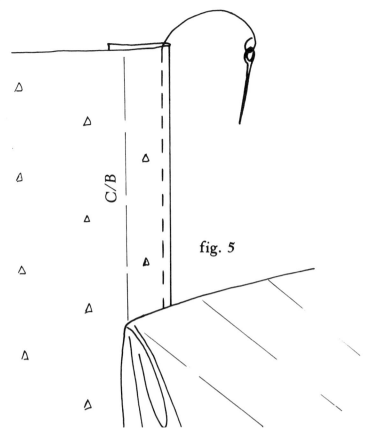

C/B

fig. 5

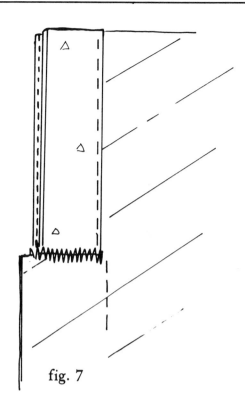

fig. 7

6. Turn the facing to the under side. Baste carefully near the edge of the outside seam line. **fig. 5.**

7. Turn the raw edge of the facing under so that the edge is at least ⅛ of an inch inside of the marked seam line. This is done so that the stitches on the facing will not show from under the top of the placket. Finish with the Invisible Slip Stitch. **fig. 6.**

8. To finish the bottom of the placket, you may zigzag the facing to the seam or turn under the facing and hem with hemming stitches. **fig. 7.**

Sew snaps to close. **fig. 8.**

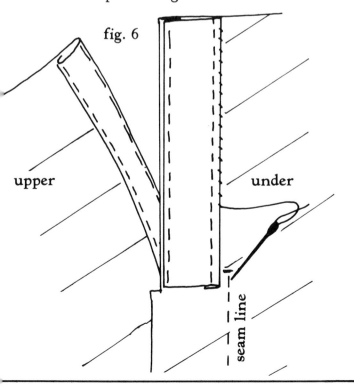

fig. 6

upper

under

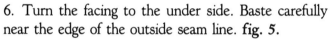

seam line

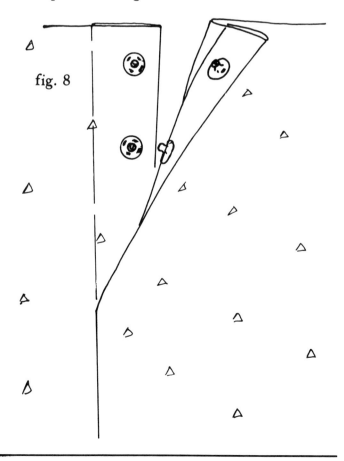

fig. 8

EXTENSION PLACKET FOR NARROW SEAMS

1. Leave open the portion of the seam desired for the placket opening. **fig. 1.**

2. Pin, press or baste to mark the seam line on both sides of the placket opening.

3. Cut a straight facing the width the placket is to be plus ⅛" for the turning and ¼" for the seam. Cut the facing 1" longer than the opening.

4. Place the right side of the facing to the right side of the garment and stitch to within ⅛" of the seam line. **fig. 2.**

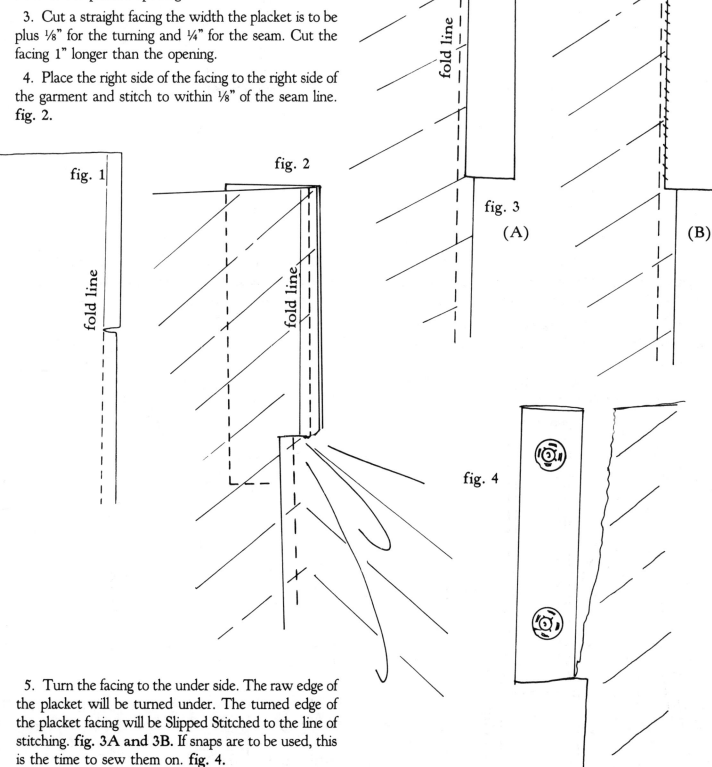

fig. 1

fig. 2

fig. 3

(A)

(B)

fig. 4

fold line

fold line

fold line

5. Turn the facing to the under side. The raw edge of the placket will be turned under. The turned edge of the placket facing will be Slipped Stitched to the line of stitching. **fig. 3A and 3B.** If snaps are to be used, this is the time to sew them on. **fig. 4.**

Fold the upper placket again on the fold line. Press. **fig. 5.**

6. For the under portion of the placket, cut the facing two times wider plus ¼" and 1" longer. This facing will be the same length as the top facing. **fig. 6.**

7. Turn under ⅛" on both of the long sides and one end. Stitch. Fold in half and press. **fig. 7A and 7B.**

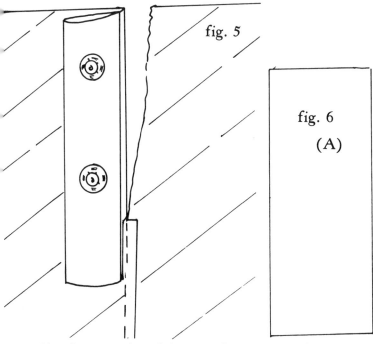

fig. 5

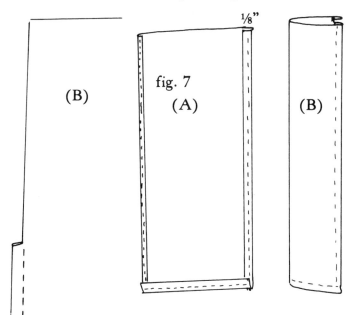

fig. 6

(A)   (B)

⅛"

fig. 7

(A)   (B)

8. Slip the raw edge of the seam between the folded facing edge and pin. Do not let the facing come nearer to the marked seam line of the garment than ⅛ of an inch. **fig. 8.**

9. Stitch the edges of this extension. **fig. 9.**

10. Sew the remainder of the snaps on at this time. The female side of the snap will be on the facing. **fig. 10.**

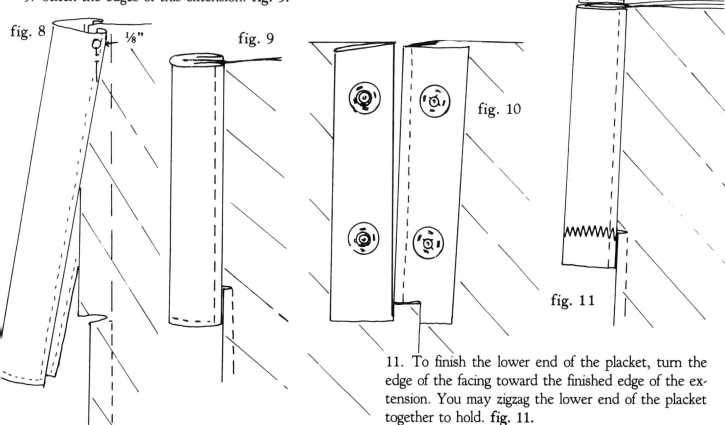

fig. 8   ⅛"   fig. 9   fig. 10

fig. 11

11. To finish the lower end of the placket, turn the edge of the facing toward the finished edge of the extension. You may zigzag the lower end of the placket together to hold. **fig. 11.**

DOUBLE LACE PLACKET

1. Measure and cut two strips of lace insertion the length needed for the opening. **fig. 1.**

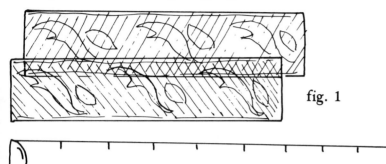

fig. 1

2. Place one piece of lace insertion on top of the other and whip together on one side. Set the machine to a zigzag setting so that the needle will just encompass the lace heading and clear the edge. Set the length so that it looks as if you have whipped it by hand. **fig. 2.**

3. Place the lace heading of the top piece of lace insertion on the seam allowance. Baste and machine stitch to hold. **Fig. 3.**

4. Underneath, whip the bottom piece of lace insertion to the stitching line. This will form the underneath placket. **fig. 4.**

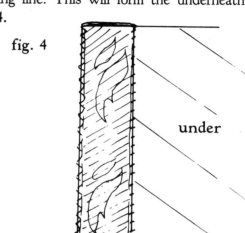

fig. 4

under

5. For the upper placket, tiny baste a strip of lace insertion onto the seam allowance. Machine stitch to secure. **fig. 5.**

6. Fold this piece of lace insertion to the underneath side and whip stitch using tiny invisible stitches. **fig. 6.**

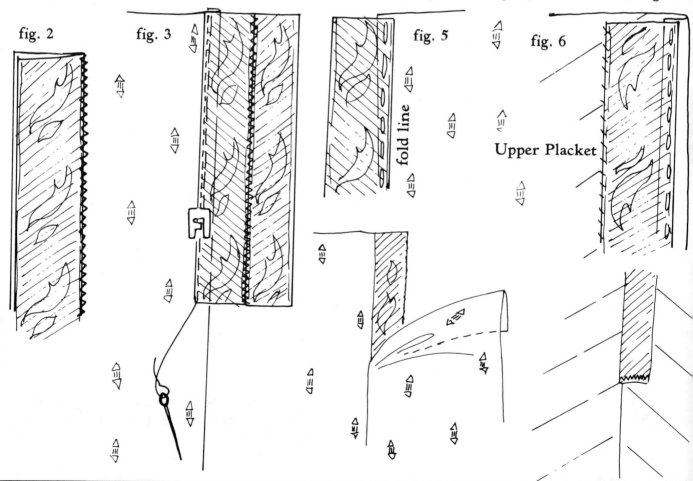

fig. 2

fig. 3

fig. 5

fold line

fig. 6

Upper Placket

This placket is good when making baby things or using fabrics which are soft and will roll and whip well.

1. Mark and then cut your placket depth at the center back of the garment. If the garment does not call for this type placket and the extra ½" has not been allowed for, add that same amount to the center back of your pattern before cutting the garment out. **fig. 1.**

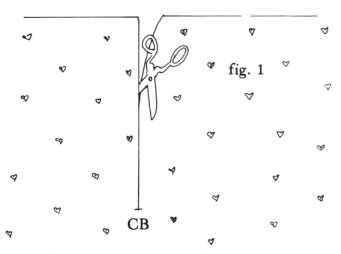

fig. 1

CB

2. Roll and whip using the widest width and a short Zigzag Stitch. As you come to the end of the placket, maneuver the right side of the placket down so that your machine can continue to the bottom. **fig. 2.**

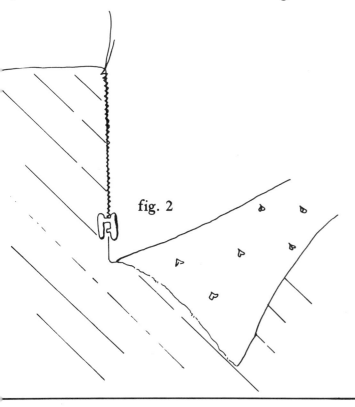

fig. 2

3. Leave your needle in the down position as you turn the garment. Take two or three stitches as you rotate. **fig. 3.**

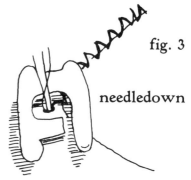

fig. 3

needledown

4. Continue rolling and whipping to the top edge of the placket. **fig. 4.**

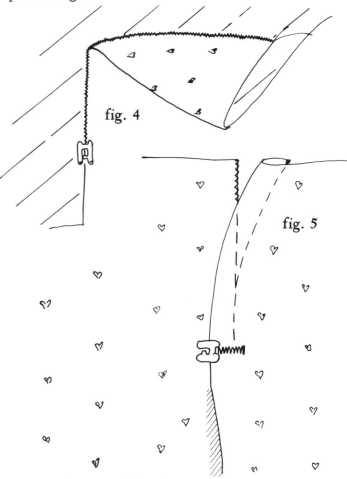

fig. 4

fig. 5

5. Bring the two rolled and whipped edges together ½" or the width you prefer your placket to be and stitch, using a narrow Zigzag Stitch. If the garment is for an infant, the placket can be as narrow as ¼", or if on an adult, even an inch is okay. **fig. 5.**

PLACKET WITHOUT A SEAM

If you choose to make a garment and you do not wish to have a center back seam when the pattern has called for one, it is necessary to *make an adjustment to the pattern* before cutting it out.

1. Place the pattern with the center back 1" from the fold of the fabric.

2. Mark the placket line the depth you wish for the placket to be. This mark will be on the fold line of the fabric.

3. At the end of the placket, with the right side of the fabric facing you, make a mark ½" to the left of the placket line and ¼" to the right of the placket line. This will be the width of the placket. **fig. 1.**

4. Cut on the marked lines. This line will be the placket line, whereas the two lines on either side will remain the center back line. Before bringing together with the placket, we will refer to them as the left and right center back. **fig. 2.**

fig. 2

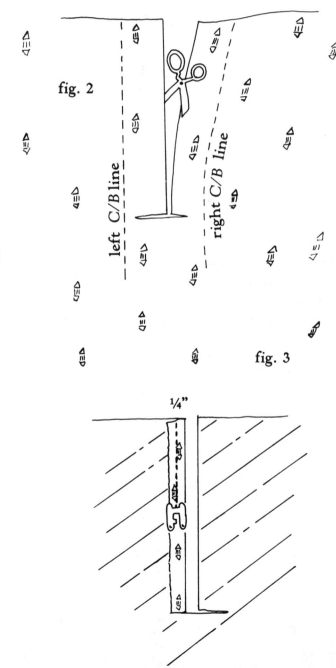

fig. 3

fig. 1

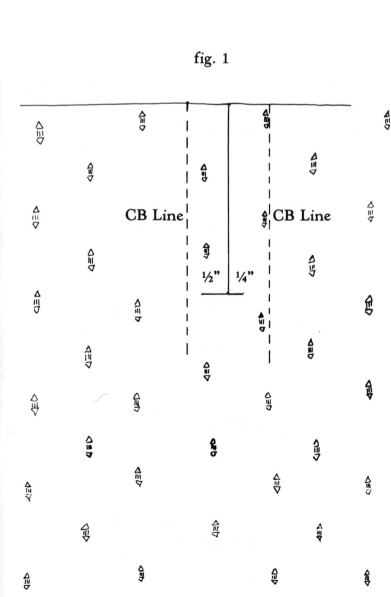

CB Line | CB Line

½" | ¼"

5. With the wrong side of the fabric facing you, turn under the raw edge ¼" and machine stitch. **fig. 3.**

6. Turn under the other side about ⅛" to ¼". Press and turn under again ¼" and slip stitch into place. **fig. 4 A and B.**

fig. 4

¼"

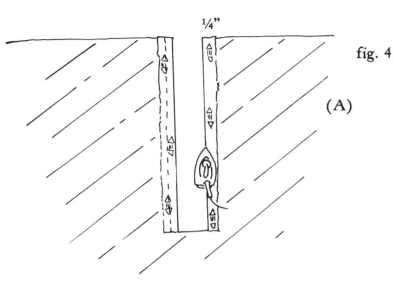

(A)

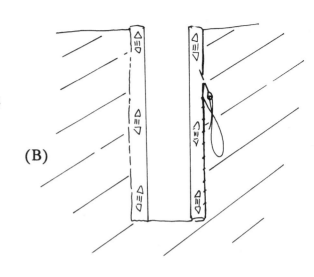

(B)

8. There will be a pleat at the end of the placket opening.

9. On the wrong side, stitch using the zigzag at the end of the placket from the center back to the edge. **fig. 6.**

7. With the right side of the garment facing you, fold on the right center back line. Bring the fold to the left and place the right center back fold line onto the left center back line. Press. **fig. 5**

fig. 5   left C/B line

right C/B line

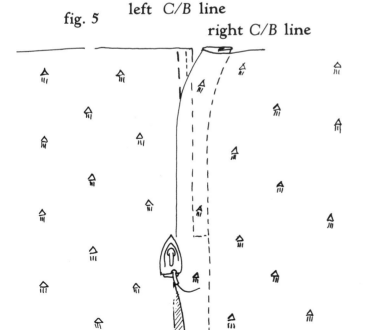

fig. 6

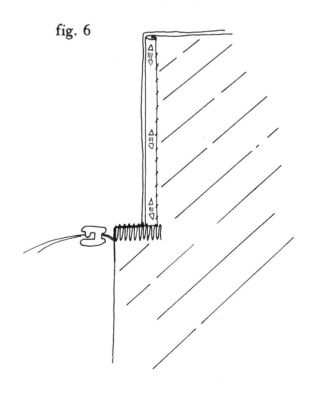

THE LAP PLACKET WITHOUT A FACING

1. The seam should be at least 1¼" wide. Leave open the top portion of the seam the length desired for the placket opening.

2. Turn under the inside edge half the seam allowance, hem. Stitch close to the fold. **fig. 1.**

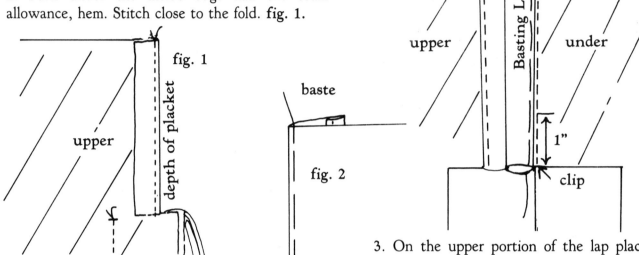

fig. 1

upper

depth of placket

1¼"

baste

fig. 2

3. On the upper portion of the lap placket, turn under *on the seam line* and baste near the edge. **fig. 2.**

5. Turn this edge to the under side. Baste carefully near the edge of the seam line. This will leave a scant ½" facing. Finish with the Invisible Slip Stitch. **fig. 4.**

6. Clip into the seam line at the end of the placket so that the seam can be pressed open flat.

7. To hold the placket in place, do a fancy hand stitch or make use of the adorable little labels and stitch one at this point. **fig. 5.**

Invisible Slip Stitch Line

fig. 4

½"

upper

Basting Line

under

1"

clip

4. To finish the under portion of the lap placket, turn under the edge ⅛" and machine stitch into place. **fig. 3**

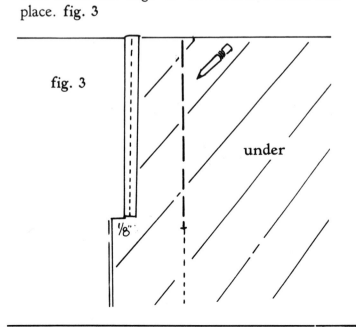

fig. 3

under

⅛"

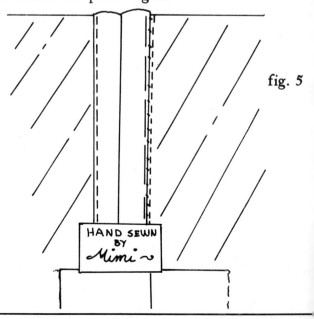

fig. 5

HAND SEWN
BY
Mimi

It is sometimes preferrable to have a Buttonhole Loop of thread extending from the edge of the fabric, to having a buttonhole for a very small button.

1. Begin with a knot hidden in the fold. **fig. 1** Make a small stitch into the fold, close to the area where the needle came out. **fig. 2.**

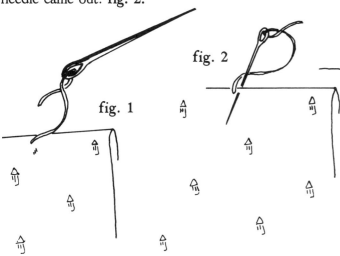

fig. 2

fig. 1

b. Pull needle down through the loop of thread and then up to form the buttonhole twist. **fig. 5.**

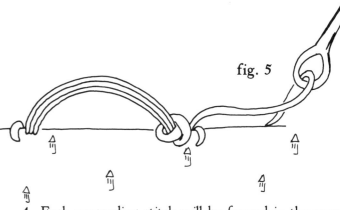

fig. 5

4. Each succeeding stitch will be formed in the same manner.

5. When you have completed doing the Buttonhole Stitch, secure the thread at the end and take the needle out through the fold. **fig. 6.**

2. Make another stitch into the fold from the first stitch leaving a loop of thread. This stitch will be made the distance of the diameter of the button to be used. You may choose to use several loops of thread to make the loop stronger and/or larger, but be sure to anchor the thread well at both ends. **fig. 3.**

3. Work over the loops with a Buttonhole Stitch.

   a. Work from the right to the left, with the point of the needle toward you. Loop the thread to the left. The needle will go down through the loop of thread and the thread which you looped to the left will be under the needle. **fig. 4.**

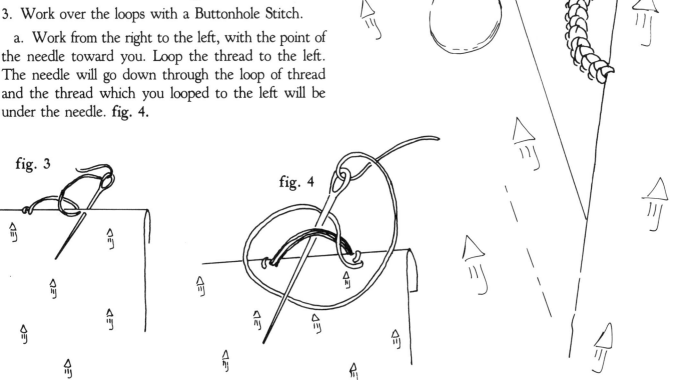

fig. 6

fig. 3

fig. 4

ELASTIC LOOPS

1. Stitch the center back seam to the point where the placket begins.

Clip straight across and press the seam open. (If using a French Seam, press the seam to one side.) **fig. 1.**

2. Cut the placket piece 1½" wide and two times longer than the placket opening.

3. Open the placket opening so that it will form a straight line.

4. Place the right side of the placket piece to the right side of the dress with the raw edges even. The placket piece will be underneath. Pin.

5. Stitch the placket to dress using a seam allowance the same as the allowance used for the back seam of the dress. **fig. 2.**

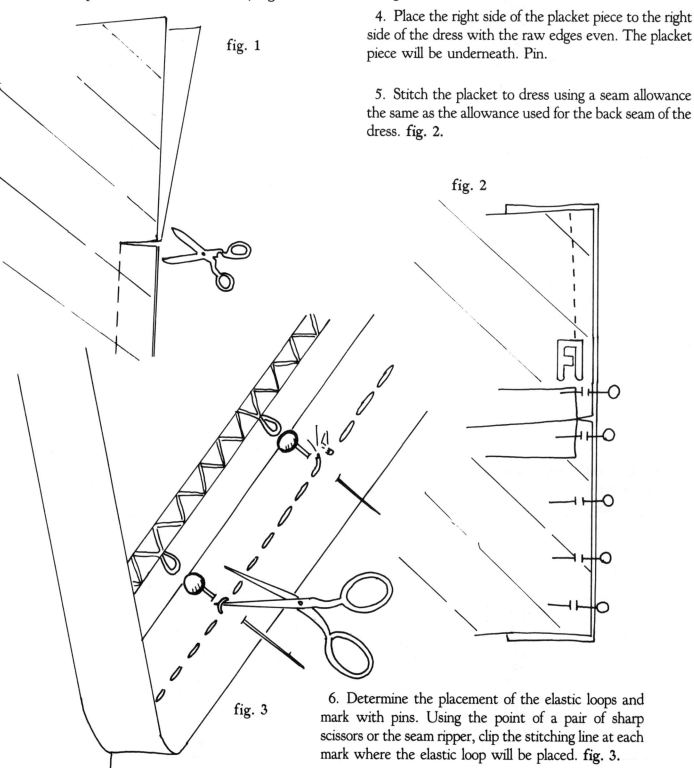

fig. 1

fig. 2

fig. 3

6. Determine the placement of the elastic loops and mark with pins. Using the point of a pair of sharp scissors or the seam ripper, clip the stitching line at each mark where the elastic loop will be placed. **fig. 3.**

7. On the inside of the seam allowance, insert each loop into the clipped stitch line. Pull the loops through and secure them with a pin to keep them from slipping out. **fig. 4.**

9. Fold the placket piece over the seam allowance. With the edge of the placket piece even with the stitching line, whip into place. **fig. 6.**

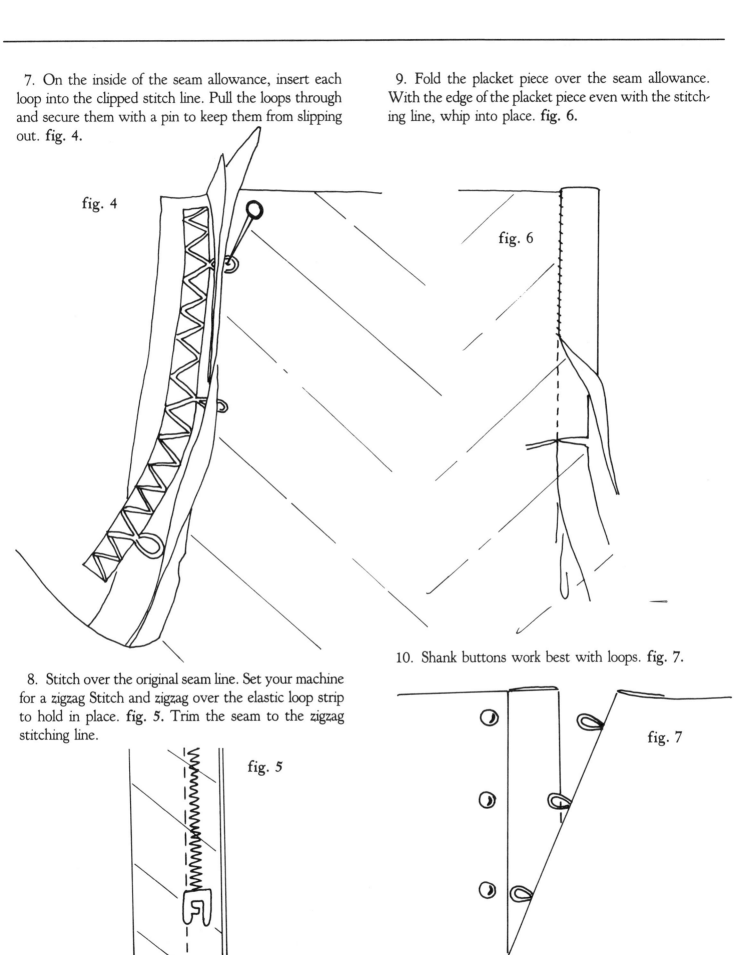

fig. 4

fig. 6

8. Stitch over the original seam line. Set your machine for a zigzag Stitch and zigzag over the elastic loop strip to hold in place. **fig. 5.** Trim the seam to the zigzag stitching line.

fig. 5

10. Shank buttons work best with loops. **fig. 7.**

fig. 7

"With Love From Me To You"

Due to last minute changes, the instructions and pattern for this dress were taken out. This dress, which won first place in the 1987 MYLACE contest, was designed by Susan York of Nashville, Tennessee.

You may contact Susan for the pattern.

Susan York
908 Patters Lane
Nashville, TN 37206
(615) 228-6994

Hope you enjoy it!
Susan York

OTHER THINGS

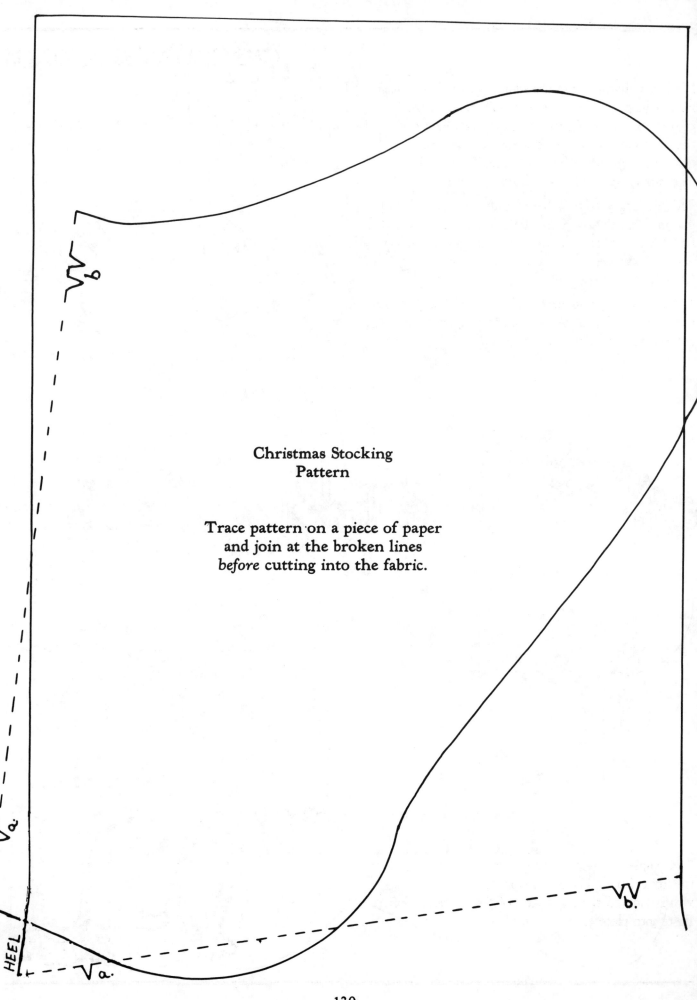

Christmas Stocking
Pattern

Trace pattern on a piece of paper
and join at the broken lines
before cutting into the fabric.

I feel that anytime I can use something small, yet useful for teaching, then the student will want to finish the project. So, round Christmas time, use the Christmas Stocking with all the fancy trims for a class to learn from the very basic French Sewing Techniques to the more advanced methods of working with laces, etc.

The stocking pattern is here for you to use. Use your imagination or copy some of the ideas here. You will find that the techniques for doing these different designs are basically the same ones used with the Church Dolls. Have fun!

1. Cut your stocking out. I like velvet, but you may use any fabric you desire. Finish the top back edge either by folding down and hemming, or you may just want to extend a piece of entredeux and lace edging on around to the back. However, it is not necessary. **fig. A.**

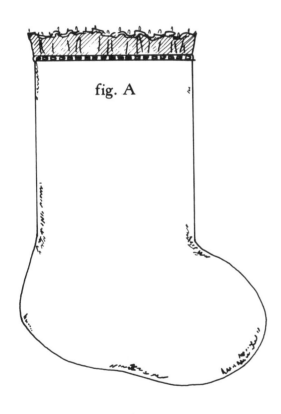

fig. A

2. Complete whatever design you are going to put on the front. Place the piece of work just finished with the wrong side to the right side of the stocking. Pin or Baste into place.

a. Cut a piece of fabric 7" wide x 8" long. **fig. 1.**

b. Mark the position where you would like the lace to be. **fig. 2.**

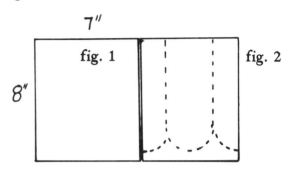

c. Beginning at the top edge, Baste the strip of lace down.

d. As you come to the bottom edge of the lace, gently pull the very top thread in the lace heading to gather the lace so that it will lie flat.

e. Baste around the curve on the outside line. **fig. 3.**

f. Continue to Baste the lace to the top.

g. Gently pull the top thread in the Lace Insertion which will go on either side of the lace panel. Place the ends of the lace under the lace panel.

h. Baste. **fig. 4.** Stitch the lace around the top side curve and up the side panel on both sides. Stitch the inside of the lace panel.

i. Trim the excess fabric from behind the lace. **fig. 5.** Gather lace edging and attach to the bottom of the lace insertion. **fig. 5**

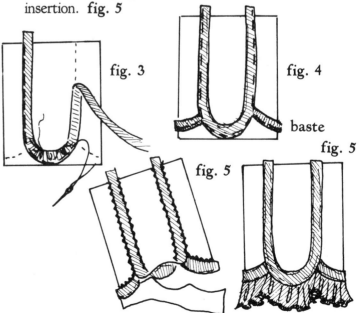

j. Gather a piece of lace edging to fit a 7" piece of entredeux.

Stitch the entredeux to the top of the stocking. Follow the techniques of attaching Entredeux to Fabric. **fig. 6.**

3. Place the two pieces of the stocking right sides together. Stitch. Clip the curves. **fig. 8.**

4. Turn and press. **fig. 9.**

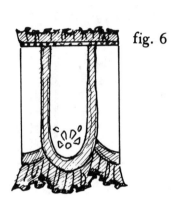
fig. 6

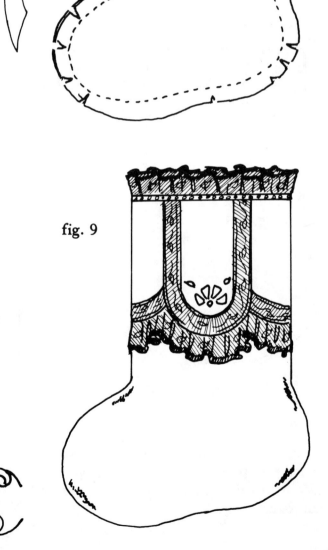
fig. 8

k. Place the design to the right side of the stocking. Baste. **fig. 7.**

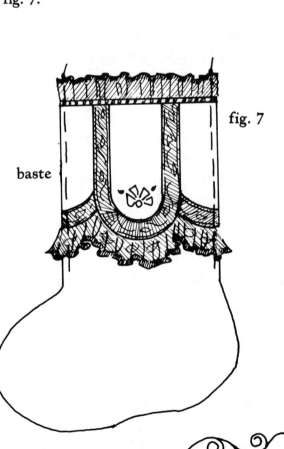
baste
fig. 7

fig. 9

This is an excellent project for teaching machine techniques and could be adapted for hand stitching as well.

Working with just a narrow strip from 1¾" to 3", plan what is to go into making up that width, which is to be used in the Fancy Band.

I personally feel that sometimes the width is just too wide for the wee sizes; however, 3" is just great for the five-year-old. The chart gives you my suggested widths and the cutting size for the back of the bonnet.

If you choose to make the band less than the width measurements given, then add some width to the back of the bonnet so that there will be enough fabric to fit the child's head.

Chart for cutting Bonnet

Age	Fancy Band	Ruffle	Bonnet Back
Infant	1¾" x 9½"	19"	5" x 26½"
6 mos.	1¾" x 12½"	19"	6" x 26½"
1	2" x 13½"	26"	6" x 26½"
2	2½" x 14"	28"	6½" x 26½"
3	3" x 14½"	29"	6¾" x 26½"
4	3" x 15¼"	30"	7¼" x 26½"
5	3" x 15¾"	30"	8¼" x 26½"

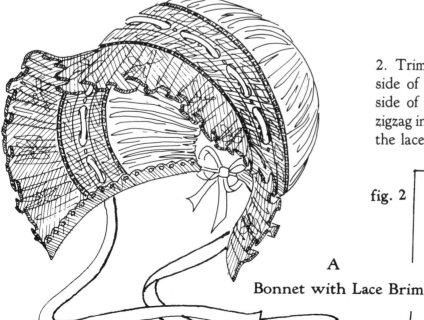

A
Bonnet with Lace Brim

You may choose to create your fancy band using something entirely different, which is just great. Just keep in mind the overall size of the bonnet. Here the directions are given for Mimi's French Bonnet, six-month-old size, construction according to Mimi's design.

Cut two pieces of entredeux 10" long.

Cut two pieces of lace insertion 10" long.

Cut one piece of lace beading 10" long.

Note: The width of the entredeux, lace insertion, and beading should not exceed 1¾" for the infant size. Choose the laces, etc. to make up the width you will need.

1. To make the Fancy Band, join the lace insertion and beading together by placing side-by-side. Set the width of the Zigzag Stitch so that the needle will go into and encompass the lace heading of each strip of insertion/beading. **fig. 1**. There will be a piece of lace insertion each side of the beading.

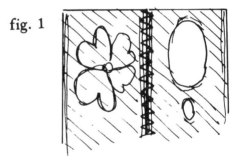

fig. 1

2. Trim one side of the entredeux and join to each side of the band of lace strips. Place the trimmed side of the entredeux to the edge of the lace and zigzag into each hole and onto the lace encompassing the lace heading. **fig. 2**.

fig. 2
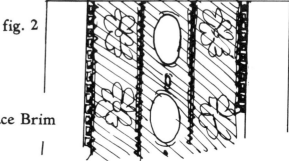

BONNET BRIM

You may choose:

(A) Just Lace Edging as a brim.
(B) Fabric with a lace edge.
(C) Fabric with a double row of lace edging.

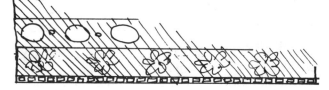

fig. 3

A. LACE EDGING

Cut a piece of lace edging 1" wide x 16" long.
Pull the top thread to fit the entredeux of the Fancy
Band. **fig. 3.**

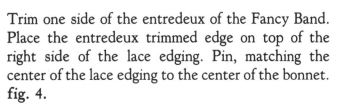

Trim one side of the entredeux of the Fancy Band.
Place the entredeux trimmed edge on top of the
right side of the lace edging. Pin, matching the
center of the lace edging to the center of the bonnet.
fig. 4.

Zigzag into each and every hole of the entredeux
and off the edge. **fig. 5.**

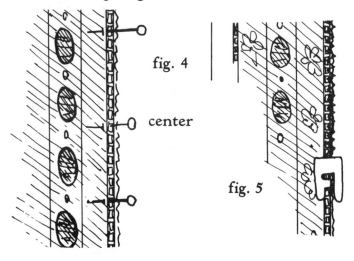

fig. 4

center

fig. 5

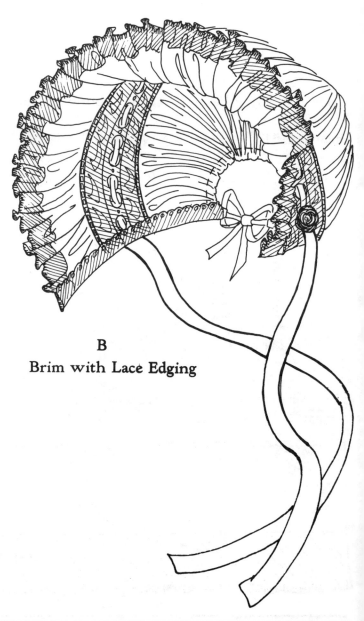

B
Brim with Lace Edging

B. FABRIC BRIM WITH LACE EDGING

Cut a piece of fabric a scant 1" wide and 16" long.
Cut a piece of lace edging ½" wide or less x 16"
long.

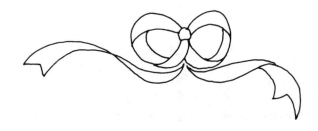

Attach the Flat Lace Edging to one long edge of the fabric. There are several methods of attaching flat lace to a straight fabric edge. Choose the method which you prefer or you may choose to Baste the lace to the right side of the fabric strip and use the Pin Stitch, a Feather Stitch, or the Hem Stitch. **fig. 6.** If using an Elna # 7000, use the stitch selector # 746, increase the tension to 9. The width should be changed so that the needle just encases the lace heading, and the width will be determined by the size of the lace heading. You may also choose to use the Wing Needle, if you want larger holes. If not, the # 16 needle will give a beautiful stitch. Trim and finish the raw edge with a Zigzag Stitch. **fig. 7.**

Place the right side of the rolled, whipped and gathered edge to the right side of one side of the Fancy Band entredeux's trimmed side. The entredeux will be on top. Set the machine so that the needle will zigzag into each and every hole of the entredeux and then clear the edge of the fabric. **fig. 9.**

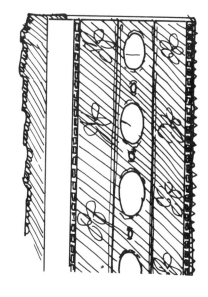

fig. 9

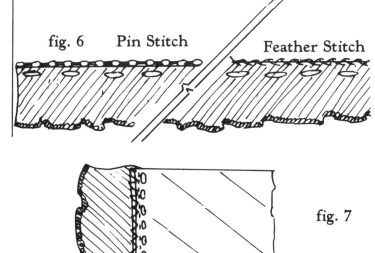

fig. 6   Pin Stitch   Feather Stitch

fig. 7

C. FABRIC WITH A DOUBLE ROW OF LACE

Cut a piece of fabric 1" wide and 16" long. Cut two pieces of lace edging 16" long.

Roll, Whip and Gather the remaining long edge of the fabric. **fig. 8.**

← center

fig. 8

Attach one piece of the flat lace edging to one long edge of the fabric by placing the right side of the lace edging to the right side of the fabric. Leave ¼" of the fabric edge exposed. Set the machine width so that the needle will encompass the lace heading and clear the fabric edge as the needle swings. **fig. 10.**

The second strip of lace edging will be attached to the fabric. This strip of lace edging will be seen only on the underneath side of the bonnet so that great care should be taken to place it *even and onto the seam line*.

Place the wrong side of the lace edging to the wrong side of the fabric strip. Let the lace heading be on the seam line of the fabric strip. Baste into place. **fig. 11.**

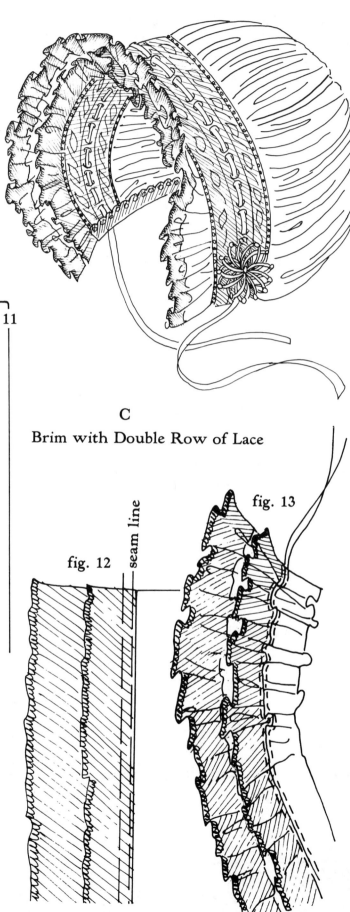

C

Brim with Double Row of Lace

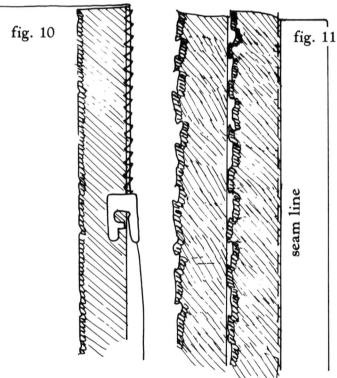

Stitch two rows of lengthened machine stitching. One row will be in the lace heading and the second row will be ⅛" to the inside (on the lace) of the first row. **fig. 12.** (This will be pulled out after the lace has been attached to the entredeux of the Fancy Band.) Pull thread up to the same length as the Fancy Band. **fig. 13.**

Do NOT trim the entredeux edge of the Fancy Band. Place the right side of the Fancy Band to the right side of the ruffle which has had the two rows of machine stitching pulled up to fit. **fig. 14.**

Be very careful to place the edge of the untrimmed entredeux so that when you Stitch in the Ditch, the line of stitching will be exactly on top of the lace heading.

Measure and mark the center of the ruffle. Match to the center of the Fancy Band, and use the method of attaching entredeux to gathered fabric.

Stitch in the Ditch. **fig. 14.**

Trim to within ⅛". **fig. 15.**

Roll and whip, letting the needle zig just to the edge of the entredeux hole and clear the fabric as it zags to the left. **fig. 16.**

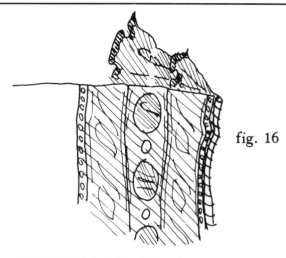

fig. 16

STITCHING FANCY BAND TO BONNET BACK

Cut the back according to the chart.

1. Roll, Whip and Gather one long edge of the back using the Quilting Thread Method.

2. Mark the center of the Fancy Band as well as the center of the back piece. Trim the batiste fabric away from the entredeux. **fig. 17.**

3. Pull up the gathers to the same measurement as the Fancy Band. **fig. 18.**

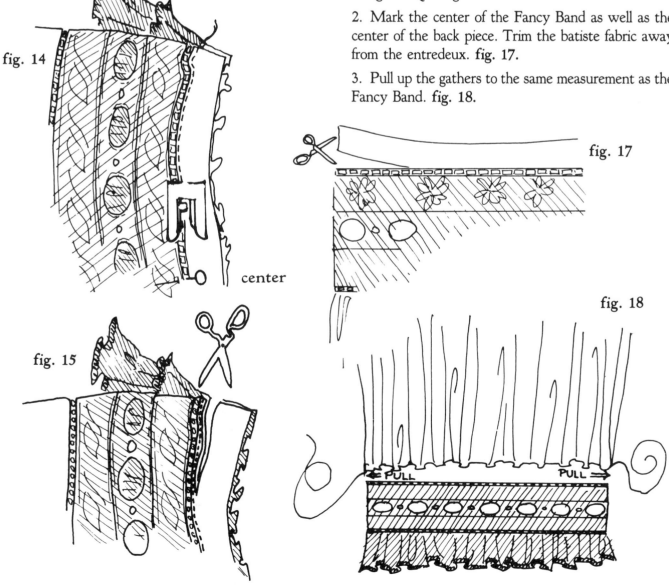

fig. 14

center

fig. 15

fig. 17

fig. 18

PULL

PULL

4. With right sides together, and matching the centers, distribute the gathers evenly. Place the right side of the Fancy Band to the right side of the rolled, whipped and gathered edge. This is the method for attaching Gathered Fabric to Entredeux. Remember to zig into each hole of the entredeux and zag off the rolled edge. fig. 19.

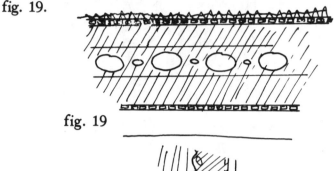

fig. 19

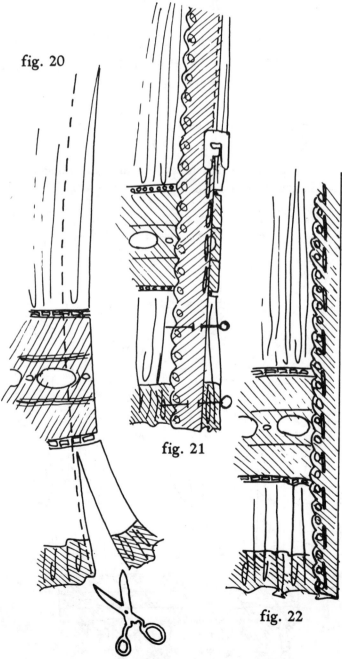

fig. 20

fig. 21

fig. 22

FINISHING THE BONNET

1. Machine stitch a straight row of stitching ¼" outside the seam allowance on both sides of the bonnet. Trim just as close as you can to the machine stitching without cutting into the line of stitching. **fig. 20.**

2. Pin, baste, and stitch a very narrow piece of lace netting or lace edging to the seam allowance on the right side of the bonnet. **fig. 21.** This lace will cover the raw edge of the fabric and ends of the laces in the Fancy Band.

3. Fold the lace net to the back with the fold on the seam allowance. Whip Stitch into place. **fig. 22.**

BACK CASING

To make the back casing, fold under ⅛" and then ⅜" to form the casing. You may machine stitch; however, I find that this is an excellent place for the Pin Stitch to be practiced. Also, it is especially pretty to place a piece of flat lace edging along this line. Choose one of the following for the back casing:

  a. Just turn and machine stitch in place. **fig. 23.**

  b. Press the raw edges under and use the Pin Stitch to hem.

  c. Press the hem in place and use the machine to Hem Stitch. For the Elna # 7000, you would use the Stitch Selector # 746. **fig. 24.**

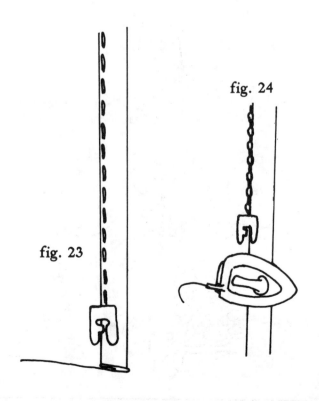

fig. 24

fig. 23

Cut a piece of ribbon ¼" wide and run through the back casing. Pull up and tie in a small bow. **fig. 25.**

Make two ribbon rosettes or flat bows for each side of the bonnet. Place the ribbon ties to each side with the rosettes on top. Anchor well.

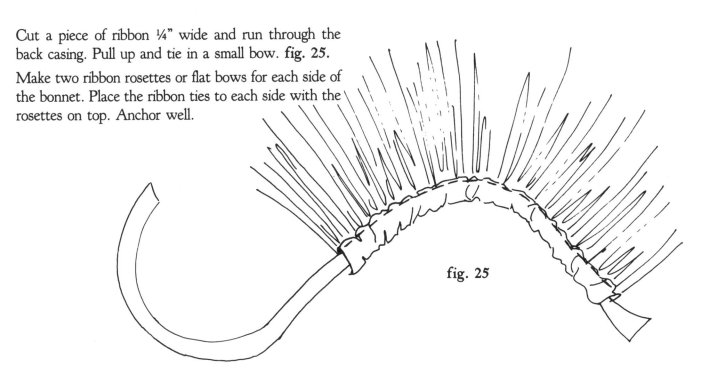

fig. 25

RIBBON ALPHABET FOR SHADOW EMBROIDERY

COVERED SNAPS

Covered snaps can add a lot to any garment using snaps at the closure. And, covering snaps is not that hard. Follow these steps:

1. Cut out a circle of fabric twice the diameter of the snap. This may be with or without a tail. If I am doing the very small snaps, I like to have the tail to hold on to. Therefore, the circle is drawn on a piece of fabric, but not cut out around it. fig. 1.

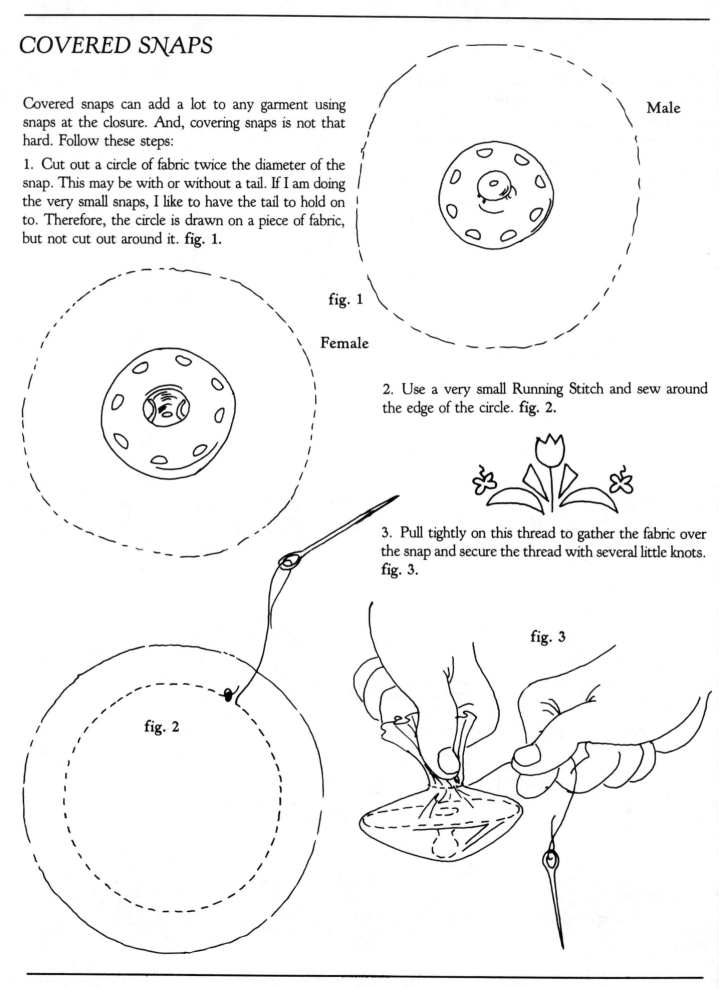

Male

fig. 1

Female

2. Use a very small Running Stitch and sew around the edge of the circle. fig. 2.

3. Pull tightly on this thread to gather the fabric over the snap and secure the thread with several little knots. fig. 3.

fig. 3

fig. 2

4. Now, if you will wrap the thread several times around the fabric and secure again, you will find that the fabric around the snap is nice and tight. Wrapping, and then leaving the thread hanging to sew the snap on later, is an idea that Susan Oliver shared with me. You can cover several snaps, leave the threads hanging, and later sew them all onto the garment. **fig. 4.**

5. Poke a tiny hole in the center of the fabric on the pointed side of the snap (male side) to let the metal point protrude. I use a stiletto, but any sharp instrument will work. **fig. 5A and 5B.**

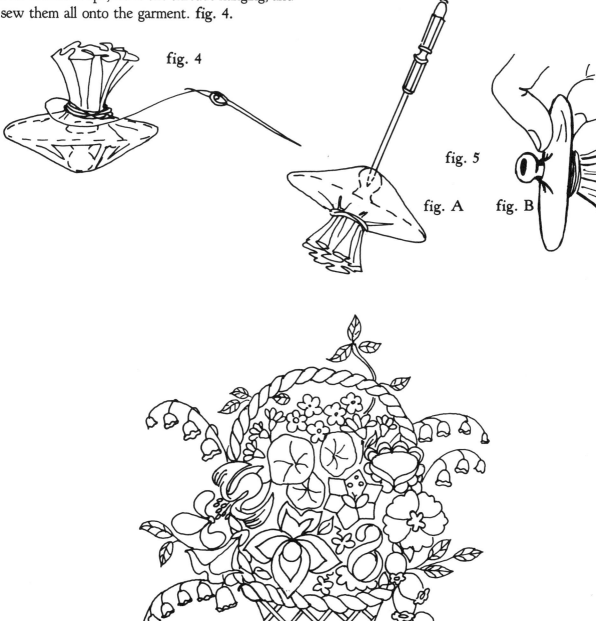

fig. 4

fig. 5

fig. A

fig. B

A THREAD CHAIN
Ribbon or Belt Carrier

If you make the thread chain small enough, it can become a button loop as well as a belt carrier. It can be as long as needed. If the chain is made longer than the distance between the markings that indicate its beginning and end, then it will have a looped shape.

1. Mark on garment where the chain begins. Bring the needle up at the mark. **fig. 1.**

2. At the beginning mark, take a small stitch and draw the thread through, **fig. 2** leaving about a 5" loop. **fig. 3.**

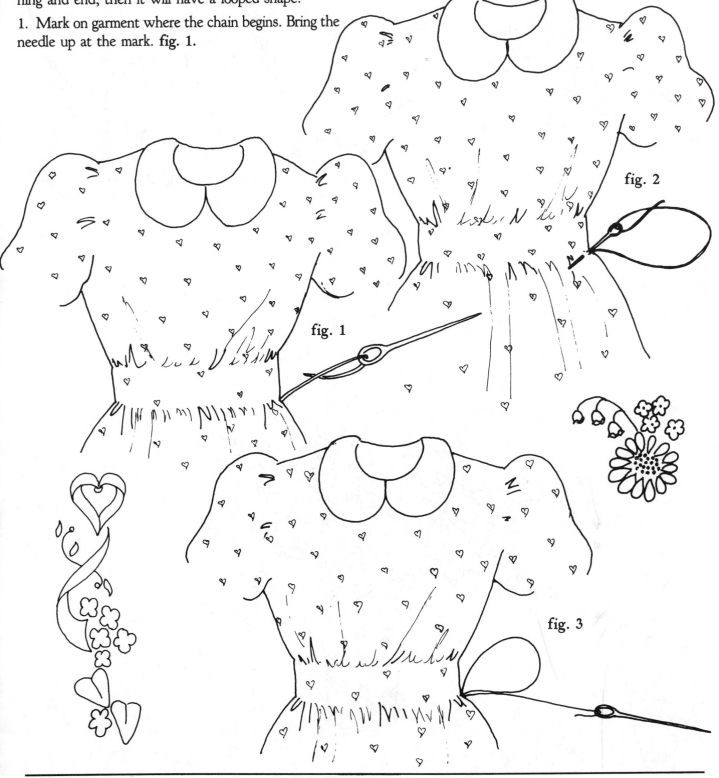

fig. 2

fig. 1

fig. 3

3. Hold the supply thread in the right hand. Leave the loop open. Reach through and grasp the supply thread with your left hand **fig. 4** to start a new loop and pull the thread through. **fig. 5.**

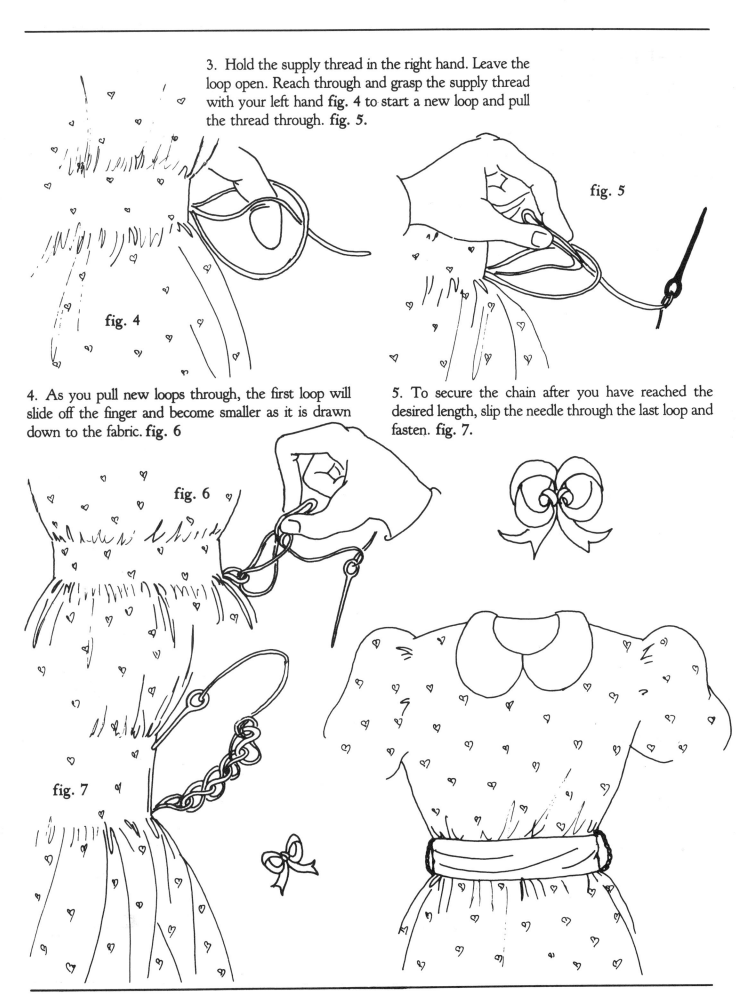

fig. 4

fig. 5

4. As you pull new loops through, the first loop will slide off the finger and become smaller as it is drawn down to the fabric. **fig. 6**

5. To secure the chain after you have reached the desired length, slip the needle through the last loop and fasten. **fig. 7.**

fig. 6

fig. 7

BULLION

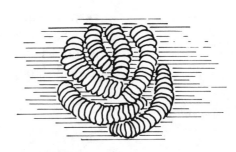

Bullion Knot: Similar to French knot but covering a length of stitches formed by wrapping the thread around the needle and passing the needle through the cloth to anchor it.

1. I prefer using the milliner's needle and no more than two strands of embroidery floss when doing the bullion stitch.

Knot the thread in the end.

2. Bring threaded needle up at point A; pull through. **fig. 1.**

Insert needle at point B and bring needle up again at point A; but, DO NOT PULL THROUGH. **fig. 2.**

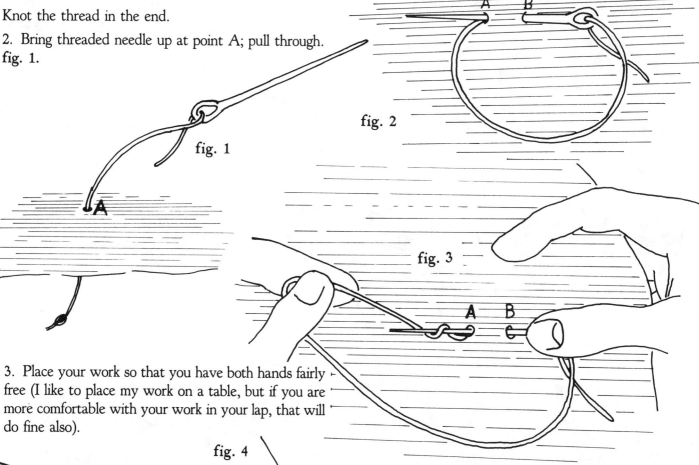

fig. 2

fig. 1

fig. 3

3. Place your work so that you have both hands fairly free (I like to place my work on a table, but if you are more comfortable with your work in your lap, that will do fine also).

fig. 4

Hold your needle so that you are holding the thread with your left hand about 2½" from point A. **fig. 3.** Mary Clark says to wrap as the "water falls" when doing bullion roses. That means that you will take the thread to the back of the needle and bring it over the top of the needle and down and back around again. Wrap the thread around the needle as many times as you need it. DO NOT wrap too tightly around the needle that it is hard to pull through. The wraps will tighten when pulled in place.

Hold the wraps in place with the index finger as you wrap. **fig. 4.**

4. Hold the wraps around the needle, between the thumb and index finger of the right hand, and pull needle through. **fig. 5.**

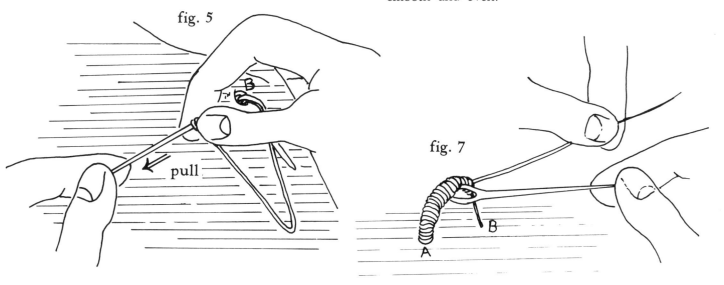

fig. 5

pull

(The left hand pulls the needle toward the left until all the thread is pulled up.)

5. To make sure that the loops are not twisted on the thread, pull the thread to the right. **fig. 6.**

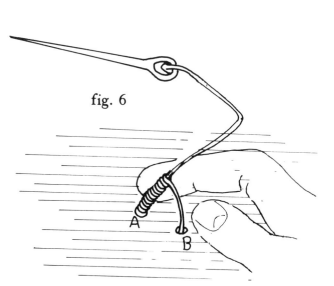

fig. 6

A
B

Note: This stitch takes practice and sometimes patience to perfect, but it is well worth the effort.

6. Insert the eye of the needle under the wraps, and pull up the stitches and straighten. **fig. 7.**
Keep pulling from underneath until they are smooth and even.

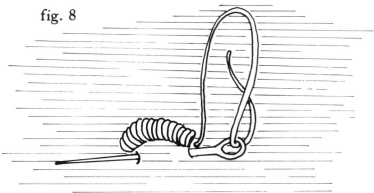

fig. 7

A
B

7. Insert the needle again at B and pull through to the back. **fig. 8.**

fig. 8

8. To make another Bullion side-by-side to the one just made, insert needle again at point B and come up at A and wrap.

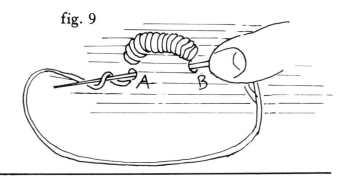

fig. 9

A   B

FRENCH SEAMS

I like using the French Seam for children's clothes, particularly as I feel that the seams are stronger and the inside of the garment is neater. The French Seam is primarily for thin materials and dainty garments. And, when I am making an infant-type garment, I make the French Seam a little bit different as far as the stitching goes.

MAKING A FRENCH SEAM # 1

1. Baste or pin the garment right side out or wrong sides together.

2. Stitch the seam ¼" outside the seam line. **fig. 16A.**

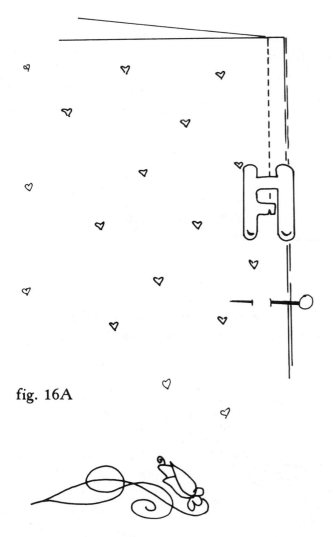

fig. 16A

3. Trim all the edges of the seam down to ⅛" of an inch. **fig. 16B.**

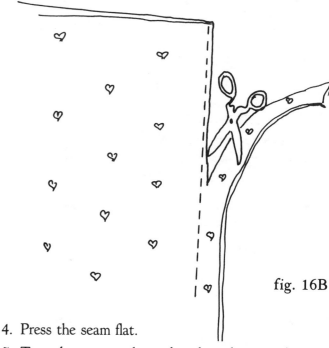

fig. 16B

4. Press the seam flat.

5. Turn the seam to the underside and encase the raw trimmed edges by basting or pinning the seam ¼" wide. The seam must be wide enough to cover the edges of the first seam so that no raw edges or threads show on the right side of the garment. **fig. 16C.**

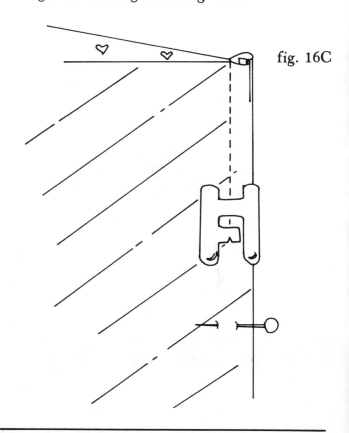

fig. 16C

1. Baste or pin the wrong sides together.

2. Stitch, using a Zigzag Stitch. The stitch will go onto the fabric edge and off the fabric causing the raw edges to be slightly rolled. You will use a setting for your machine which will give you a wide zigzag and a stitch length which will not be real short. For the Elna 7000, I use the width setting of 4.4 and the length setting of 1.2, and the needle will only be taking about 1/16" bite of the fabric. There will be no need to trim the edges when using this method. **fig. 17A.**

3. Press the seam and turn to the underside.

4. Encase the zigzagged edge into the seam using a seam allowance just wide enough to encase the edges. With the Elna 7000, if the B Foot is used, the zigzagged edge will ride in the groove and makes it very easy to get a very small and straight seam. There will be no fuzzies showing using this method, as they are all held in place with the Zigzag Stitch. **fig. 17B.**

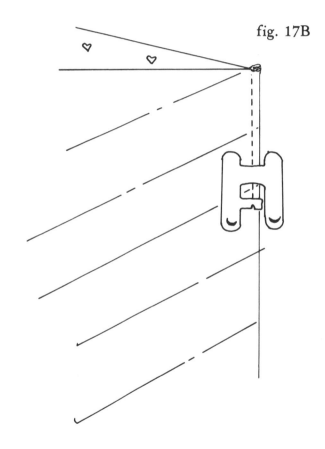

fig. 17B

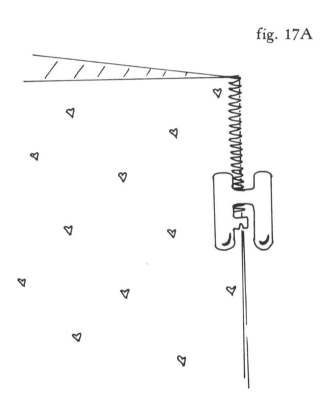

fig. 17A

THE FEATHER STITCH

Feather Stitch: A tiny decorative surface embroidery loosely resembling a vine, often found on infant garments. May also be done as double or triple feather stitch.

I love using the Feather Stitch on garments and there are several different kinds of Feather Stitches.

BASIC FEATHER STITCH

The Basic Feather Stitch is worked with the stitches alternating to the right and left.

Work the stitches from the top to the bottom.

1. Bring the needle up at 1 in the center. **fig. 1**

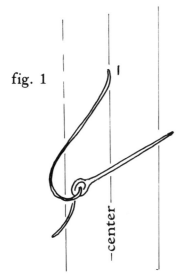

fig. 1

center

2. Insert to the needle at 2, which is slightly lower and to the right of the thread brought up in the center.

3. Angle the needle and come out at 3, which is along the center line. The length of the stitch is determined by this stitch. **fig. 2.**

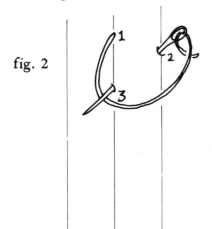

fig. 2

Note: Watch the thread so that when the needle comes up at 3, the thread is under the point of the needle.

4. Insert the needle at 4 and angle to the center. Bring the needle up at 5, which is along the center line. Make sure that the thread is under the needle. **fig. 3.**

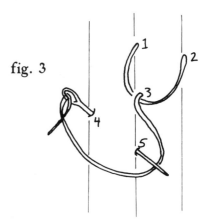

fig. 3

5. Continue, alternating the angle of the looped stitches.

6. To end the row of Feather Stitching, take a small stitch over the last loop. **fig. 4.**

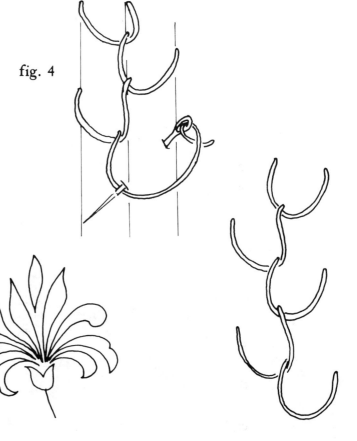

fig. 4

LONG-ARMED FEATHER STITCH

The Long-armed Feather Stitch is just like the Basic Feather Stitch, with the exception that the longer half of each loop is on the outside, rather than in the center.

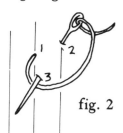

1. Bring the needle up at 1 and in center. **fig. 1.**

fig. 1

2. Insert the needle at point 2, which is slightly higher and to the right of point 1.

3. Angle the needle out at 3 along the center line. **fig. 2.**

4. Carry the thread under the needle point and pull through. **fig. 3.**

fig. 2

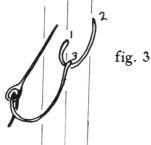

fig. 3

5. Insert the needle at point 4, which is slightly higher and to the left of point 3, and then out at 5 along the center line. **fig. 4.**

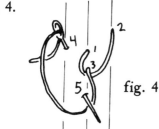

fig. 4

Note: The distance between 1 and 2 and 4 and 3 should be equal.

6. Make sure that the thread is under the needle and pull through.

7. Repeat 1 - 7 to end.

OPEN-CLOSED FEATHER STITCH

I think this is so pretty when doing very tiny stitches.

The Open-Closed Feather Stitch is a simple variation of the Basic Feather Stitch.

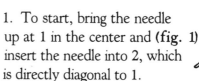

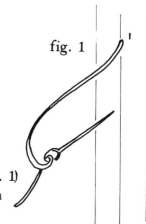

fig. 1

1. To start, bring the needle up at 1 in the center and **(fig. 1)** insert the needle into 2, which is directly diagonal to 1.

2. Emerge the needle at 3, keeping the thread down and under the needle. **fig. 2**

3. Pull the needle up and insert it at 4, which is directly across from 3.

Take the needle down and up at 5, again keeping the thread down and under the needle when pulling the needle up and out. **fig. 3**

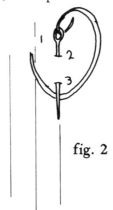

fig. 3

fig. 2

4. Continue to repeat in this manner until the Feather Stitching is completed. **fig. 4**

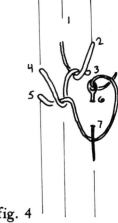

fig. 4

DOUBLE FEATHER STITCH

This stitch makes a very pretty zigzag border.

Instead of single-looped stitches placed alternately left and right, with the double Feather Stitch, two stitches are made consecutively to one side and then to the other. Keep the loops even.

1. To start, bring the needle up at 1, which is in the center. **fig. 1.**

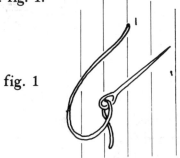

fig. 1

2. Insert the needle directly across. Angle the needle to the left and out at 3. **fig. 2.**

fig. 2

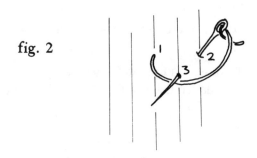

3. Bring the needle up with the thread under the point and pull.

4. Insert the needle at 4, directly across from 3.

5. Angle the needle to the right and out at 5, and carry the thread under the needle and pull. **fig. 3.**

fig. 3

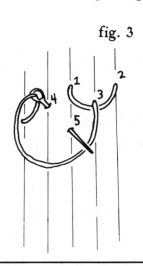

6. Insert the needle at 6.

7. Angle the needle to the right, coming out at 7. **fig. 4.**

8. Again, make sure that the thread is under the needle when you pull.

fig. 4

1. Insert needle at 8 directly across from 5 and below 3.

2. Angle left and out at 9.

Carry the thread under the point of the needle and pull. **fig. 5.**

fig. 5

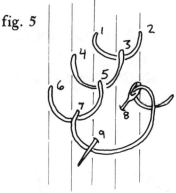

Two sets of looped stitches are made. **fig. 6.** Repeat the sequence from the start. **fig. 7.**

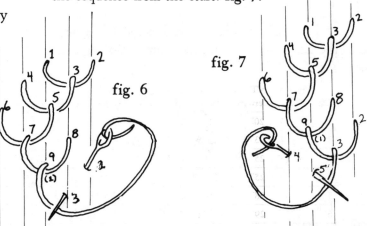

fig. 6

fig. 7

Note that the point of 9 of the last sequence is point 1 of the new sequence.

Continue with 1 to 9 until the row is complete.

THE BISHOP DRESS

This, the Bishop Dress, is especially for my students at the community college. This is all their lessons compiled for The Bishop Dress Construction Before Smocking.

1. Select appropriate fabric.
   100% Cotton
   Poly/Cotton
   Small Prints
   Fabric of your choice

2. Select trims (laces, buttons, etc.) floss, smocking plate, etc. **fig. A.**

fig. A

MATERIALS NEEDED

SIZE	YARDAGE FOR DRESS	TRIM FOR SLEEVES ONLY	TRIM FOR SLEEVES AND NECK
1	1½ yd.	1 yd.	1½ yd.
2	1¾ yd.	1 yd.	1½ yd.
3	2 yds.	1 yd.	1¾ yd.
4	2 yds.	1⅛ yd.	1¾ yd.
5	2⅛ yds.	1⅛ yd.	2 yds.
6	2¼ yds.	1¼ yd.	2 yds.
7	2½ yds.	1¼ yd.	2⅛ yds.
8	2½ yds.	1¼ yd.	2¼ yds.

REMEMBER:

1. To be sure about neck, sleeves, and hem length, measure your child. These sizes are average.

2. Measurements include ½" seam allowance.

3. For back and sleeves you cut two pieces.

3. Make template for size needed. **fig. 1.**
(Use Template Armhole Curve Pattern)

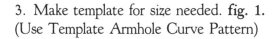

CHART FOR CUTTING BISHOP DRESS

fig. B

(Sizes 1-8 given)

SIZE	FRONT Width/Length	BACK Width/Length	SLEEVES Width/Length	PLACKET Width/Length	NECK BIAS Width/Length	GUIDE FOR SLEEVE	HEM ALLOW-ANCE	NO. OF ROWS FOR SMOCKING
1	23" x 20"	(2) 13" x 20"	(2) 14" x 7"	2" x 11"	1¼" x 12½"	4¾"	3"	8
2	27" x 23"	(2) 14" x 7½"	(2) 14" x 7½"	2" x 11"	1¼" x 13"	5¼"	3	8
3	28" x 25"	(2) 16" x 25"	(2) 16" x 8½"	2" x 11"	1¼" x 13½"	5½"	4"	8
4	30" x 25"	(2) 17" x 25"	(2) 16" x 9"	2" x 11"	1¼" x 14"	5¾"	4"	8
5	36" x 28"	(2) 21" x 28"	(2) 20" x 9½"	2" x 12"	1¼" x 14½"	6"	4"	10
6	37" x 29"	(2) 21½" x 29"	(2) 20" x 10"	2" x 12"	1¼" x 15"	6¼"	5"	10
7	38" x 31"	(2) 21½" x 31"	(2) 21" x 10"	2" x 12"	1¼" x 15½"	6¾"	5"	10
8	38" x 33"	(2) 21½" x 33"	(2) 21" x 11"	2" x 12"	1¼" x 16"	7"	5"	10

Template Armhole Curve Pattern fig. 1

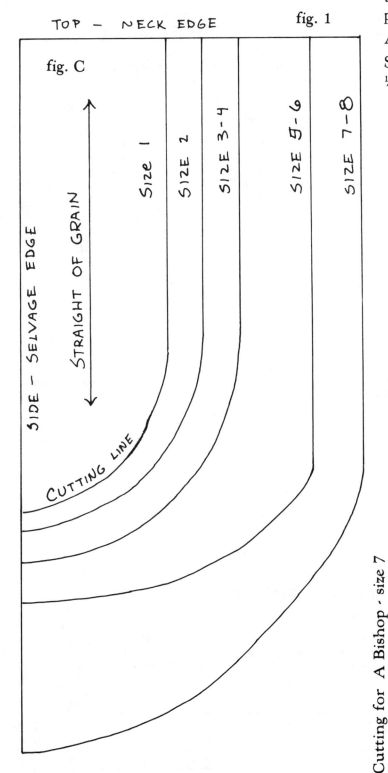

fig. 1

TOP — NECK EDGE

fig. C

SIDE — SELVAGE EDGE

STRAIGHT OF GRAIN

Size 1

SIZE 2

SIZE 3-4

SIZE 5-6

SIZE 7-8

CUTTING LINE

4. Check to see that your fabric has been cut from selvage to selvage on a true straight line. If the ends have been torn, you know that the ends are straight. This is necessary, as the dress is cut from measurements and not a pattern.

5. Cutting Bishop Dress

For an example, a size 7 requires 2½ yards of fabric for the dress. The sleeves, backs, front, neck bias and placket are all cut from the 2½ yards.

A diagram of how/where the pieces are cut. **fig. 2.**

Seam allowances are included in these measurements. ½" seams are allowed.

fig. 2

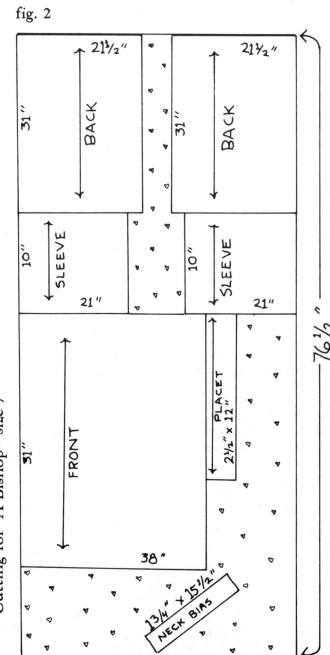

Cutting for A Bishop · size 7

CUTTING FOR A BISHOP

A. THE BACK

Two pieces are to be cut. Measure down the selvage 31" and tear across. **fig. 3**. The total width of the two pieces is 43". Pull a thread to remove excess fabric, (If you need help in how to pull a thread, see How To Pull A Thread in the Techniques section of this book) lengthwise of the fabric, so that the width will be 43", or less if you desire. **fig. 4**.

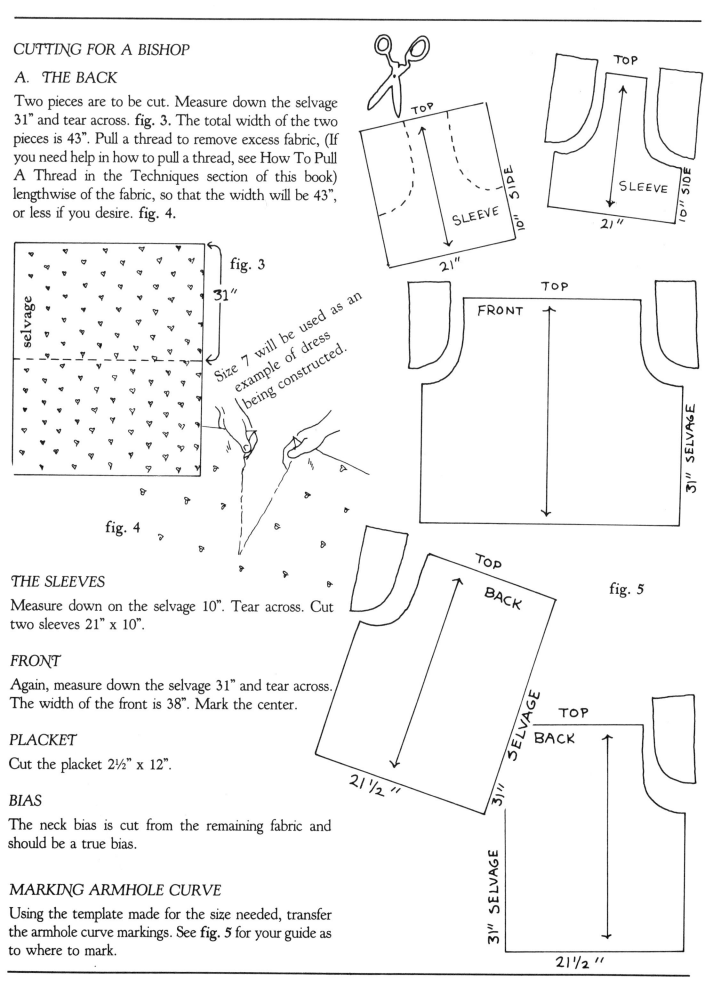

fig. 3

31"

Size 7 will be used as an example of dress being constructed.

fig. 4

fig. 5

THE SLEEVES

Measure down on the selvage 10". Tear across. Cut two sleeves 21" x 10".

FRONT

Again, measure down the selvage 31" and tear across. The width of the front is 38". Mark the center.

PLACKET

Cut the placket 2½" x 12".

BIAS

The neck bias is cut from the remaining fabric and should be a true bias.

MARKING ARMHOLE CURVE

Using the template made for the size needed, transfer the armhole curve markings. See **fig. 5** for your guide as to where to mark.

ADJUSTING THE CENTER FRONT AND BACKS

To prevent the front and back of the Bishop from dipping, remove ½" from the front and back.

a. To re-draw the neck edge, place a rule ½" from the raw edge of the fabric at the center front and back, and let the rule edge touch the raw edge of the fabric at the armhole. **fig. 6.**

This is a very gentle curve and it will not affect the pleating.

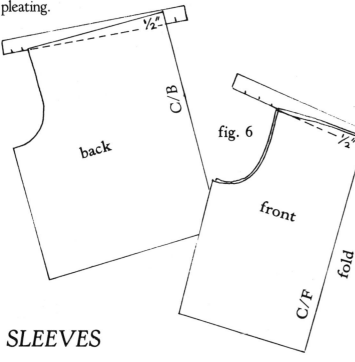

fig. 6

SLEEVES

FINISHING THE SLEEVE EDGE

It's easier if the sleeve edge is finished and the sleeve pleated before stitching the sleeve to the front and back.

Choose the style and method you want for your sleeve. Some suggestions:

a. Roll, Whip and attach lace to the bottom edge by machine or hand.

b. Attach lace with the use of hem stitching or entredeux.

c. Use the Mock French Roll and finish bottom edge of sleeve.

d. Scallop the bottom edge of the sleeve.

Machine Settings for the Scallop:
Elna # 7000, Stitch Selector # 10, 11 or 12
(all make pretty scallops)
Bernina # 1130, Stitch # 25

PLEATING THE SLEEVE

Measure 1½" from the bottom edge of the finished sleeve, and this will be the first gathering thread or pleating thread. Three rows of smocking makes for a pretty smocked sleeve; however, it is wise to always pleat two extra rows. The extra rows just make smocking easier.

After you have pleated the sleeve, flatten out the pleats. **fig. 7.**

fig. 7

FRENCH SEAMS

It is very important when making French Seams in the Bishop Dress that the seams be very neat and very small, so that the dress will go through the pleater.

It is much easier when making French Seams in the Bishop to follow these steps *before* beginning to stitch.

See Making French Seams # 2 if illustrations are needed.

(Follow diagrams for Folding The Bishop to make handling of fabric easier.)

1. Baste or pin the wrong sides together.

2. Stitch, using a Zigzag Stitch. The stitch will go onto the fabric edge and off the fabric causing the raw edges to be slightly rolled. You will use a setting for your machine which will give you a wide zigzag and a stitch length which will not be real short. For the Elna 7000, I use the width setting of 4.4 and the length setting of 1.2, and the needle will only be taking about 1/16" bite of the fabric. There will be no need to trim the edges when using this method.

3. Press the seam and turn to the underside.

FOLDING THE BISHOP

1. Place the wrong side of one of the backs up.

2. Place the wrong side of the sleeve to the wrong side of the back, with the armhole edges even. **fig. 8.**

3. Fold the sleeve so that the front of the armhole is also on the back armhole. Do not pin this side of the sleeve at this time. **fig. 9.**

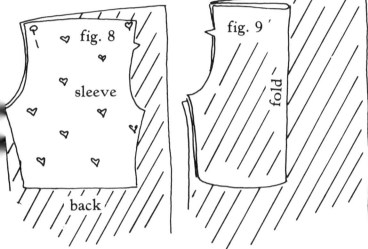

4. Place the front of the dress, wrong side, to the wrong side of the sleeve. Pin. **fig. 10.**

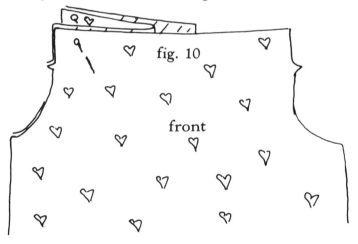

5. Fold the front of the dress in half, so that the other front armhole is placed on top of the armhole edge just pinned. **fig. 11.**

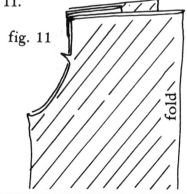

6. Place the remaining sleeve, wrong sides, to the wrong side of the front and pin into place. **fig. 12.**

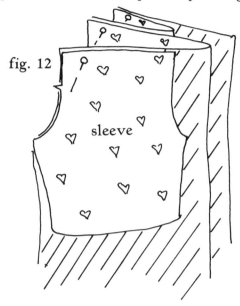

7. Fold the sleeve so that the back of the sleeve arm-hole will be on top of the front side of the armhole. **fig. 13**

8. Place the remaining back armhole edge to the sleeve armhole and pin. **fig. 14.**

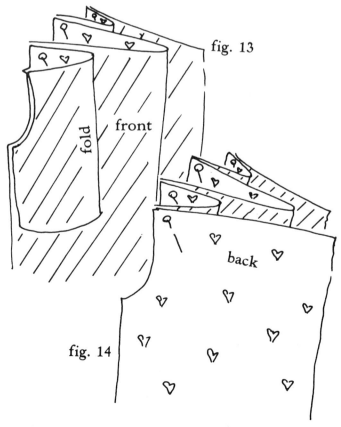

9. With all the pieces of the Bishop Dress pinned and still folded so that all the armhole edges are on top of one another, begin stitching the first stitching row of the French Seam.

Fold all the armhole edges back except for the very first one. See **fig. 15**. Stitch.

When that one row of stitching is completed, fold it back out of the way and then bring the next armhole to be stitched. **fig. 16**

Continue in this manner until all four of the armhole edges have been stitched. **fig. 17A and 17B.**

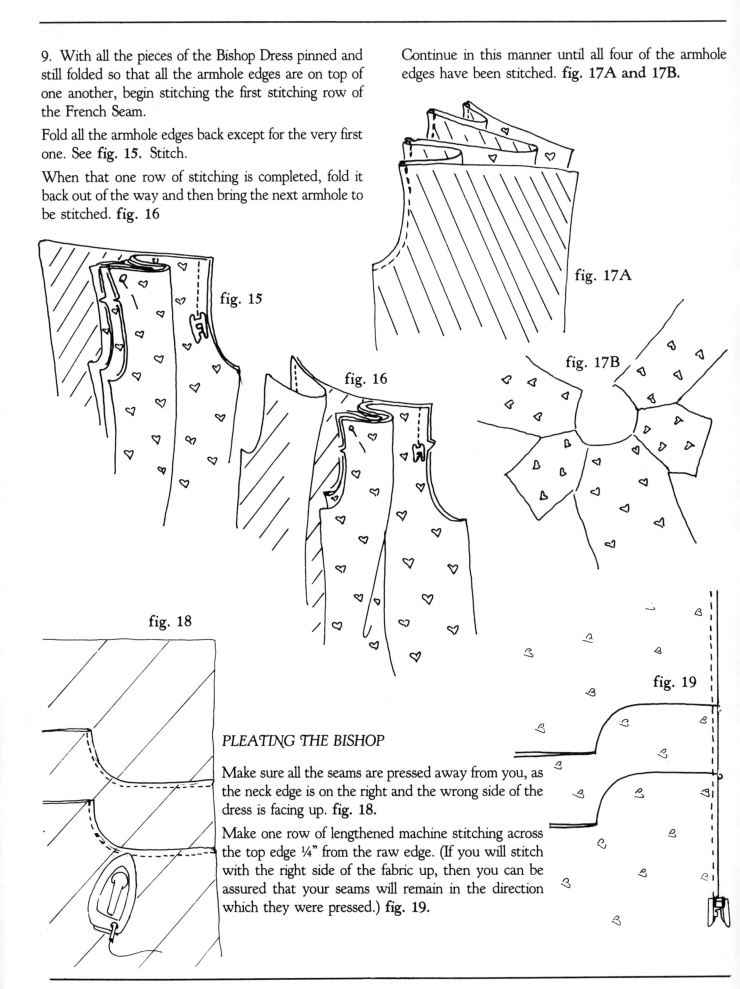

fig. 17A

fig. 17B

fig. 15

fig. 16

fig. 18

fig. 19

PLEATING THE BISHOP

Make sure all the seams are pressed away from you, as the neck edge is on the right and the wrong side of the dress is facing up. **fig. 18.**

Make one row of lengthened machine stitching across the top edge ¼" from the raw edge. (If you will stitch with the right side of the fabric up, then you can be assured that your seams will remain in the direction which they were pressed.) **fig. 19.**

1. Place the dress right side down and the neck edge toward the right.

Place the dowel on the dress lengthwise grain, letting the dowel extend the length of the sleeve, at least. **fig. 20.**

Keep the seams parallel to the dowel, and the dowel parallel to the lengthwise grain of the fabric.

The skirt will hang out of the pleater and should rest on the table as you pleat, so as not to pull on the fabric in the pleater.

Note: See chart for number of rows to be pleated.

3. Place the dress, which has been rolled on the dowel, into the pleater. **fig. 21.**

The neck edge is to the right, with the dowel extending through the ends of the pleater. The skirt of the dress is beyond the pleater to the left.

4. Be very careful as the seam passes through the roller. Go very slow, and keep the neck edge feeding through at the same guide point all the time. Keep the grain straight as it comes off the dowel into the roller of the pleater.

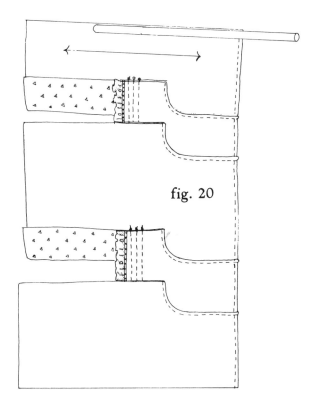

fig. 20

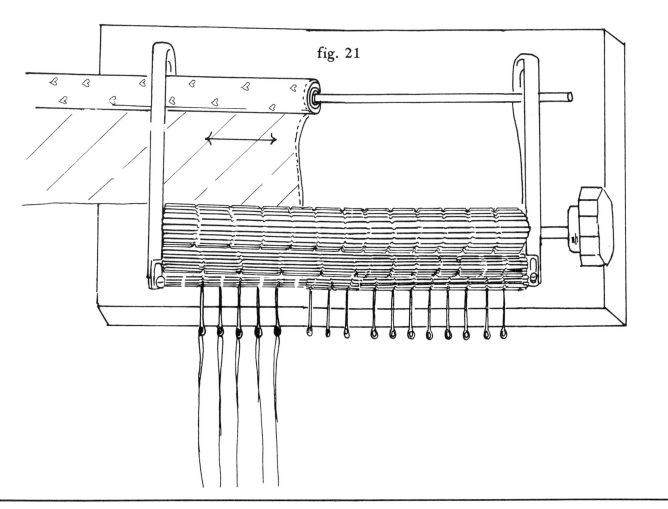

fig. 21

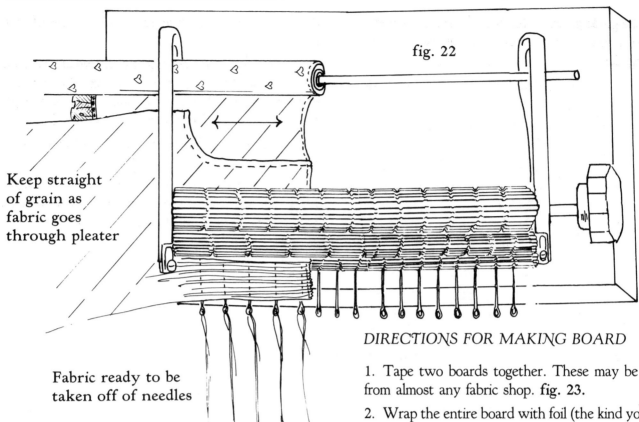

fig. 22

Keep straight
of grain as
fabric goes
through pleater

Fabric ready to be
taken off of needles

TYING OF PLEATER THREADS

Pulling up and tying off the pleater threads is important! A guide has been given for your use.

Note: I use two empty fabric bolts taped together to aid in tying off.

DIRECTIONS FOR MAKING BOARD

1. Tape two boards together. These may be secured from almost any fabric shop. **fig. 23.**

2. Wrap the entire board with foil (the kind you find in your kitchen).

3. Make a muslin slip cover for the board, or use an old pillow slip. **fig. 24.**

You will find a hundred uses for this board! Use the Bishop Guide (located at the end of this section) or use the beautiful guide which Cathy Crisp has, and just pin it to the board. Cathy's guide is printed on pellon and is great to use.

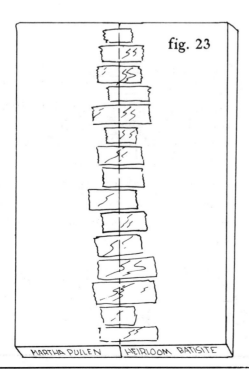

fig. 23

MARTHA PULLEN   HEIRLOOM BATISTE

BOARD

fig. 24

SLIP COVER

If using the guide given in this book, transfer the markings onto a piece of paper and pin the paper to the board. **fig. 25.**

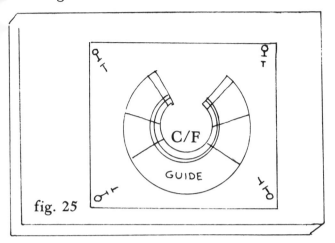

fig. 25

a. Place the dress, right side up, onto the paper guide with the center front of the dress to the center front of the paper guide.

b. The neck edge of fabric should be placed on the appropriate line for your dress size. **fig. 26.**

c. Pin back edges and sleeve seams to the paper guide.

d. Pull the gathering threads until the fabric is nice and flat to the guide.

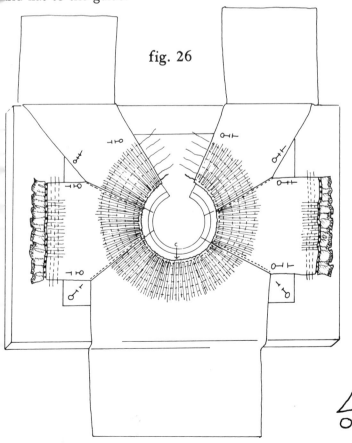

fig. 26

When you have the yoke nice and flat, tie off the threads.

e. Beginning at the neck line, tie off two at a time on the left side. Tie off at the right edge. Pull up the machine stitching. Remember to pull the bobbin thread. Adjust the gathers, distributing evenly.

Tie off the sleeve gathering threads using the measurement chart.

At this point, I use spray starch and saturate the yoke. Let dry naturally, or you may speed the process with the use of the hair dryer. **fig. 27.**

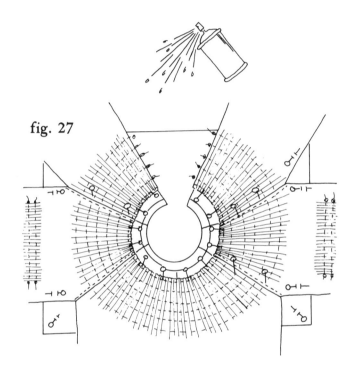

fig. 27

BACK SMOCKING

Back Smock on the first pleating thread at the neck edge. To Back Smock, simply do a Cable Stitch on the wrong side of the fabric, using embroidery floss to match the fabric.

The purpose of Back Smocking is to make the pleats stand evenly, and is used as a guide for stitching the neck bias. The Back Smocking will be covered by the seam.

BACK SEAM

1. Sew back seam. I prefer a French Seam for children's clothes.

Be sure to back stitch at the top of seam to secure and then clip to the stitching line. **fig. 28**. Press.

2. The knot of the gathering threads should just come to the seam line. Stitch, beginning at the top. Keep the same seam allowance all the way to the other end. The seam allowance is determined by the distance from the center point of the placket to the outside edge of the Placket.

3. The clip you made at the top of the French Seam will enable you to continuously sew the Placket. Be careful not to leave a hole at the point where you leave the needle down to turn the fabric. **fig. 30**. The needle will only catch 2 or 3 threads.

4. After you have the fabric maneuvered behind the needle, continue to stitch to the end. **fig. 31**.

5. Trim the Placket seam to ¼". Press seam toward Placket strip.

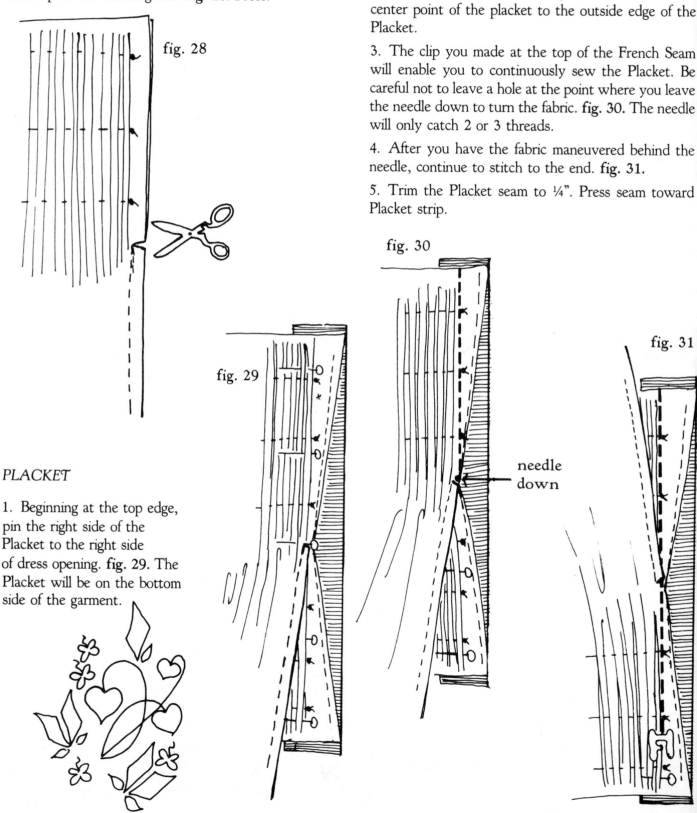

fig. 28

fig. 29

fig. 30

fig. 31

needle down

PLACKET

1. Beginning at the top edge, pin the right side of the Placket to the right side of dress opening. **fig. 29**. The Placket will be on the bottom side of the garment.

6. Turn the raw edge under about ⅛" to ¼". fig. 32.

7. Fold and Baste the Placket over the seam you have just stitched. Slip Stitch to hold in place. fig. 33.

To hold the Placket flat and turned correctly, stitch across the bottom of the Placket diagonally. fig. 34.

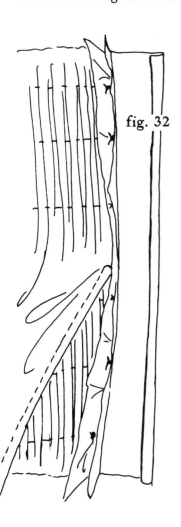

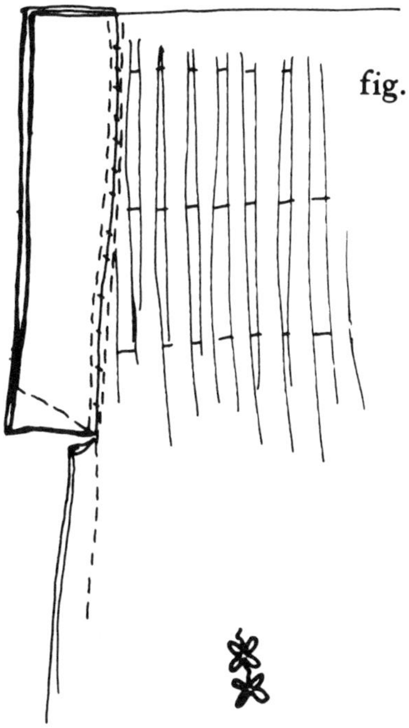

fig. 32

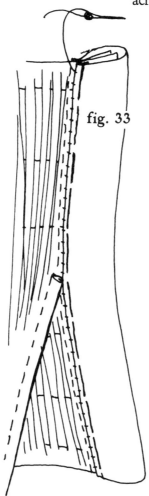

fig. 33

fig. 34

8. The left Placket extension will extend out from the dress just enough to sew the female side of snaps. This side will fit under the right side, which has been turned under on the seam line, and will have the male side of the snaps sewn. fig. 35.

NECK BIAS

1. Fold the bias strip in half lengthwise. fig. 36.

2. Check and make adjustments, if necessary, so that the neck measures the same as the bias strip.

fig. 36

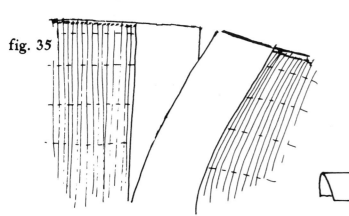

fig. 35

Mark the center of the bias strip and match to the center of the dress. **fig. 37**. With right sides together and the raw edges of the bias even with the edge of the neck, pin and baste very carefully.

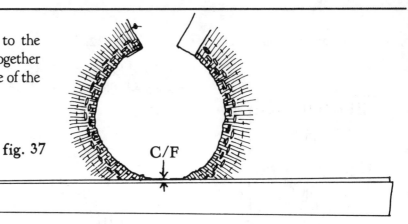

fig. 37

C/F

The ends of the bias strip extend about 1" on each side. **fig. 38**.

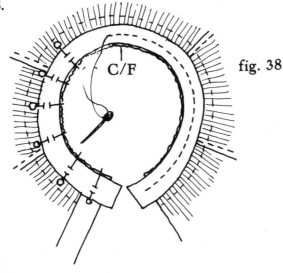

C/F

fig. 38

3. After securing the bias piece, turn and wrap the end pieces. **fig. 39**.

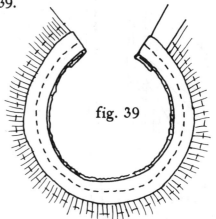

fig. 39

Turn bias over and pin folded edge over seam line. Whip Stitch the bias down using tiny invisible stitches. **fig. 41**.

5. Sew snaps onto Placket. Make sure there is a snap even with the last row of Pleating. Finish the closure off with the use of a small shank button and thread loop at the very top placed on the neck bias strip. **fig. 42**.

4. With the bias strip on the bottom and the row of Back Smocking on top, machine stitch.

Use the row of Back Smocking as a guide.

The first row of Pleating should be about ⅜" from the raw edge of the neck edge. The bias strip edge is even with the neck edge, so the stitching line will be ⅜" from the raw edge and on top of the Back Smocking. **fig. 40**.

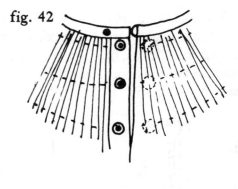

fig. 42

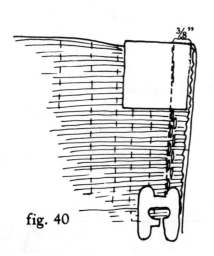

⅜"

fig. 40

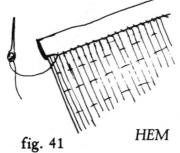

fig. 41

HEM

Turn under ¼" of the raw edge and press. You may choose to machine stitch this turn or not. Overcasting of the raw edge is also acceptable.

Measure and turn up hem. Pin and baste into place. Take great care to make small invisible hemming stitches.

BISHOP GUIDE

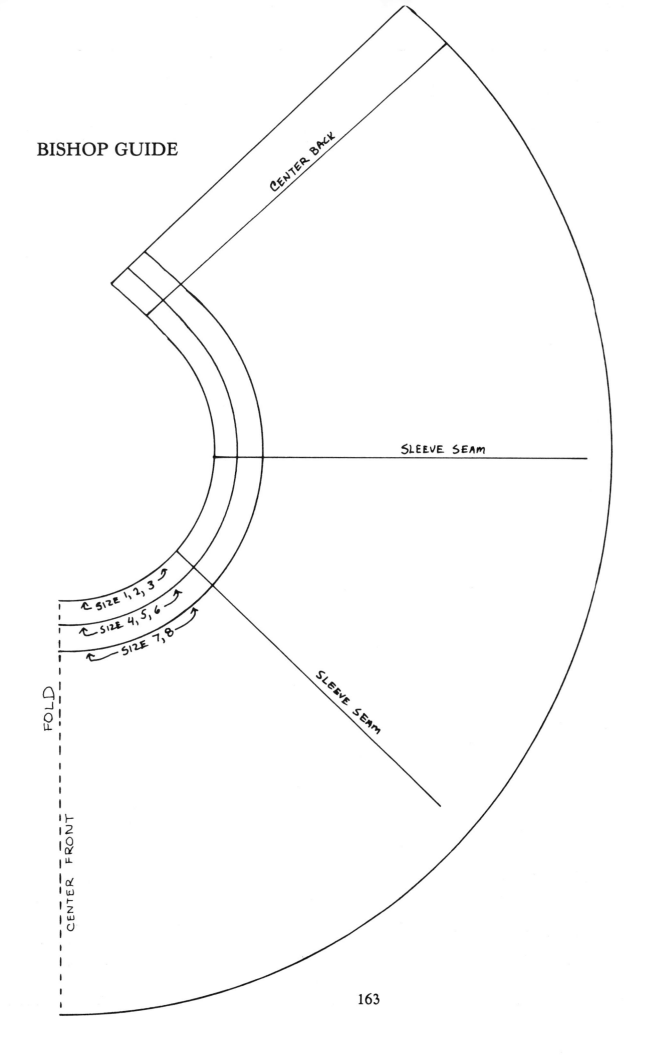

CENTER BACK

SLEEVE SEAM

↖ SIZE 1, 2, 3 ↗
↖ SIZE 4, 5, 6 ↗
↖ SIZE 7, 8 ↗

SLEEVE SEAM

FOLD

CENTER FRONT

163

MIMI'S HEART DRESS

MIMI'S HEART DRESS

Mimi's Heart Dress has a slightly raised waistline and gathered skirt, with hearts on the hemline. The dress has puffed sleeves with a fancy band and a ribbon sash with buttons in the back to close.

I. FRONT AND BACK SKIRT

1. Tear two pieces of fabric 36" wide for the size two, or 45" or more for the remaining sizes, and the desired length for your child.

II. PLACKET

1. Cut a 3 - 5" slash down the center back skirt. fig. 1.

2. Cut a lengthwise strip of fabric 2" wide and two times longer than the slash just made in the center back.

3. Place the right side of the Placket strip to the right side of the opening and stitch. fig. 2.

4. Stitch ¼" from the raw edge. Stitch from the top to the bottom of the opening.

5. Use the needle as a pivot at the bottom of the slash. fig. 3.

Stitch up the other side. fig. 4.

6. Turn under raw edge of the Placket strip and Whip to the wrong side over the machine stitching. fig. 5.

7. Make a diagonal stitch across the end (on the inside of the Placket) to prevent pulling fig. 6.

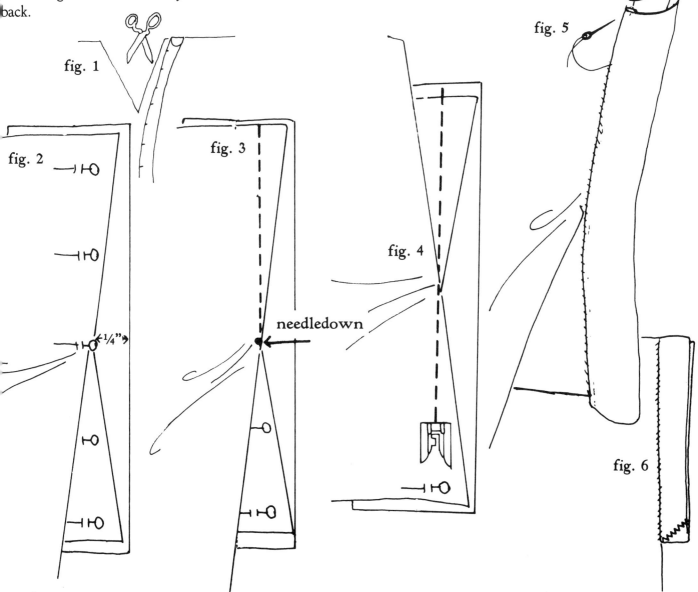

fig. 1

fig. 2

fig. 3

fig. 4

needledown

fig. 5

fig. 6

III. CONSTRUCT COLLAR

1. Draw the collar shape onto the fabric. DO NOT CUT! fig. 7.

2. Cut one piece of Lace Insertion 20½" long. Transfer the markings from the lace guide to the piece of Lace Insertion. See the lace guide "A". The lace will look something like this with the markings. fig. 8.

3. Using a very narrow and short Zigzag setting, stitch the lace together at the marks which you have made on the lace. You will actually be stitching a small dart in one end, and just stitching diagonally on the other, to join the two ends together. fig. 9.

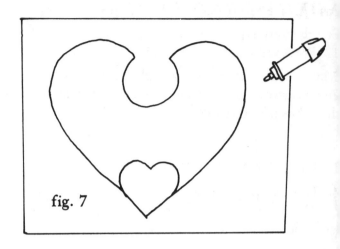

fig. 7

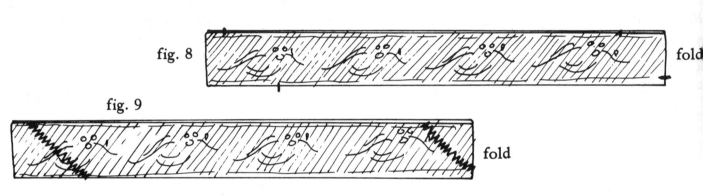

fig. 8

fold

fig. 9

fold

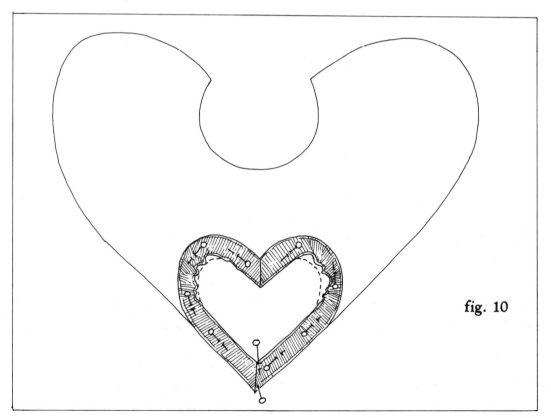

fig. 10

4. Place the lace heart, right sides up, onto the collar fabric at the bottom front. Carefully pin and then Baste onto the fabric. fig. 10.

Baste on the outside edge of the Lace Insertion. **fig. 11.**
Pull the very top thread to make the lace lie flat. **fig. 12.** Press well on the wrong side of the fabric.

5. Set your machine for a very narrow and short Zigzag Stitch. Stitch on the lace heading on the inside of the heart *only*. **fig. 13.**

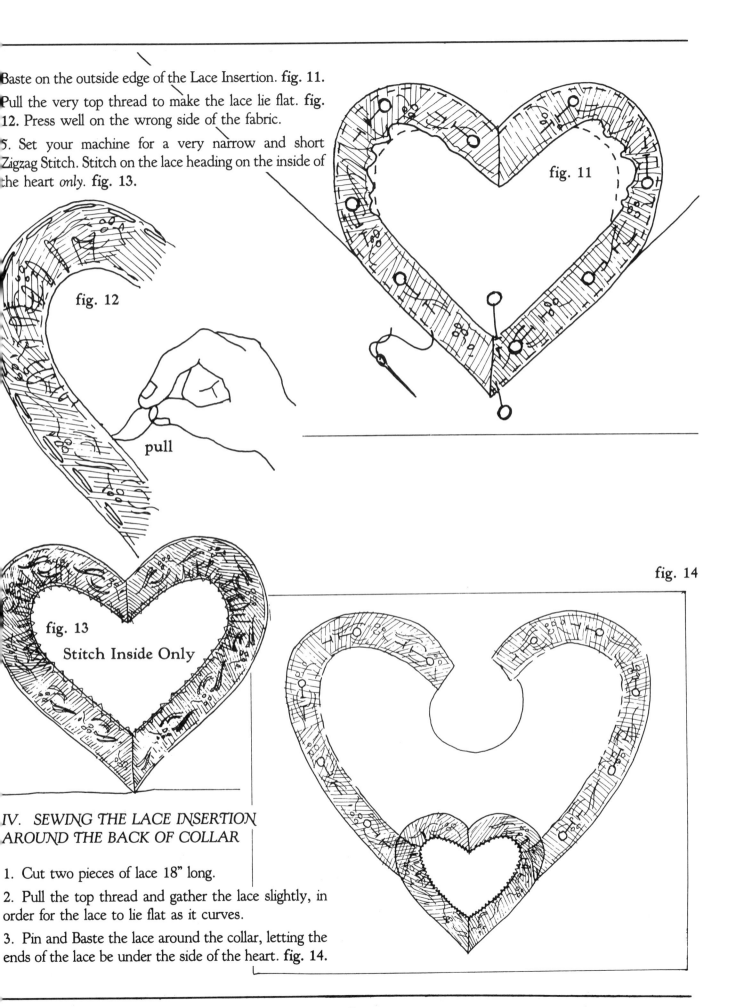

fig. 11

fig. 12

pull

fig. 14

fig. 13

Stitch Inside Only

IV. SEWING THE LACE INSERTION AROUND THE BACK OF COLLAR

1. Cut two pieces of lace 18" long.

2. Pull the top thread and gather the lace slightly, in order for the lace to lie flat as it curves.

3. Pin and Baste the lace around the collar, letting the ends of the lace be under the side of the heart. **fig. 14.**

Set your machine for a very narrow and short Zigzag Stitch and stitch around the collar on the inside edge of the Lace Insertion and around the top side of the heart. fig. 15.

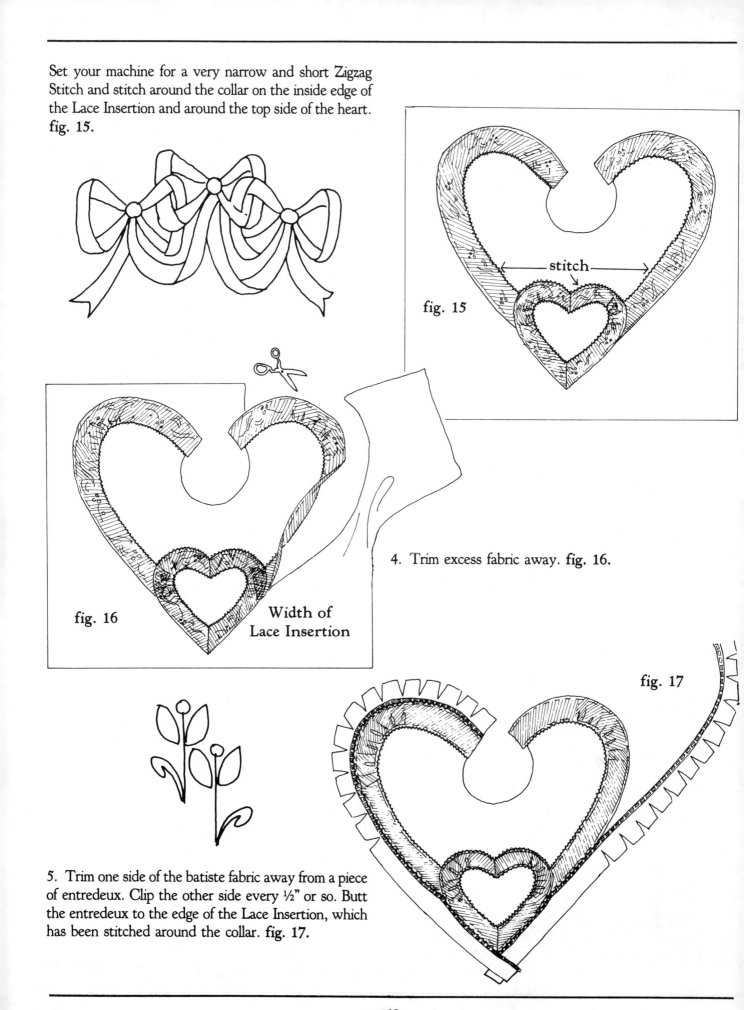

fig. 15

stitch

fig. 16

Width of Lace Insertion

4. Trim excess fabric away. fig. 16.

fig. 17

5. Trim one side of the batiste fabric away from a piece of entredeux. Clip the other side every ½" or so. Butt the entredeux to the edge of the Lace Insertion, which has been stitched around the collar. fig. 17.

Zigzag into each and every hole and onto the Lace Insertion edge. Be sure to miter the entredeux at the point of the collar.

For mitering entredeux, (a) Zigzag into each of the entredeux holes and encompass the lace heading. As you approach the corner, continue to Zigzag onto the entredeux for about ½". Cut your entredeux at this point. fig. 18.

fig. 18

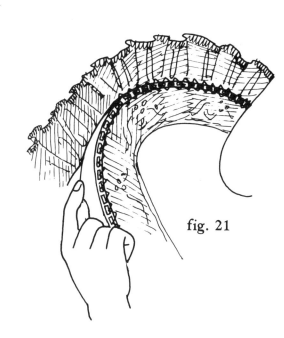

fig. 21

(b) Place the second piece of trimmed entredeux to the edge of the lace and on top of the entredeux which has already been stitched. I like to use a little fabric glue under the corner of the batiste fabric to hold in place until I stitch. fig. 19.

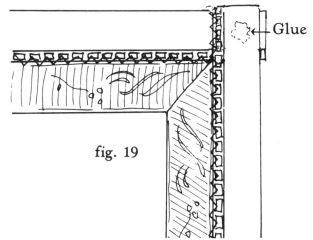

←Glue

fig. 19

(c) Zigzag into each hole and off onto the entredeux fabric until the lace end is reached. Continue stitching into each hole of the entredeux and onto the lace heading. Trim the remaining side of the entredeux. fig. 20.

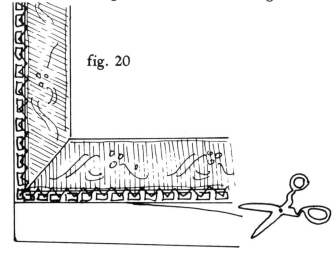

fig. 20

6. You may gather the lace edging or leave it flat. I prefer to use gathers, except at the point where the lace is mitered.

Begin at the back and use the Butt Method. Gather the lace edging slightly, holding the gathering thread in front of the stitching. Zigzag into each hole and off to encompass the lace heading of the lace edging. fig. 21.

As you come to the point of the Heart, flatten out the lace for about an inch before the point. Leave the needle in the down position in the very last hole as you miter the lace. (Refer to the Technique section on how to Miter Lace Edging - The Diamond Church Doll)

Continue stitching the lace edging until the lace is all the way around the collar.

V. BODICE

1. Stitch front shoulder seam to back shoulder seam, making a French Seam. Press the seam to the back. fig. 22.

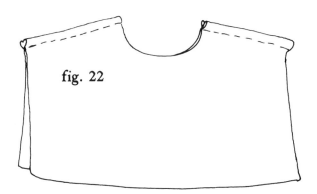

fig. 22

5. I prefer to sew buttons on the left-hand side and make buttonholes in the right side of the bodice at this time.

6. French Seam the underarm side seam. **fig. 27.**

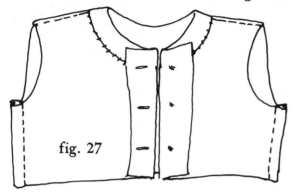

fig. 27

VI. CONSTRUCT SLEEVE

1. Stitch two rows of lengthened machine stitching across the top of the sleeve. **fig. 28.**

2. Roll, Whip and Gather the bottom edge of the sleeve. **fig. 29.**

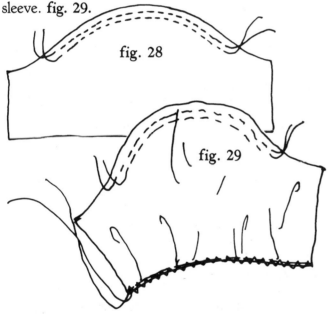

fig. 28

fig. 29

VII. MAKING THE FANCY SLEEVE BAND

1. Cut two pieces of entredeux the correct arm measurement. This measurement should be the arm measurement, plus about 1½" for ease and ½" for seam allowance.

Trim one side of the entredeux and attach it to both sides of the wide lace beading. A pretty wide beading insertion is pretty on the sleeve. If you do not have available such a piece of beading, it is very easy to make it by joining two pieces of Lace Insertion to both sides of the entredeux, and then the entredeux to each side of the insertion/beading band.

Butt the entredeux to the lace. **fig. 30.**

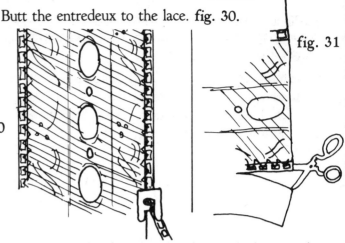

fig. 30

fig. 31

2. On one side of the lace beading with the entredeux attached, trim the remaining entredeux fabric away. **fig. 31.**

Gather the lace edging 1½ to 2 times the length of the entredeux.

Attach to the entredeux using the method of placing the Right Sides Together, entredeux on top, and stitching into each and every hole and clearing the fabric on the other side. **fig. 32.**

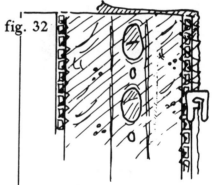

fig. 32

3. Trim the remaining side of the entredeux on the other side of the lace beading.

Attach this Bancy Band to the bottom edge of the sleeve, which has been Rolled, Whipped and Gathered to fit the fancy arm band, by placing the Fancy Band and the sleeve right sides together. **fig. 33.**

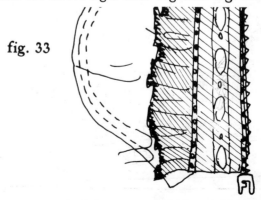

fig. 33

2. Pin and Baste the collar to the neck edge. Place the collar so that the back of the collar (the edge of the trim) stops at the center back line.

Fold the facing back over the collar and Baste. **fig. 23.**

3. Cut a bias strip 1" wide by 12" long.

Stitch bias to dress and collar using a ¼" seam. Stitch a second row of stitching 1/16" to the outside from the first line of stitching. Trim and clip the seam. **fig. 24.**

fig. 23

fig. 25

4. Turn the bias strip inside over the raw edge. **fig. 25.** Anchor the bias strip using small hand stitches. **fig. 26.**

fig. 24

fig. 26

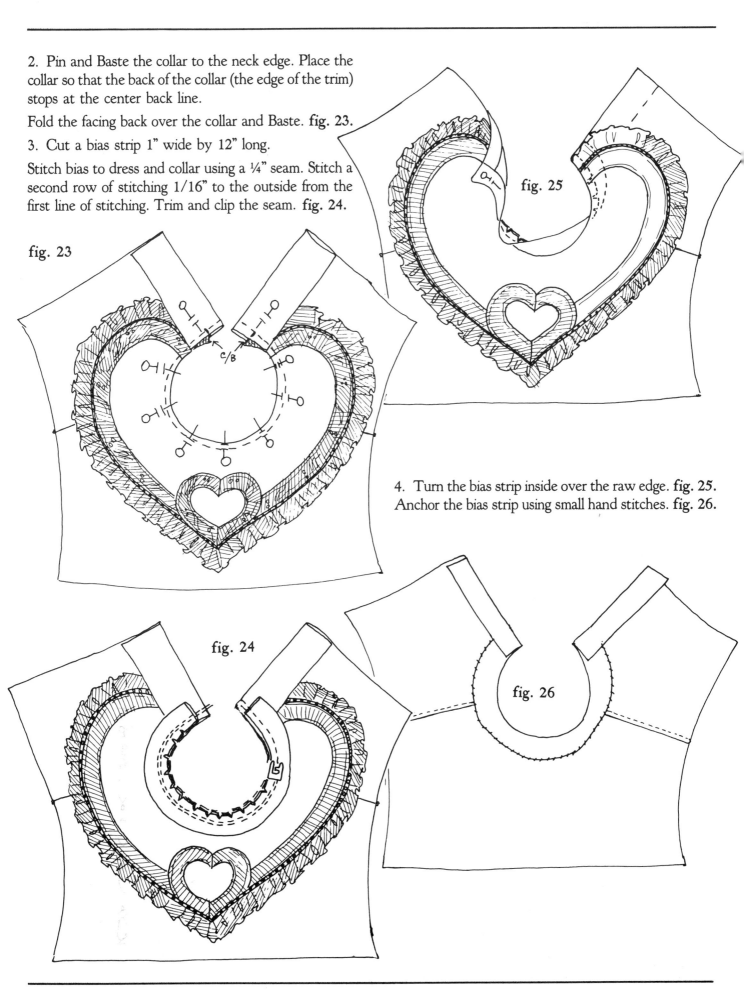

With this method you will have your machine set for a wide Zigzag setting, and your needle should go into each hole of the entredeux and off the fabric edge.

4. French Seam the underarm seams. The sleeve is now ready to be stitched into the garment. **fig. 34.**

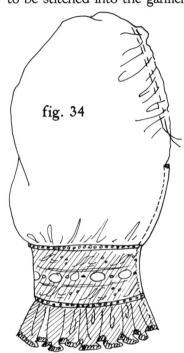

fig. 34

VIII.   *SET-IN SLEEVE USING A FRENCH SEAM*

1. Work from the right side of the garment, and with the wrong side of the sleeve to the wrong side of the garment. Pin or Baste the sleeve in. Match underarm side seams to underarm sleeve seams, shoulder seams to center of sleeve, etc. Make sure raw edges are even. Pull gathering threads in the top of the sleeve until the sleeve fits the arm opening. **fig. 35.**

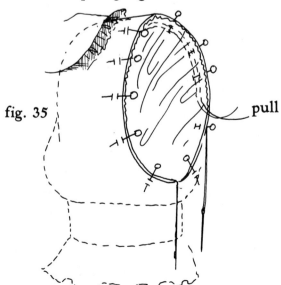

fig. 35   pull

2. Stitch ¼" from edge. **fig. 36.** Trim to a scant ⅛". **Note:** I like to do a Zigzag Stitch on and off the edge of this seam, as it keeps all the fuzzies in the French Seam. **fig. 37.**

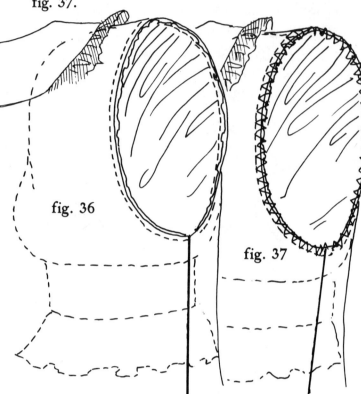

fig. 36

fig. 37

3. Turn the sleeve and bodice wrong side out and finger press the first seam until it rolls out. Complete the French Seam by stitching again ¼" from the edge. **fig. 38.**

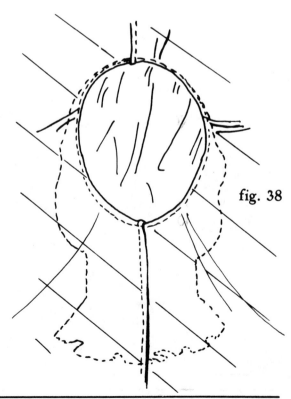

fig. 38

IX. HEARTS ON THE BOTTOM OF THE SKIRT

Make as many hearts as you need to go around the bottom of your skirt.

Each large heart is 8½" wide at the widest point, using the width of Lace Insertion and measurements which are here; however, lace will stretch, a different width of insertion may make a difference, etc. The lace width used for these directions is ⅝" wide.

Take the width of your heart and divide it into the width of the fabric which you are using. This will give you the number of hearts you will need to go all the way around the bottom edge of your garment.

For an example, when using 45" wide fabric, you will use 5 hearts. For the smaller dress with a width of 36" fabric, you will probably choose to use the small heart, which is 6" wide and you will be able to use 6 hearts.

1. Use the lace guide "B" and transfer the markings to the number of 32" strips of lace needed for the hearts.

2. Follow the steps for making the Heart for the Collar for making the hearts for the bottom of the skirt. Steps 3 through 5 and **figs. 9 - 13.**

The hearts for the bottom of the skirt will be placed side-by-side. **fig. 39.**

Place the lace hearts to the bottom edge of the skirt fabric. **fig. 39.** If there should be a difference in the amount of fabric which your heart required and the fabric you have allowed for in your skirt, just cut off the difference. Complete bottom of hearts with entredeux and lace edging and in the same manner as for Collar. **figures 17-21.**

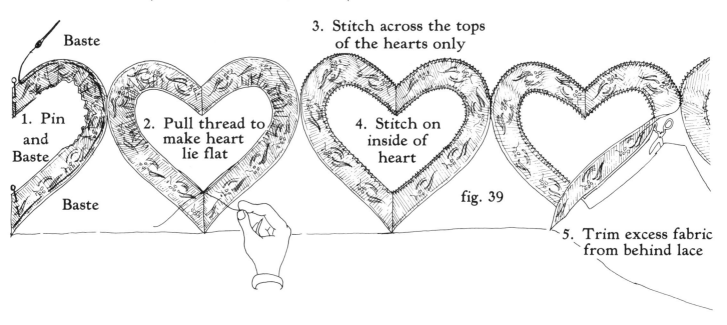

Baste

3. Stitch across the tops of the hearts only

1. Pin and Baste

Baste

2. Pull thread to make heart lie flat

4. Stitch on inside of heart

fig. 39

5. Trim excess fabric from behind lace

X. ATTACHING SKIRT TO BODICE

1. Run two rows of gathering threads along top edge of the skirt. **fig. 40.**

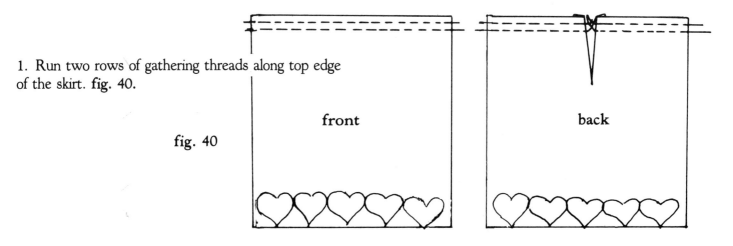

fig. 40

front

back

2. French Seam the two side seams. **fig. 41.**

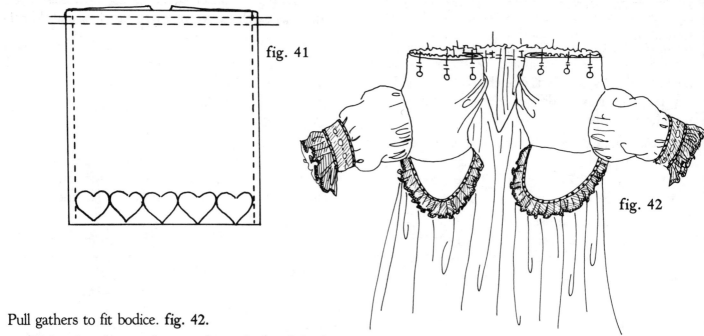

fig. 41

fig. 42

Pull gathers to fit bodice. **fig. 42.**

3. With right sides together, pin skirt to bodice. Match side seams, center front and center backs. **fig. 43.**

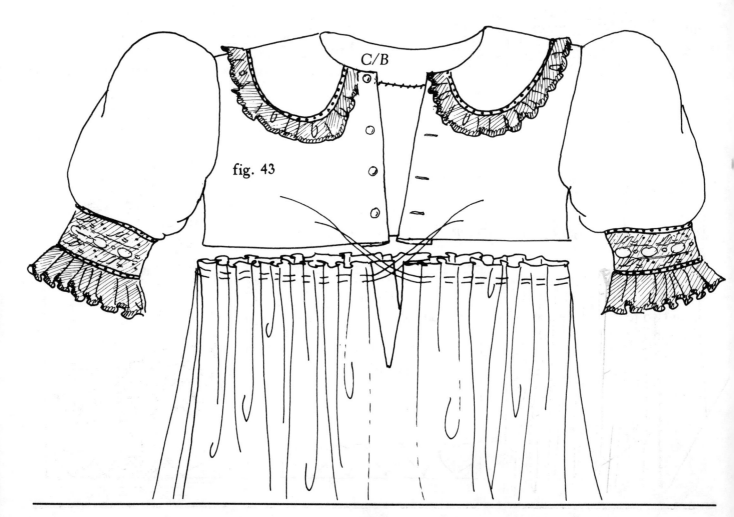

C/B

fig. 43

4. Fold the bodice back extensions over the skirt Placket so that the skirt Placket will be sandwiched between the extensions and the bodice. Stitch, using a straight machine stitch. Stitch another row of stitching ⅛" to the outside of the first line of stitching. **fig. 44.**

5. Trim and finish the seam, either with a piece of lace to encase the seam, or Zigzag, letting the needle of your machine touch the second row of stitching and clear the fabric as it Zigzags back and forth. **fig. 45.**

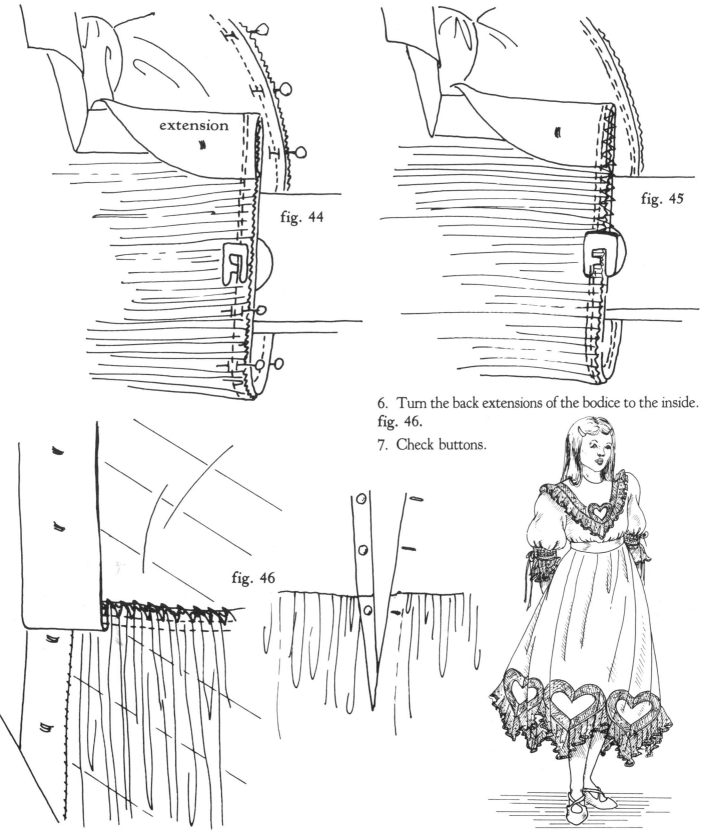

extension

fig. 44

fig. 45

6. Turn the back extensions of the bodice to the inside. **fig. 46.**

7. Check buttons.

fig. 46

Heirloom Sewing, Smocking and Quilting supplies may be obtained by mail order
from the shop of Mildred Turner. Write:

Mimi's Smock Shoppe, Inc.
502 Balsam Road
Hazelwood, NC   28738
(704) 452-3455